JOBS AND JUSTICE
Fighting Discrimination in Wartime Canada, 1939–1945

T0317138

Despite acute labour shortages during the Second World War, Canadian employers – with the complicity of state officials – discriminated against workers of African, Asian, and Eastern and Southern European origin, excluding them from both white-collar and skilled jobs. *Jobs and Justice* argues that, while the war intensified hostility and suspicion towards minority workers, the urgent need for their contributions and the egalitarian rhetoric used to mobilize the war effort also created an opportunity for minority activists and their English Canadian allies to challenge discrimination.

Juxtaposing a discussion of state policy with ideas of race and citizenship in Canadian civil society, Carmela K. Patrias demonstrates how these activists brought national attention to racist employment discrimination and eventually garnered its official condemnation. Extensively researched and engagingly written, *Jobs and Justice* offers a new perspective on the Second World War, the racist dimensions of state policy, and the origins of human rights campaigns in Canada.

CARMELA PATRIAS is a professor in the Department of History at Brock University.

CARMELA PATRIAS

Jobs and Justice
Fighting Discrimination in Wartime
Canada, 1939–1945

UNIVERSITY OF TORONTO PRESS
Toronto Buffalo London

ISBN 978-1-4426-4236-2 (cloth)
ISBN 978-1-4426-1128-3 (paper)

Printed on acid-free, 100% post-consumer recycled paper with
vegetable-based inks

Library and Archives Canada Cataloguing in Publication

Patrias, Carmela, 1950–
Jobs and justice : fighting discrimination in wartime Canada, 1939–1945 /
Carmela Patrias.

Includes bibliographical references.
ISBN 978-1-4426-4236-2 (bound)   ISBN 978-1-4426-1128-3 (pbk.)

1. Discrimination in employment – Canada – History – 20th century.
2. Discrimination in employment – Government policy – Canada.   3. Minorities –
Employment – Canada – History – 20th century.   4. Minorities – Civil rights –
Canada – History – 20th century.   5. Canada – Race relations – History – 20th
century.   6. Racism – Canada – History – 20th century.   7. Canada – History –
1939–1945.   I. Title.

HD4903.5.C3P38 2012   331.13'3097109044   C2011-906624-6

University of Toronto Press acknowledges the financial assistance to its publishing
program of the Canada Council for the Arts and the Ontario Arts Council.

 Canada Council   Conseil des Arts
for the Arts   du Canada

 ONTARIO ARTS COUNCIL
CONSEIL DES ARTS DE L'ONTARIO

University of Toronto Press acknowledges the financial support of the Government of
Canada through the Canada Book Fund for its publishing activities.

This book has been published with the help of a grant from the Canadian Federation
for the Humanities and Social Sciences, through the Aid to Scholarly Publications
Program, using funds provided by the Social Sciences and Humanities Research
Council of Canada.

For Wayne

Contents

Acknowledgments

Thanking all those who helped with the research, writing, and production of a monograph is one of the great pleasures that accompanies its publication. My greatest debt is to Ruth Frager and Wayne Thorpe. Ruth introduced me to the history of human rights activism in Canada. The idea of writing this book developed during our collaboration on a project on the social origins of human rights legislation in Ontario. Since then, despite her many commitments, she generously took the time to discuss the project, read drafts of the manuscript, share her expertise on computers, cameras, and software, and help in innumerable other ways. I am deeply grateful for her friendship and support. Wayne listened patiently while I developed my ideas for this project and offered advice, encouragement, the healing powers of his irreverent sense of humour, afternoon espressos, and early evening spritzers. His comments on the manuscript helped immensely to clarify my thoughts and improve my writing. My friends and colleagues at Brock University, especially Pat Dirks, Tami Friedman, Heidi Klose, Jane McLeod, Danny Samson, and Larry Savage, have made it possible for me to work in a stimulating and supportive scholarly community for almost twenty years. I thank them all.

This book could not have been written without the assistance of archivists and librarians from across Canada. It is a pleasure to acknowledge with gratitude the help of staff at the Esther Clark Wright Archives, Acadia University; the Canadian Jewish Congress Charities Committee National Archives in Montreal; Library and Archives Canada; Queen's University Archives; Archives of Ontario; the University of Toronto Archives; Ontario Jewish Archives; United Church Archives; McMaster University Archives and Research Collections; Brock University

Library and Special Collections; St Catharines Public Library, Special
Collections; Windsor Community Archives; Saskatchewan Archives
Board, Regina; University of Saskatchewan Archives, Saskatoon; Glen-
bow Archives, Calgary; UBC Special Collections; and City of Vancouver Archives. A Standard Research Grant from the Social Science and
Humanities Research Council of Canada provided generous financial
support. Len Husband and Frances Mundy at the University of Toronto
Press helped to make the transformation of the manuscript into a book
pleasant and smooth.

Jobs and Justice is dedicated to Wayne Thorpe, whose early experience with too many jobs and too little justice honed the commitment to
equity that guides him.

JOBS AND JUSTICE

Introduction

Sometime in 1941 a group of 'Slavic' workers travelled from Alberta to Ontario in search of skilled jobs in war industries. All the workers were Canadian-born and all had been trained under the government's War Emergency Training Programme. Yet, despite shortages of skilled labour in Ontario, they were unable to obtain work. Upon learning their names, Ontario employers refused to hire them, and the workers were eventually forced to return to Alberta.[1] The rejection of these workers, despite their Canadian birth and training, baffles the contemporary reader. Were these workers of Polish, Ukrainian, Czech, Slovak, Serbian, or Croatian descent? Did they trace their origins to countries at war with Canada or ones allied with it? Ontario employers apparently considered such information irrelevant. Not the national heritage of these 'Slavic' workers but their 'race' convinced prospective employers that they were unfit to work in war industries.

In 1941 'foreign' names were widely understood as markers of racial difference. The introduction to the *Eighth Census of Canada, 1941*, for example, stated that 'knowledge of one's racial origin,' could be 'perpetuated in a family name.' Census analysts found it necessary to explain the criteria by which 'racial origin' could be known because the basis for racial classification in the census varied for different groups. 'Colour' was the basis for classifying the 'Indian, Eskimo, Negro, Hindu, Chinese and Japanese races,' religion for classifying Jews, and language for classifying Ukrainians. For some groups 'racial origin' implied 'geographical area – the country from which the individual himself came or that which was the home of his forebears.' In the case of groups of European descent, racial origin was traced through the father. This meant that the offspring of mixed marriages would be assimilated into their father's

CARTER?
CARON?
CAPLAN?
CANAKOS?
CANTROWICZ?
CANADIAN

Wartime Information Board, Propaganda Poster.
Artist: Harry Mayerovitch, 1944.
Library and Archives Canada, C-115712

group. By contrast, children of 'mixed blood' – those born of mixed marriages between whites and 'Negro, Japanese, Chinese, Hindu, Malaysian etc.' – were classified as belonging to those racial groups if either parent belonged to the 'black, yellow or brown races.' The racial designation for people of mixed 'white and Indian blood' was 'Half-breed.'[2] People of colour were thereby defined as unassimilable.[3]

That the names of the 'Slavic' workers from Alberta signified 'racial' difference of sufficient magnitude to disqualify them from obtaining work in war industries suggests that, however imprecise its definition, the racial origin designation was economically and socially very significant. One goal of this study is to examine the nature and extent of racist employment discrimination during the Second World War. It will show that, in wartime Canada, racializing minority groups – attributing to them substantial, inborn distinguishing characteristics – greatly disadvantaged group members in the labour market and prevented their full incorporation within the body of the nation.[4] A second and related goal is to demonstrate that although the government officially prohibited employment discrimination based on race, nationality, and religion during the war, state officials colluded with racist employers and workers in such discrimination.

Studying employment discrimination affords a particularly broad view of the treatment of racialized minorities because minority group members of all classes faced such discrimination. Many white-collar jobs were closed to the educated among minority groups, and poorly educated minority women and men were by and large relegated to unskilled, ill-paid, insecure blue-collar and service sector jobs. The focus on the war years offers a unique opportunity for studying racist employment discrimination because evidence of such discrimination on the home front abounds. Unprecedented intervention by the federal government in the labour market generated a good part of this evidence. State officials intent on maximizing labour productivity during the war were forced to pay close attention to employment discrimination because members of racialized minority groups constituted an indispensable source of labour. On the one hand, discrimination threatened productivity both by creating tensions among workers and by excluding some of them from certain occupations. On the other hand, after 1942, when employment was plentiful and menial jobs went unfilled, racialization could be useful in channelling workers into undesirable yet essential jobs. This study draws extensively on the records of federal government agencies.

Studying employment discrimination during the war can do more, however, than illustrate the nature and significance of racism between 1939 and 1945. That the national heritage of the 'Slavic' workers from Alberta made so little difference to Ontario employers suggests that employment discrimination on the home front owed far less to wartime alliances on the international stage than to longstanding association between 'race' and suitability for certain types of employment and for citizenship in Canada. To be sure, state officials anticipated – and some of them shared – security concerns about the participation of 'enemy aliens' in home defence and war production. As we shall see, however, many employers, workers, and state officials also racialized Canadian-born and naturalized people of Chinese, Japanese, central, eastern, and southern European, and Jewish origin: many Canadians saw these racialized groups as 'foreigners,' suspected them of disloyalty, and therefore believed that they were undeserving of certain economic and political rights. The war also brought sharply into focus and even intensified racist assumptions that African Canadians, eastern and southern Europeans, and Native people were suitable only for menial jobs and that other groups, the 'aggressive' and 'greedy' Jews, Chinese Canadians, and Japanese Canadians, constituted unfair competition for 'true' Canadians because they placed economic gains above patriotic duty. Such racist assumptions served to legitimize the marginalization of minority groups in Canadian society.

The inclusion of minority groups of southern and eastern European parentage – such as the 'Slavic' workers introduced above – as well as of African, Asian, and Native Canadians, is central to the analysis of the meaning and impact of race offered here. Some of the most influential recent studies of racism in Canada make clear that characterizing groups that we would describe today as 'white' as racially distinct and inferior reveals the social construction and hence fluidity of racial classification.[5] Even in these studies, however, the attention given to 'visible' minorities generally outweighs examinations of the racialization of groups of European origin. Such a focus is understandable because people of colour have been the targets of the most extreme and most overtly state-sanctioned racism in Canada, in the form of immigration restrictions, denial of the franchise, and legal exclusion from certain types of jobs. It is also easier to study such racism than the less formalized racialization of groups of European descent. This study's focus on employment discrimination allows us to explore the meaning and impact of racist ideas and practices for minority groups of 'peripheral' European as well as African, Asian and Native parentage because the mobility of all these groups in the labour force was impeded during the war.[6]

The debate among American historians concerning the racial classification of immigrant workers of southern and eastern European descent offers useful insights for studying similar groups in Canada. According to James Barrett and David Roediger the status of such workers in turn-of-the-twentieth-century America was ambiguous. Before the First World War, when non-white immigrants were barred from entering the United States, the national government classified immigrants from the 'peripheries' of Europe as white, allowing them to immigrate to the United States in large numbers and to become naturalized and thus enfranchised. The imposition of restrictions against them in the 1920s reflected the intensification of racism against such European immigrants. Their ability to become 'white' over time, however, despite the fact that both social science and popular culture regarded them as 'nonwhite,' reflected their 'inbetween' status: above African and Asian Americans, whose purported colour kept them at the bottom of the prevailing system of racial hierarchy, but below native-born whites and immigrants from northwestern Europe, whose purported whiteness placed them at the top of that hierarchy. The changing classification of southern and eastern European immigrants and their children formed part of the process of their Americanization, itself the result both of the willingness of the dominant racializing groups to perceive them as white and of their self-identification as white.[7] By contrast, Eric Arnesen, among others, questions the utility of 'whiteness' as an analytic concept, arguing that whiteness scholars misrepresent the racialization of European immigrants in the United States in the nineteenth and early twentieth centuries by reducing this 'complex, many faceted' process to 'the matter of "becoming white."'[8]

Some of the arguments of both whiteness scholars and their critics apply to Canada as well. In the late nineteenth and early twentieth centuries, here, as in the United States, the status of groups of eastern and southern European descent was above that of groups of African, Asian, and Native descent, and below that of people of northwestern European descent. Moreover, in Canada as in the United States, the status of people from the 'peripheries' of Europe was ambiguous. Encouraged to come by the hundreds of thousands prior to the First World War, such immigrants were classified 'non-preferred' during the interwar years. This classification indicated their inferiority to 'preferred' groups from Great Britain and northwestern Europe. Eastern and southern Europeans were allowed into Canada before the Great Depression only in the numbers thought to be needed to perform work that Canadian residents avoided. Although immigrants were not labelled 'non-preferred' in public documents, both the term and its implications were sufficiently well known to elicit complaints from 'citizens of standing' in 'non-preferred' countries,[9] and from the 'non-preferred' immigrants themselves.[10]

One clear expression both of the perceived inferiority of people of eastern and southern European origin in Canada and of the distinct conditions that shaped racial classification in the United States and Canada was the exclusion of 'peripheral' Europeans, along with immigrants of Asian and African descent, from 'better neighbourhoods' in Canadian cities by legally accepted covenants. Canadian scholars have yet to analyse these instruments of residential segregation systematically. James Walker's study of a Canada-wide collection of restrictive covenants by legal scholar Walter Tarnopolsky suggests important regional variations, based on the population make-up of different provinces. Walker suggests that in Nova Scotia such covenants were directed mostly against Blacks, while in British Columbia they targeted people of Asian descent first and foremost.[11] Whether restrictions in these provinces extended to some groups of European descent is not clear. In central Canada such covenants did target eastern and southern Europeans as well, including Jews. A 1936 study of restrictions against Jewish ownership and tenancy in Hamilton by the Council of Jewish Organizations of Hamilton and the Canadian Jewish Congress (CJC) reveals the character of restrictions against minorities of European origin. Some of the covenants barred 'any person of objectionable race.' Others named the 'objectionable races': 'Negroes, Asiatics, Italians, Bulgarians, Austrians, Servians, Roumanians, Turks, Armenians, Jews or Greeks.' Very significantly, not one of the nineteen surveys examined – mostly from the interwar period – limited restrictions to people of colour. Covenants concerning modest neighbourhoods tended to specify a narrower range of groups: one excluded 'any person of the Polack, Italian or any Colored Race,' another, 'Italians, Poles, Hungarians or any person of a colored race.' The exclusion only of foreign-born Italians, Greeks, and Jews in some of the Hamilton covenants implied that these groups – presumably because of their capacity to assimilate into Canadian society – were perceived as superior to people of colour, all of whom, even the Canadian-born, were excluded.[12] Yet these Canadian covenants did not reflect the type of collaboration among all groups of European descent to keep people of African descent out of 'white' neighbourhoods in the United States. David Roediger believes that what prompted realtors and developers in American cities to include groups of European origin in 'all inclusive white neighbourhoods' was neither a liberal impulse nor a decline of their suspicion of southern and eastern European groups, but their perception of groups from any part of Europe as superior to African Americans. Minorities of European descent, for whom home ownership was extremely important, learned the advantages of 'whiteness' from such covenants; they became participants in, rather than the victims of, campaigns of residential segregation.[13] These different responses reflected the differences in the ethnic make-up of the populations north and south of the border, not the absence or weakness of racism in Canada. The number of African Canadians was far too small to elicit the type of fears aroused by the migration of African Americans to the northern United States. The 1941 census classified African Canadians, along with other numerically small groups, under the catch-all category of 'other.' In many Canadian cities, including Hamilton, the number of people of colour was thus quite small. Here, 'peripheral' Europeans represented the main danger of depreciating land values in the neighbourhoods where they settled. Similarly, in most cities they were the ones whose habits and practices were deemed objectionable: their cooking was deemed to create odours and their entertainments on Sundays to generate noises offensive to 'Canadian' residents.[14]

As Constance Backhouse has argued, although the racial identity of the dominant white group was splintered in many directions, a 'racial chasm' separated such subgroups from people of African, Asian, and Native descent.[15] Not surprisingly given Canada's imperial connections, the proximity of the United States, and the easy access to both British and American publications, Anglo-Canadians were not oblivious to the privileges of 'whiteness.' Anecdotal sources reveal that eastern and southern Europeans were at times denigrated as being non-white. Yet, with the exception of the 1917 elections, when even naturalized members of European minority groups lost their franchise, European immigrants could secure citizenship rights. Such rights were denied to people of Asian descent, although not to African Canadians. As noted above, moreover, the 1941 census classifications traced the racial designation of most children through the father, but underscored the unassimilability of people of colour by assigning children to the 'black, yellow or brown races,' if either their fathers or their mothers belonged to those 'races,' and describing children of mixed 'white and Indian blood,' regardless of the gender of the Native parent, as 'Half-breeds.'

Yet, although skin colour was so significant to racial assignment in Canada, purported racial inferiority and superiority were most often not expressed in terms of colour. Even more tellingly, colour was not central to the self-definition of 'inbetween' people. Indeed, given the uneven geographical distribution of people of colour in Canada, eastern and southern Europeans were the only significant groups of racialized 'others' in many communities. The differences between the make-up of the populations of Canada and the United States go a long way towards explaining the differences in racial discourse in the two countries. Most importantly, the weakness of the institution of slavery in Canada's past along with racist immigration policies meant that, in contrast to the United States, the number of people of African descent in Canada remained small until the last decades of the twentieth century. Consequently, the type of black-white polarization that some scholars place at the core of American racial thought did not develop in Canada. To claim that immigrants from the 'peripheries' of Europe were initially perceived as 'non-white,' and that they 'became white' in the course of their integration into Canadian society, would be, to use Arnesen's terms, to oversimplify a complex and multifaceted process of racialization. This study examines the construction of racial classification in wartime by Anglo-Canadian (and to a lesser extent French Canadian) state officials, employers, and workers, and the impact of such classification on minority workers. It also explores minority workers' self-identification in response to such racialization.

Because French Canadians occupied a unique position in the classification of Canada's peoples in wartime, they do not figure prominently in this study. Although some of them complained of discrimination in the labour force and in the armed forces, they did not organize protests against employment discrimination.[16] At the same time, moreover, French Canadians also occupied prominent positions governing state-minority relations. From 1942 to the end of the war, for example, a French Canadian, Major-General L.R. LaFlèche, headed the Department of National War Services, which oversaw relations between the state and minority groups. Other French Canadians held positions in the agencies established by the government to mobilize minorities behind the war effort.[17] Access to such positions, which were closed to members of racialized minorities, offers a clear example of the difference between French Canadians and the minority groups discussed here. French Canadian leaders could advocate more effectively for disadvantaged members of their group. In 1941, when he was still associate deputy minister of the Department of National War Services, for example, Major-General LaFlèche advised officials in the Department of Labour that skilled French Canadians were denied positions in war industries because they did not speak English. Such exclusion, he noted, reflected the dominance of Anglo-Canadians in the ownership and management of armament factories. The Department of Labour responded by offering French Canadian applicants pre-employment classes in technical English.[18]

By illuminating state complicity in the racialization of workers, this study's focus on racist employment discrimination sheds new light on the role of the state in wartime Canada. Up to now, studies of the relationship between the state and minority groups during the Second World War have concentrated largely on the Nationalities Branch of the Department of National War Services and the Committee on Cooperation in Canadian Citizenship. Because these two agencies were created by the federal government specifically to mobilize minority groups behind Canada's war effort and to increase group harmony by familiarizing English and French Canadians with minority groups and their contributions to Canadian society, their records offer rich and readily accessible sources for studying state-minority relations in wartime. Some scholars believe that such endeavours marked the first step in citizenship training or in Canada's progress towards a tolerant and inclusive national policy of multiculturalism.[19] Others characterize these undertakings as Eurocentric and ineffectual.[20] The most recent analysis maintains that the government, dissatisfied with the work of the Nationalities Branch, adopted a new and different approach to citizenship education by the end of the war.[21] Whatever their conclusions, the focus of scholars on the Nationalities Branch and the Committee on Cooperation offers only a partial view of state-minority relations in wartime. The officials of many other government departments and agencies also dealt with racialized minority workers, and as this study will show, their collusion with racist employers and workers helped to block the mobility of minority workers in the labour force throughout the war. The state's complicity both reflected and legitimized racist views widely held in Canadian society both prior to and during the Second World War.

By adopting a top-down approach to state-minority relations in wartime, existing studies also obscure the role played by minority group members – educated elites and ordinary workers – in challenging employment discrimination. Educated elites among minority group members were able to respond to discrimination in a highly articulate way. Newspaper owners, journalists, lawyers, clergy, teachers, and some labour organizers had the education, confidence, and means to protest against discrimination and articulate views on integration into Canadian society. They knew English, were familiar with Canadian laws and institutions, and were the most likely to have connections to mainstream society. Their views offer an important insight into how these relatively privileged segments of minority groups envisioned integration into the labour force, and into Canadian society more broadly.

An important component of the protest against employment discrimination consisted of documenting its nature and extent. Minority activists believed that the blatant contradiction between Canada's declared war aim of fighting the racism of the Nazis and racist discrimination at home, combined with the high demand for labour and state control over the labour force, created propitious circumstances for challenging employment discrimination. The records of voluntary organizations established by racialized minority groups, especially by Jews and African Canadians, compose the second important body of evidence on which this study relies. These sources, some of them located in smaller archives, and many written in languages other than English or French, are less well known than the records generated by state agencies. Yet they are essential for understanding employment discrimination and ideas of identity and the rights of citizenship from the perspective of minority group members. Unlike most studies on state-minority relations in wartime Canada, this book juxtaposes state policy and ideas of race and citizenship in civil society. It adopts the methods of social historians – often neglected in recent times in favour of linguistic or discourse analysis focused on leaders, policy makers, and educated elites – to study this relationship from the vantage point of targeted minorities, thereby offering a new perspective of state policy. Through the examination of the role of various segments of civil society – such as middle-class, educated, and politically conservative or liberal minority group members; radical racialized workers and activists; and English Canadian critics of various ideological leanings – this study also reveals the limitations and contradictions of the different sources on this topic.

Perhaps no feature reveals the value of sources generated by minority group members themselves than the light they shed on the wartime experience of minority women in the workplace. These sources reveal that women, as well as men, suffered from and challenged racist employment discrimination. Yet, because studies of gender discrimination during the Second World War (such as Ruth Roach Pierson's 'They're Still Women After All': The Second World War and Canadian Womanhood and Jennifer Stéphen's Pick One Intelligent Girl: Employability, Domesticity, and the Gendering of Canada's Welfare State, 1939–1947) focus largely on the role of the state and the attitudes of policy makers and of the professionals in their employ, these studies say little about the additional racist barriers that minority women faced.[22] State officials in charge of women's employment during the war appear to have been unconcerned about the race or ethnicity of women workers, probably because they assumed that women would withdraw from paid employment at war's end. Perhaps because they saw only 'foreign' men as potential threats, officials in charge of protecting national security were equally unconcerned about minority women. Conversely, sources generated by minority groups that shed light on racist employment discrimination and the protest against it say nothing about the gender-based discrimination that minority women faced. The silence of the sources on this subject reveals that, as Ruth Frager and Alice Kessler-Harris argue, both in Canada and in the United States the focus on racism most often overshadowed discrimination against women in the workforce even among minority group activists, male or female.[23] Consequently, gender-equity and anti-racist campaigns seldom intersected.

To draw attention in the mainstream press to racist employment discrimination and to their campaigns against it, minority activists succeeded in harnessing both wartime egalitarian rhetoric and demand for labour. This study thus also relies on wartime newspapers and magazines. Large numbers of relevant newspaper clippings can be found in the repositories of government departments and voluntary associations. A systematic examination of a series of newspapers for the war years supplements these more specialized collections: *Le Devoir*, *Globe and Mail*, *Hamilton Spectator*, *Montreal Gazette*, *Niagara Falls Review*, *St. Catharines Standard*, *Toronto Star*, *Welland Tribune*, *Winnipeg Free Press*, *Canadian Forum*, and *Saturday Night*.[24]

Educated elites, however, were not the only members of minority groups who protested against employment discrimination. Working-class women and men, who faced the consequences of employment discrimination on a daily basis, also fought against it. Admittedly, they were generally poorly educated peasants or workers whose brawn had opened Canada's doors to them. Long hours of hard labour and frequent searches for jobs allowed them little opportunity to learn English or familiarize themselves with Canadian ways outside the workplace. The spread of industrial unions in wartime Canada, however, offered an avenue of protest even to those whose command of English and understanding of Canadian laws and institutions were limited. Organized labour courted minority group support, and minority protest was an important force in the great expansion of organized labour – industrial unions in particular – during the war years. The impact of minority protest within the labour movement not only influenced the orientation of union leadership, but also played a part in state building in the late 1940s by laying the foundations for anti-discrimination legislation and human rights commissions. In a recent re-evaluation of his path-breaking book, *Labor's War at Home*, Nelson Lichtenstein questions the book's characterization of the consequences of the wartime bargain between labour and the state as detrimental for ordinary workers. He now believes that the harnessing of wartime patriotic egalitarianism by increasingly organized workers, especially African Americans and Mexicans, and the opening of avenues for the expression and redress of grievances by minority workers (through such state institutions as the National Labor Relations Board, the National War Labor Board, and especially the Fair Employment Practices Committee) combined to constrain management's freedom. Through grievance and arbitration procedures, 'workplace contractualism' offered advantages to most workers in most places. Although it did not eliminate seniority systems designed to protect the advantages of white workers, the new system created a significant breakthrough in rights consciousness among African American workers in particular, and hence in their struggle for citizenship rights.[25] This book suggests a similar need to focus on the negotiation between minority workers and the state to understand industrial relations in Canada.

The Co-operative Commonwealth Federation (CCF) and the Communist Party of Canada (CPC), both of whom saw their main constituency as the working class, joined the anti-discrimination campaigns of labour unions. They too sought and gained support among minority group members by targeting employment discrimination specifically. Consequently, in addition to the press and archives of labour organizations, the records of these left-wing parties constitute important sources for this study.

Civic-minded intellectuals of more conservative and liberal leanings also recognized the injustice of racist discrimination. Some of them noted that such discrimination expressed itself in denying work to racialized minorities altogether or in restricting the types of jobs that were open to them. Many of these intellectuals were concerned primarily about minority groups of European origin, sometimes because they had little contact with any other racialized groups, and sometimes because they too subscribed to the racist notion that certain groups, especially people of colour, were incapable of performing any but menial jobs. Since these men and women belonged to privileged middle-class circles, they were not familiar with the circumstances of racialized workers. That is why many of them thought of ending employment discrimination as a gradual process rather than a matter of great urgency. They could thus hold on to their notion that equal opportunity for all could be attained in Canadian society through familiarizing English and French Canadians with the 'special gifts' of minority groups and the contributions they made to Canadian society, and through citizenship education for minority group members. Some of these advocates of greater tolerance, moreover, were themselves suspicious of the political left, of organized labour, and of state regulation of economic and social life. Such suspicions pitted them against the aspirations and strategies of minority group members and their labour and left-wing allies.

This study begins by exploring the nature and extent of racist employment discrimination in Canada during the Second World War. Part I also analyses the extent of and reasons for state collusion with such discriminatory practices. Part II focuses on minority group resistance to employment discrimination. Chapter 2 considers resistance and protest by Jews, whose anti-discrimination campaigns were the most highly organized and hence the best documented among the campaigns mounted by the victims of employment discrimination. The next two chapters look at resistance by other 'racialized' groups: Chapter 3 considers African Canadians, eastern and southern Europeans, and Chapter 4 looks at the disenfranchised Chinese, Japanese, and Native Canadians. Part III focuses on the support anti-discrimination campaigns received from members of Canada's dominant ethnic groups, especially English Canadians. The views and actions of conservative and liberal critics of racism form the subject of Chapter 5, while Chapter 6 analyses the participation of the CCF, the CPC, and organized labour in the fight against discrimination. The final section (and chapter) returns to a consideration of relations between the state and minority groups. It attempts to explain why the Nationalities Branch and the Committee on Cooperation in Canadian Citizenship, state agencies designed to integrate minority groups into Canadian society, had apparently little knowledge of, and hence contact with, campaigns by minority group members to achieve the same ends.

PART ONE

Invidious Distinctions

1

Employment Discrimination and State Complicity

The Denial of Employment and Relief

Calls for the dismissal of 'foreigners' from their jobs arose almost immediately after the outbreak of the Second World War and intensified in 1940, following the sudden and rapid successes of German troops in western Europe and Italy's entry into the war. Thousands of people across Canada lost their jobs. They came from a wide variety of occupations: miners in Cape Breton, steel workers in Hamilton, department store and hotel employees in Toronto and Winnipeg, municipal employees in Windsor and Calgary, and shipyard workers in Vancouver. They included not only workers who were born in, or could trace their origins to, countries now at war with Canada, such as Germany, Italy, and Japan, but also men and women born in, or whose ancestors were born in, countries allied with Canada. They also included both naturalized British and foreign subjects.[1]

The difficulties of many of these 'foreign' workers were compounded by their inability to obtain relief. Many dismissed able-bodied workers were denied relief on the grounds that they were capable of working. This placed them in a 'state of suspended animation with no means of support,' in the words of T.C. Davis, associate deputy minister of the Department of National War Services (DNWS).[2] Because immigrant workers had been disproportionately represented among the unemployed during the Great Depression, the hardship caused by the combined loss of jobs and the denial of relief was great, especially in Ontario and Alberta, where the provincial governments decided to cut off relief to all non-naturalized immigrants.[3]

The ostensible reason for dismissals and the denial of relief was that these workers were potentially disloyal – enemies capable of all manner of subversive activity, including sabotage. Reports from Europe concerning fifth column activity in the Netherlands and Norway fired the imagination of many Canadians – private citizens, public servants, and elected officials – and convinced them of the need to be vigilant.[4] Some of them harboured quite specific fears: that Japanese Canadian women employed in British Columbia fish canneries would poison herring intended for British soldiers, that Finnish loggers would destroy lumber required for making airplanes, or that German miners with Nazi sympathies would sabotage Nova Scotian mines.[5] Others expressed more sweeping distrust of all 'foreigners.' Premier Mitchell Hepburn of Ontario justified denying relief to resident aliens by arguing that payments to these 'potential enemies' would draw relief away from 'the citizens of Ontario.' Mayor Ralph C. Day of Toronto explained that even resident aliens who were willing to take an oath of allegiance would still not have the same obligations as a citizen of Canada. Providing them with relief would thus be tantamount to preferential treatment. He suggested that resident aliens should have to work in exchange for relief.[6] E.A. Horton, Ontario's director of unemployment relief, stated publicly that there should be no discrimination among relief recipients, even as he enhanced suspicion against foreign-born relief recipients by urging municipal and provincial relief administrators to increase vigilance by more frequent investigations of relief recipients' homes. Even the naturalized among the foreign-born, Horton argued, still retained 'considerable sympathy for the cause of the enemy at war with His Majesty the King.' He called upon relief administrators to report any subversive statements or sympathies to the Ontario Provincial Police or the RCMP without delay and gave them discretionary powers to discontinue relief assistance 'to proven "agitators" or "sympathizers."'[7] A Saskatoon relief officer put the lesser eligibility of people of central European origin in explicitly racist terms in the fall of 1940, when he argued that 'there should be two scales of relief, one for central Europeans and one for "white people."'[8]

The reasons for the participation of municipal and provincial governments in anti-alien campaigns at the war's outset are not difficult to find. Both levels of government stood to gain materially and politically from denying relief to 'foreigners.' In 1939, when large numbers of Canadians were still unemployed, responsibility for relief was split among the three levels of government: municipal, provincial, and federal. When Ontario Premier Hepburn and Toronto Mayor Day spoke out against foreign-born recipients they may have been hoping to force the federal government to assume the costs of caring for resident aliens. The premier may also have been influenced by anti-foreign letters, such as the one from the town council of Kenora, declaring that precious resources should not be spent in wartime on the foreign-born who did not see fit to assume the responsibilities of citizenship.[9] Whatever their motivations, the public statements of such influential figures as the Ontario premier and the Toronto mayor were clearly inflammatory. They could not have been unaware that their official communications and public statements could fuel anti-foreign sentiments. They may even have been counting on the appeal of such sentiments to Anglo-Canadian voters.

A clear indication that more than war-created anxiety concerning enemy aliens was at work in the years between 1939 and 1941 was the vulnerability of people with accents or foreign-sounding names, even if they were born in Canada or in countries allied with Canada. These women and men lost their jobs because employment was still scarce in Canada in the early war years, and many Canadians of British descent believed that they had greater claim to them than so-called foreigners.[10] Their anti-foreign sentiments were based on their understanding of race, not nationality. The author of a letter to the *Windsor Daily Star*, for example, drew no distinctions among them when he asked why 'the foreign element such as Italians, Jews, Russians, Pol[es were] all working and holding down good jobs, while ... English-speaking boys [were] on welfare, walking the streets.'[11] Many Canadians believed that some groups of immigrants were less deserving of jobs because they did not – indeed could not – form part of the Canadian nation. Allegedly inherent, or racial, differences from Canada's two 'founding races,' the British and the French, relegated such workers to perpetual 'foreignness.'

The case of mine workers of Italian origin in Nova Scotia, dismissed from their jobs following Italy's entry into the war in June 1940, sheds light on the nature and causes of such discriminatory attitudes as well as on the hardship they created. While District 26 of the United Mine Workers of America voted to allow foreign-born men to return to work, Anglo-Canadian miners in two collieries refused to work with them. That summer the unemployed 'foreigners' provided for themselves and their families by supplementing their small relief allowances with the produce of their gardens. By the fall of 1940, however, the workers were finding it impossible to subsist. As winter approached, their children's clothing was so threadbare that some were unable to go to school.[12] Clarence Gillis, CCF MP for Glace Bay South, Nova Scotia, believed that for local, young Anglo-Canadian men, who had never had any work because of the Great Depression, Italy's participation in the war provided an excuse to throw 'foreigners' out of work. They resented the fact that 'such a large number of foreigners [were] gainfully employed while they, the natives of the country, [were] walking the. street.'[13]

The seriousness of this type of discrimination – even after the economic boom generated by war eliminated unemployment – came to light as part of a study conducted by the Manpower Labour Supply Investigation Committee, established in July 1941. The committee put at 15,096 in rural Manitoba alone the number of men of Polish, Russian, Ukrainian, Czech, and Slovak descent who should be considered 'as one' with Canadians in the war effort because they were 'of the same stock as the races actively engaged in fighting the Axis Powers in Europe.' Yet, even when shortages in skilled labour began to develop, eastern Canadian employers resisted hiring such workers. Employers interviewed for the Manpower study declared that they would not hire these men unless they were 'forced to do so by circumstances.'[14] The case of the 'Slavic' workers from Alberta who were unable to find skilled work in Ontario illustrates the implication of surnames as signifiers of racial difference.[15] In the context of wartime Canada, this perceived difference meant that not only the loyalties but also the skills of Canadians bearing 'foreign' names were suspect. There was a noteworthy correlation between the groups deemed unqualified to take jobs in war industries and those designated as 'non-preferred' by immigration officials before the war and admitted to Canada only to fill the least desirable jobs in agriculture, construction, domestic service, lumbering, mining, and railway maintenance.[16] Because such immigrants and their children had traditionally filled menial jobs, many Canadians came to question their suitability for more skilled work.[17] In Winnipeg employers attributed the decline in quality of job applicants to the increased numbers of 'Non-Anglo-Saxons' among them.[18] A Toronto machinery company employer reported that 50 per cent of the persons seeking work at his gate bore foreign names, and were not employed by him.[19]

Canada's leading newspapers took notice of this type of discrimination and clearly identified it as racist. In December 1941, for example, both the *Globe and Mail* and the *Montreal Star* reported the case of Myrm Chknoski, convicted in the Toronto Police Court of a breach of the National Resources Mobilization Act. The act required registration by all Canadian residents over the age of sixteen, men and women alike. The purpose of national registration was to create an inventory of the mechanical and industrial skills of Canada's workforce, as well as of men available for home defence. Racial origin formed part of the information sought by the government, and was duly noted on the card each worker received upon registration. In principle, only those possessing registration cards were eligible for employment. Although Chknoski complied with the act and obtained a registration card, his 'foreign-sounding name' prevented him from getting work. He was arrested and tried because in desperation he gave himself an 'Anglo-Saxon' name on a second card, on which he forged the signature of a deputy registrar. A *Globe and Mail* editorial sympathized with Chknoski's plight and ascribed the inability of men like him to obtain work to 'racial prejudice.'[20] The *Montreal Star* also stressed that such discrimination, which was not uncommon, reflected 'a state of national adolescence,' a refusal to recognize 'that Canada is no longer a private preserve for Anglo-Saxons and French Canadians, but a partnership of all of the races of Europe and many of Asia, pledged to a common effort, to a common ideal and moving towards a common destiny.'[21]

The Unpatriotic and Dangerous 'Foreigners'

The widely held – though inaccurate – belief that foreigners were not volunteering to serve overseas and were not required to train for home defence exacerbated hostility towards them. The *Vancouver Sun*, for example, reported that:

> While Canadian young men are volunteering and having to enter training for home defense ... many hundreds, perhaps some thousands of alien youths are having a good time in British Columbia. They are taking the jobs of the Canadian boys. They are earning better pay than they have ever known before. They are acquiring new skills that will serve them well when the war is over. They are digging in.

The article went on to suggest that foreign-born males who could be trusted be conscripted, and those who were not trustworthy be compelled to perform some other public duty, lest this state of affairs breed racial hatred.[22] The complaints of some Vancouver residents, that Chinese Canadians were becoming rich because of the war and now refused to remain within the confines of Chinatown, confirmed the *Vancouver Sun*'s predictions about the intensification of racial hatred.[23] Without knowledge of enlistment figures, many English Canadians concluded that while their sons were away fighting, the sons of 'foreigners' were staying home and making money.[24] Members of the Vancouver Island Farmers' Council, for example, maintained that 'Oriental' farmers benefitted from unfair advantages over 'European' farmers because they did not have to train for home defence and were not enlisting in the armed forces. They wrote: 'The result has been that large numbers of white farmers have had to plant their land to grass while the Oriental ... is taking up land formerly used by European farmers.'[25] Farmers around Cooksville, Ontario, were 'stewing' because their sons and husbands were 'in the thick of war while those damn foreigners [Jews and Italians]' were 'running Toronto markets and fruit stands and growing rich.'[26] Suspicions that Jews were profiteering through black market activities instead of enlisting were especially widespread.[27]

Some employers found it advantageous to stoke the flames of anti-alien sentiments. Blaming 'foreigners' for labour activism and unrest was a convenient way to discredit the labour movement, especially the Congress of Industrial Organizations (CIO) which was making inroads among Canadian workers. In 1941, when the Packinghouse Workers' Organizing Committee (PWOC) successfully enlisted workers at the Canada Packers plant in Toronto, for example, J.S. Willis, the company's personnel director, accused the union of attempting to sabotage the war effort by slowing down production so that 'Canadian' men who could have been at the front were held back in Canada. His 'proof' of union disloyalty to the allied cause was the assertion that about 70 per cent of the men who chose to support the PWOC rather than the company union already in place were 'foreigners,' and that one of their leaders, Adam Borsk, was of German origin and sympathetic to the German cause. Based on surveillance of the plant, the RCMP supported Willis's allegations.[28] Police reports described Borsk as a 'White Russian' Nazi sympathizer, and warned that he was in a position to set the pace of production in the plant.[29] Fears about the influence of 'foreigners' at Canada Packers receded, but only after the CIO's organizing efforts were defeated by the company's insistence that the vote on the union be conducted in all its plants and by the dismissal of Adam Borsk.[30] By then, however, the publicity surrounding the case no doubt intensified suspicions against foreign-born workers.

In the fall of 1941, members of Local 199 of the United Auto Workers (UAW) voted to strike at McKinnon Industries of St Catharines. The efforts of management to exploit anti-alien sentiment to discredit both the union and the strike were so transparent that they failed to enlist some of the Anglo-Canadian workers they targeted. The company's representative, known to workers in St Catharines as Major Carmichael, or the Digger, enlisted group leaders and other Anglo-Canadian workers in a secret organization, the Inner Circle Counter-Sabotage Committee, ostensibly to combat any form of sabotage in the plant. In meetings held under cover of darkness in a field on the outskirts of town, the Digger began by advising all those present to watch for possible sabotage by employees of 'foreign extraction.' The foreign-born, according to Carmichael, were the 'Quislings' and the 'fifth columnists.' Most of what he had to say, however, was directed against the CIO. He attempted to discredit the UAW by claiming that Local 199 was dominated by 'foreign-born' people and arguing that strike action in the plant would be tantamount to sabotage. Fred Steeve, a McKinnon employee who had been invited to the meeting, believed that members of the Inner Circle Counter-Sabotage Committee were responsible for putting signs up in different plants and throughout St Catharines reading 'We are at war. Speak English only.' Donald Schoures, another pro-union worker invited to the secret meetings, soon concluded that the Inner Circle Counter-Sabotage Committee was set up as an anti-union organization rather than an anti-sabotage group.[31]

In their effort to discredit the rival CIO, even some officials of the Canadian Federation of Labour (CFL) purported to see links between 'foreigners,' the CIO's organizing drives in Canada, and the threat to war production. They used the term 'foreigner' to describe both American control of the CIO and the workers it sought to organize. CFL secretary-treasurer W.T. Burford claimed that the recruitment by the United Mine Workers of America, a CIO affiliate, of 'a thousand men, mostly foreigners and farm hands' who worked seasonally in Saskatchewan's lignite coal mines, prevented the CFL from honouring its commitment to the dominion government to avoid labour disputes.[32] Such accusations fell on receptive ears because many Canadians believed in the political untrustworthiness, and especially proclivity to radicalism, of people of southern and eastern European descent.[33]

Canada's powerful minister of munitions and supply, C.D. Howe, blamed a strike at the Arvida Aluminum Smelter, which produced almost half of the aluminum for the allied powers, on a man reported to be of German origin, and ordered the military to intervene. Fortunately, the local commander refused, stating that 'a strike of Canadian workers in Canada was not an illegal action.' Intelligence assessments of the short-lived strike later revealed that it was caused by low wages and the intense heat in the 'pot room,' staffed by newly hired men who could not 'stand up to it like experienced men.'[34]

Jews and African Canadians

Racism was clearly at work when Canadian-born Jews and African Canadians, who could hardly be accused of harbouring loyalties to Canada's wartime enemies, were barred from certain types of employment. Such racism, of course, predated the war, but it came to light during the war because activists in these two minority groups believed that the incongruity of calling upon them to make sacrifices on behalf of the nation through enlistment while simultaneously denying them the right to equal treatment in the labour market created a unique opportunity to fight against racism and discrimination in Canada. For ammunition in this campaign, they actively collected evidence of employment discrimination.

The Joint Public Relations Committee of the Canadian Jewish Congress and B'nai B'rith (JPRC), established in 1938 to oppose anti-Semitism specifically and racial and religious discrimination generally, decided to take action because state-owned or crown companies as well as private industry involved in war production 'consistently refused employment to Jews solely on racial or religious grounds.'[35] The JPRC assembled copies of job application forms that included questions about the 'race' and 'religion' of prospective applicants, and solicited information from Jews who had experienced or witnessed employment discrimination. Despite fears that such testimony could render them unemployable, Jews in various lines of work responded. Some of them, probably those less proficient in English, provided oral accounts and then signed affidavits, while others wrote letters describing their experiences.

The cases of Hy Lampert and Gertrude Green illustrate the nature of discrimination against Jewish blue-collar workers. Lampert responded to a 1942 newspaper advertisement for general help in a machine shop of a Toronto plant, for which he had both training and some experience. When he identified himself as Jewish in response to a question concerning his religion, he was informed that the job was filled. Yet advertisements for the same position continued to appear in Toronto newspapers. Wary of anti-Semitism, Gertrude Green inquired whether a 'Jewish girl would be employed' before going to an interview for a job at Canadian Acme Screw and Gear in Toronto. The answer she received was unequivocal: 'they had never done so and had no intentions of hiring them [Jews] in the future,' and therefore, she should not bother going in for an interview.[36]

According to the Ontario division of the Canadian Jewish Congress (CJC), the extent of employment discrimination against Jews was best illustrated by their 'infinitesimally' small numbers in war industries.[37] H.M. Caiserman, of the CJC's head office in Montreal, identified Canadian Marconi, RCA Victor, Royal Typewriters, and Canadian Car & Foundry as some of the Montreal companies not hiring Jews.[38] As late as the spring of 1943, the CJC claimed that because the National Selective Service (NSS) was not sending them to jobs consonant with their skills and goals, thousands of Jewish men, boys, and girls were standing in line for hours at the Montreal Selective Service to obtain open permits which would allow them to approach places of employment on their own.[39]

African Canadians also publicized, and protested against, employment discrimination. War production actually somewhat reduced the segregation of Blacks within the labour force. For example, some African Canadian women, the majority of whom were forced to work as domestic servants until the 1940s, could now find employment in factories. As one of them explained, 'We weren't allowed to go into factory work until Hitler started the war, and then they would beg you, "Would you like a job in my factory?"'[40] Yet by no means did all factories welcome African Canadian workers. A *Globe and Mail* reporter discovered in October 1942 that only a small number of the four thousand African Canadians in Toronto were able to find work in industry. Although their own acceptance of racist stereotypes played an important part in job allocation, employers sometimes blamed objections raised by other employees for this type of discrimination.[41] Automobile manufacturers, for example, sought Black men specifically for employment in physically demanding jobs in the powerhouses and foundries. When they found too few in Ontario, they travelled to Nova Scotia in search of African Canadian male workers. As for African Canadian women, racism combined with gender-based discrimination kept them out of automobile factories.[42]

White-Collar Work

Even as a booming economy enhanced chances for upward mobility for many other Canadians starting by 1941, racism continued to block Jews, African Canadians, and people of eastern and southern European descent from white-collar occupations. Reverend Harvey Forster, superintendent of the All People's Missions in the Niagara peninsula, reported such discrimination in Welland, an industrial community with an exceptionally high proportion of people of eastern and southern European descent. Officials of a war plant, seeking clerical workers at the end of the school year in 1942, requested the names of the best high school graduates from the local school board, on which Forster served. The list sent by the board included the names of pupils of central European origin. 'Don't send us foreigners; send us white men!' responded war plant officials.[43] In Ontario, Canadian-born teachers of eastern European descent were refused employment by 'Anglo-Saxon' school boards.[44] Jewish teachers were generally not hired by rural schools, and such discrimination made it difficult for them to get jobs in big cities, since city schools preferred to hire teachers with experience.[45] In Quebec, where Jewish pupils attended Protestant schools, the Protestant school board did not hire Jewish male teachers. It hired Jewish 'girls,' but only for schools where Jewish pupils predominated.[46]

The entry of Jewish women and men into other white-collar occupations was similarly restricted. During the war years, Jews were employed by state agencies. They found it difficult to obtain professional jobs in private businesses, however, even those engaged in war production. For example, after trying unsuccessfully to enlist in the armed forces, Norman Cowan, a trained accountant, sought work in Toronto. Six different firms turned him down, despite Cowan's excellent references from previous employers and auditors. Three of the six, including Price Waterhouse, told him outright that they did not employ Jews. Small wonder that the disappointed Cowan wrote the JPRC about a 'boycott against the Jews.'[47]

Adeline Natanson had similar experiences. An interviewer at the war plant of the John Inglis Company in Toronto, having declared that her educational background and experience qualified her for the job, was

ready to hire her as a typist. As an afterthought he inquired as to her
'nationality and racial origin.' When she told him that she was Jewish,
he replied that 'unfortunately, for simply *that* reason *only*,' he would
be unable to hire her, explaining that he had to abide by office policy.
The interviewer apparently regretted turning Natanson away and tried
to place her by calling a friend who managed a department of another
war plant, only to discover that concerning the employment of 'those of
Hebrew nationality for clerical work' the Small Arms Branch adhered
to the same policy as the John Inglis Company.[48]

African Canadians also continued to be barred from white-collar
occupations. In Montreal, Janet Long, field secretary of the Girls' Cot-
tage School, protested publicly on behalf of 'coloured girls.' 'Most employers did not wish coloured employees for office work,' she stated.[49]
Frances E. Upton, registrar and school visitor of the Association of
Registered Nurses in Quebec, explained restrictive practices in nursing
in Montreal by observing that if 'Negroes were admitted to the pro-
fession, white mothers would decline permission to their daughters to
train as nurses.' She added that coloured girls did not work as hard
as white girls, did not like to be disciplined, and would not bring the
same 'refinement' to their jobs.[50] In Toronto, Black university graduates
used the pages of the *Globe and Mail* to publicize their inability to obtain
white-collar jobs.[51]

State Intervention

We will never know the precise number of those affected by dismissals,
the denial of relief, and restriction to menial jobs. The problem was sufficiently great, however, to concern Canada's ministers of labour, justice,
and national war services, and such leading civil servants in Ottawa as
Norman Robertson, deputy minister of external affairs, and T.C. Davis,
associate deputy minister of the DNWS. These officials recognized that
those affected included many naturalized British subjects and so-called
friendly aliens.[52] Officials in charge of the federal-provincial War Emergency Training Programme also complained about employment discrimination. In November 1941, J.H. Ross, regional director for Alberta,
wrote to alert R.F. Thompson, supervisor of training in Ottawa, that a
difficult situation was developing in Alberta and northern Saskatchewan because employers would not accept 'Canadian born trainees'
who were 'of foreign but naturalized parentage.' 'This action is most
unfair,' he added, because such men 'are accepted without question for

the Armed Forces.' Thompson in turn thought the matter grave enough to inform the Department of Munitions and Supply.[53] A few months later, at a conference of the training programme directors in Ottawa, several directors, lamenting that those born in Canada of 'non-Anglo-Saxon parentage' found it impossible to obtain employment, formally resolved to notify the proper authorities in order to challenge such discrimination.[54]

Since a large proportion of Canada's labour force was facing employment discrimination, Ottawa could simply not afford to ignore their plight. Officials in the Department of External Affairs (DEA) were among the first to consider acting against employment discrimination. Although only the fate of nationals of other countries fell within their mandate, they knew that such discriminatory treatment was not limited to enemy aliens but extended to naturalized Canadians of German and Italian origin and even to Canadian residents of other European origins, 'irrespective of their status under the Naturalization Act.'[55] By 1940, a small, interdepartmental committee under the leadership of the DEA – consisting of representatives of the DNWS, the RCMP, the Censorship Branch, the Custodian of Enemy Property, and others – started meeting to explore the possibilities of facilitating fuller and smoother participation of these groups in the war effort.[56] They focused almost exclusively on groups of European descent.

One of the first proposals of the committee was to create labour battalions in which men, unemployable because of their nationality or 'race' 'could be enlisted and put to useful work of national importance for the duration of the war.' The plan both acknowledged the existence of employment discrimination and sidestepped it. The proposed battalions would be open to individuals other than enemy aliens, who 'for one reason or another could not be usefully employed either in the defense forces, on essential war work or [in] public work.' The battalions would offer advantages both to those enlisted in them and to the government. Enlistees would have the opportunity to demonstrate their loyalty to Canada. The government would benefit because the battalions would provide labour in the country's defence such as 'coast defense work, camp construction, preparation of air training fields, completion of the trans-Canada and other arterial highways, possibly even the Alaska–British Columbia highway.' These units could additionally serve as agencies for assimilating immigrants, a responsibility which according to Norman Robertson had been neglected by the Canadian government. In the end this plan was not adopted, probably owing to fears that the battalions would displace other workers and thus intensify resentment against 'foreigners.'[57]

Another early plan called for the minister of labour to approach employers through the Canadian Manufacturers' Association, the Canadian Chamber of Commerce, the Canadian Association of Boards of Trade, and labour unions to put a stop to employment discrimination against workers of foreign extraction.[58] The Department of Labour issued a circular on 14 March 1941 urging employers and secretaries of trade unions not to discriminate against persons of foreign name or birth, whether citizens or residents, so long as they had demonstrated unquestioned loyalty to Canada.[59]

These state plans, however, were designed to deal only with the problems of workers of European descent. Although the circular stated that the help of 'various nationalities ... regardless of creed or racial origin' would be required to win the war, the fate of people of Asian origin – Japanese Canadians especially – was considered separately throughout the war. This was ostensibly because their concentration in British Columbia distinguished them from other minority groups. In fact, however, their distinct treatment had to do with the intensity of racism against Asian Canadians. The Committee on the Treatment of Aliens and Alien Property, for example, stated that the loyalties of Japanese Canadians were 'racial not national.'[60] A Special Committee on Orientals in British Columbia considered the establishment of separate civilian labour battalions for Japanese Canadians, after it decided that Chinese Canadians, 'East Indians,' and Canadian-born and naturalized people of Japanese descent should not be trained for home defence because an obligation to participate in such training would entitle them to enfranchisement. Those committee members most sympathetic to Canadians of Asian origin, such as Professor Henry Angus of the University of British Columbia, were the strongest supporters of the civilian battalion plan. Angus believed that such service would show the world that Canada was not racist and prove to Canadians that people of Japanese origin 'wished the triumph of the democratic countries.' Debates over remuneration, however, led first to the postponement and eventually to the abandonment of the formation of the battalions.[61]

Racism against people of Asian descent was also a key reason for Ottawa's failure to consider legislative remedies for employment discrimination. When the Department of Labour proposed an order in council in 1942 that would prohibit racial discrimination in war industries, Henry Angus, now an official of the Department of External Affairs, advised that such an order would conflict with pre-war provincial legislation limiting the employment of 'persons of the Chinese race' and of 'persons of other races by Chinese.' Angus added that such an order would place employers in a difficult situation if their employees, customers, or communities harboured racist attitudes towards Japanese Canadians.[62]

State Complicity

Not only did government officials not stop racist employment discrimination, they often actively colluded in racist practices, including ones that targeted people of eastern and southern European descent. As we have seen, the directors of the War Emergency Training Programme complained in 1941 that racist employment practices undermined the efficacy of the programme. But instead of challenging such exclusion, officials in charge of vocational training in some cases reinforced it by barring members of some racialized minority groups. During the first two years of the war, for example, some of those who trained young men for skilled work in the armed services believed there was no point in training 'Asiatics' and members of the 'coloured races' since they would not be admitted into the Royal Canadian Air Force (RCAF) in any event.[63] In 1942, employment discrimination led those in charge of training in Toronto to classify 'Jews, Negroes, Chinese' as 'problem cases,' along with 'Canadian children not of British origin (e.g., Canadian children of Italian or German origin),' 'people with relatives in the warring countries,' and 'people with foreign-sounding names.' In order not to 'waste time and money,' applicants from these groups were admitted to the training programmes only if they were sponsored by future employers.[64] Thus, minority workers could not always avail themselves of government training programmes to move out of the marginalized sectors of the economy to which they had been relegated.

Officials of the NSS, an agency established in 1942 to mobilize and ensure the most efficient use of the civilian labour force in war production, also collaborated with discriminatory employers, as did employees of the Unemployment Insurance Commission (UIC), whose offices were formally incorporated into the NSS structure. In principle every potential worker required the permission of an NSS officer to enter any new employment. Recent research suggests that many Canadians ignored NSS officers altogether, moving from one job to another on their own.[65] But some minority workers whose occupational mobility was constrained by racism attempted to use government offices to find better jobs. All too frequently they were sorely disappointed.

Guided by prevailing racial stereotypes, some NSS officials used information on 'racial origin' to discriminate against minority group members. In Windsor, for example, although the UAW district council pointed out that 'Chinese' were 'doing an excellent job of work in Ford,' NSS officials were sending Chinese workers to work in restaurants and laundries.[66] In Montreal, an NSS officer who was trying to rehabilitate Italians released from internment in 1943 maintained that 'Italians are adaptable to foundries, smelters and such kind of work.' He added that placing Italian workers in this type of heavy labour would not only give them the opportunity to earn decent wages but also help to 'relieve a shortage of certain fields for which they are most suitable.'[67] Racist stereotypes were even more damaging in the case of African Canadians. When the executive director of the Negro Community Centre in Montreal consulted the head of the city's NSS about employment of African Canadians, he was told, 'I can't do anything for your people, their I.Q. is too low.'[68] Such attitudes no doubt explained why 'coloured boys and girls' were being offered 'menial jobs, without regard for qualifications.'[69] Anti-Semitism led some NSS officials in Montreal to direct Jewish applicants only to jobs in 'lower or lowest brackets.'[70] It could not have been irrelevant in all these cases that the lower-paid, lower-status occupations were becoming more and more difficult to fill.

To be sure, not all NSS officials were racist. Some of them even belonged to racialized minority groups. A few Anglo-Canadian officials, moreover, spoke up against racist discrimination. For example, Verna McClure, an employment and claims officer for NSS, chaired the London Japanese Advisory Committee, which protested against racism that prevented Japanese Canadians from contributing to national life by earning a living in the occupations for which their training and experience qualified them.[71] Some Montreal NSS officials, not all of them Jewish, supplied the Canadian Jewish Congress with evidence of the anti-Semitic attitudes of their colleagues and with lists of employers who specified that they were unwilling to employ Jews.[72]

Many more state officials, however, who may or may not have subscribed to racist ideas, accepted such requests as 'no aliens and no Jews' from prospective employers.[73] The clearest evidence of such official collusion came from Jewish employers who sought to fill positions through the NSS or the UIC. UIC employees on several occasions asked prospective employer J.H. Gringorten of Canada Motor Products

Limited in Toronto, a plant for the assembly of aircraft and automobile fuses, 'whether nationality made any difference.' Upon receiving
a negative response, they added 'not even if they are Jewish?' These
questions troubled Gringorten, who believed that they planted the idea
of discriminating against prospective Jewish employees in the minds of
otherwise neutral employers. When he confronted one of the officials,
she explained that the questions were asked in the interest of the Jewish
applicants, 'who all too often' had been sent to 'places whose practice
was to discriminate against them, and it simply meant a waste of time
and carfare and general disillusionment for the applicant.'[74]

Targeted minorities, especially Jews and African Canadians, protested against such discrimination. In November 1942, representatives
of labour unions with large Jewish memberships such as the International Ladies' Garment Workers' Union and the Fur Workers' Union,
along with community activists, presented evidence of discrimination
against Jews to Elliott M. Little, who as chief of the NSS Board stood at
the helm of civilian and military mobilization in Canada. Percy Bengough, acting president of the Dominion Trades and Labour Congress,
accompanied the delegation. African Canadian community organizations, church groups, and youth clubs similarly publicized discrimination through interviews with the press and petitions and delegations to
the federal and provincial governments. Given what we know about
the complicity of their employees in racist employment practices, the
scepticism with which NSS authorities initially greeted these allegations appears disingenuous, to say the least.[75] The ensuing publicity
nevertheless convinced the NSS to warn employers that it would not
tolerate discrimination 'for reasons of race, color or creed.'[76] The NSS
prohibited the inclusion of questions concerning race and religion on
official registration and employment forms and warned employers that
'the practice of discrimination' might mean a 'shutting off of all labor
supplies for their plants.'[77]

Even after such classification on official forms was prohibited, however, employers continued to express their racial preferences, and NSS
officials attempted to comply. They inquired about the background of
applicants not in writing, however, but over the telephone or during interviews. About a year after discrimination based on race was officially
prohibited, the director of NSS issued an internal directive encouraging
such collusion with the racist requirements of employers. The new directive suggested that applying the anti-discrimination provisions too
rigidly had 'caused embarrassment both to applicants and employers.'

'Where good judgement would indicate that there is some possibility of real difficulty in the assimilation of the applicant into the organization of the prospective employer,' the instructions suggested, 'a preliminary enquiry should be made preferably by telephone to determine whether there are insurmountable obstacles in the way of acceptance of the applicant.'[78]

Whatever the motivation of NSS officials, state intervention in the labour market in wartime Canada had the effect of reinforcing the racialization of minority workers. As late as 1943, H.C. Stratton, manager of the Unemployment Insurance Commission in Windsor, seemed to see nothing wrong with following racist instructions received from prospective employers. In response to a complaint from Alvin McCurdy, president of the African Canadian Amherstburg Community Club, Stratton explained that when employers placed 'an order in this office for their help requirement' and specified 'age, weight, height, sometimes religion, race, etc.,' officers of the UIC had 'to choose applicants to meet these requirements' the best they could 'before making referrals.' 'I think you will see that our hands are more or less tied,' he added, 'because we are only a bureau to bring together the employee and employer, and according to our present regulations we still have not the right to insist that the employer must take any particular person, so that if an applicant calls at this office we can only place them in proportion to the orders on hand and considering the qualifications to fill that particular job.'[79]

Equally blatant racialization was state complicity with efforts to channel Chinese, Japanese, and Native Canadians into farm labour, lumber work, light industries, and service jobs, precisely those sectors of the economy that other groups were abandoning for more lucrative employment elsewhere. Although skilled and white-collar jobs in many parts of Canada remained closed to Jews, African Canadians, and other minorities from eastern and southern Europe, by 1942 the expanding wartime economy did offer them some new employment opportunities. Such workers could and did abandon seasonal or temporary, ill-paid, dangerous jobs or those in isolated areas, to which they were relegated before the war, in favour of more regular, better-paid work in war industries. Women who had earned livings as domestic servants, in seasonal employment picking fruits and vegetables, or working in canneries, now sought employment in factories. Women and men who worked in low-paid jobs in the textile, clothing, and food-processing industries also moved to better-paid jobs in war industries. Men from remote mining communities and lumber camps sought employment in urban areas. Their ranks were joined by men and women migrating to central Canada from less industrialized prairie and maritime provinces.[80]

Consequently, serious labour shortages developed in agriculture, food processing, lumbering, mining, railroad maintenance, and service sectors – the very sectors staffed by 'non-preferred' immigrants before the war.[81] Since the war had put a stop to immigration, worried government officials were desperately searching for new sources of labour to fill such jobs. Alarmed by crops left rotting in the fields, uncultivated farmlands, the closure of food processing plants, and declining production in the resource sector, state officials increasingly turned to those groups most marginalized by racism in the Canadian economy.

In the case of Chinese Canadians, the state's desperation to fill various undesirable jobs was at least partly responsible for Ottawa's failure to tackle the resentment created by their exclusion from training for home defence. NSS director Arthur MacNamara argued in 1943 that 'Chinese' were probably more useful in civilian jobs than they would be in the military. A year later, just before some Chinese Canadians were recruited to help with covert military operations in the Pacific, MacNamara still proposed that perhaps they should be called up, found unfit, and then sent to NSS for alternative service. The advantage of such a plan, which was never implemented, would have been that those designated for civilian work would be obligated to stick with it.[82]

Japanese Canadians

In the case of Japanese Canadians, state collusion with racist attitudes, policies, and practices was even more flagrant. Here racist attitudes eventually converged with labour needs. After the removal of Japanese Canadians from coastal British Columbia deprived them of their means of livelihood, the British Columbia Security Commission (BCSC), charged with the removal, faced a Herculean task: to make Japanese Canadians self-supporting so they would not constitute a financial burden for the federal government when most Canadian communities adamantly opposed the settlement of Japanese Canadians within their boundaries. Its initial plan entailed the separation of families. Women, children, and unemployable men were moved into ghost towns in the interior of British Columbia. Only a few men of prime working age

'View of workers from a road camp on the Hope-Princeton Highway.'

University of British Columbia Library, Rare Books and Special Collections, Japanese Canadian Photograph Collection, JCPC 3.0007.

were allowed to accompany them, to make the towns liveable. Most Japanese Canadian men between the ages of eighteen and forty-five, whether Japanese nationals, naturalized, or Canadian-born, were moved to road camps. Canadians who refused to let the men move into their communities were quite happy to allow them to build new highways under strict government supervision. The men were expected to stay in the road camps, unless given permission to leave by the RCMP. They were not free to take commercial employment, and were required to assign $20 from their monthly earnings (unskilled labourers earned 25 cents per hour) for the maintenance of their dependants, a sum supplemented by the government by no more than $5 per dependent child per month.[83] The government supplement was used to justify paying less than minimum wage to Japanese Canadian road workers.[84]

At the time of the evacuation, the only way that Japanese Canadian families could stay together was to agree to go to the sugar beet fields of Alberta and Manitoba.[85] Nearly four thousand Japanese Canadians were sent to such fields in Alberta, Manitoba, and eventually Ontario.[86] Because the work was seasonal, the Japanese Canadians required either additional work or government assistance for part of each year. Initially, only males could find additional work in northern lumber camps. Although jobs deemed appropriate for women in canning and domestic service were available in communities near the beet fields, Japanese Canadian women could not take up such work because they were formally excluded from such communities as Lethbridge.[87] Eventually, some communities did allow Japanese Canadians to undertake some of this work, in canning factories, for example, on condition that they return to sugar beet farms at the end of the work season.[88]

The BCSC and the Department of Labour allowed a small number of British Columbia's Japanese Canadians to move east of the Rocky Mountains on their own. To allay public fears, however, all people of Japanese descent required permits to change residence or travel across provincial boundaries. To prevent permanent settlement, they were prohibited from purchasing or leasing land and growing crops. Those who chose to move east faced additional restrictions from local authorities. Particularly onerous for the small business owners among them was the refusal to issue business licenses to Japanese Canadians. Such formal restrictions, along with great difficulty in finding employment and housing, rendered Japanese Canadians dependent on government plans for them.

By the end of 1942, at least in part because of the development of great shortages of labour throughout Canada, the federal government decided that 'dispersal' east of the Rocky Mountains, especially in areas of lumbering and agriculture, was the solution to the Japanese Canadian 'problem'. State officials chose to place Japanese Canadians in localities and occupations where they would not 'compete seriously with white workers' and where they would not be required to meet the public regularly. Occupations for young women initially included jobs in domestic work, basketmaking, dress factories, laundries, and canneries, and for young men, gardening, domestic work, truck driving, painting, garages, tanneries, foundries, lumbering, and railway work as section men and repairmen.[89] One plan for Japanese Canadian families included settlement on abandoned farms, where they would grow specialized crops. These were largely the jobs abandoned by all who could find more lucrative employment in war production. As one BCSC official put it, the Japanese Canadians 'have been and are being placed in industries where we have found it utterly impossible to find suitable labour.' 'None of the positions,' he added, 'are at all classified as attractive,' pointing out that the Japanese Canadians could remain at these jobs even after the war, because they would not have displaced other workers.[90]

Federal government officials – even those who protested that these workers could not be treated like indentured labour – at times used travel permit requirements to direct Japanese Canadians to or keep them in undesirable jobs. They advised, for example, that travel documents be withheld from families seeking to leave sugar beet fields in Manitoba.[91] In principle, of course, all Canadians of working age required permission to change employment starting in 1943. But while many other Canadians ignored this requirement, Japanese Canadians could not do so.[92]

Not surprisingly, Reverend K. Shimizu, the United Church minister serving Japanese Canadians in southern Ontario and Montreal, reported in June 1944 that occupational maladjustment was one of the main reasons that Japanese Canadians were not satisfactorily resettled. They could not engage in independent enterprise and very few white-collar jobs were open to them. Because 'every Japanese Canadian has been reduced to being a wage-earner,' he noted, almost all of them regarded their present jobs as temporary, and the 'feeling of "temporariness" in the most basic need of man – earning one's living – is not conducive to settlement.'[93]

Native People

Another racialized group of workers over whom the state exercised an
exceptional degree of control was Native Canadians. Although all Native people were still officially wards of the federal government during the war years, and some state officials viewed them as so marginal
to the economy that they exempted 'Indians' from national registration, their employment patterns, and hence the ability of the Indian
Affairs Branch (IAB) to control their participation in the labour force,
varied greatly. By the 1940s, Native peoples who lived in proximity to
white settlements in Canada and the northern United States had well-
established traditions of working for wages away from their reserves.
These patterns continued and even strengthened during the war. They
worked in steel plants in Sorel, Sault Ste Marie, and Michigan; an aluminum plant in Massena, New York; a foundry in Fort William; munition plants in Owen Sound and New Toronto; a synthetic rubber plant
and other industries in Sarnia. They harvested wheat on the Prairies
and hops in Oregon; they worked in fishing, ranching, and shipyards in
British Columbia. In some areas where Native people had been denied
employment during the Great Depression on the grounds that they
were the responsibility of the federal government, labour shortages
now reopened doors to them.[94]

On remote reserves, however, poverty was so great that Native
people seeking employment away from home were unable to relocate
without IAB assistance. On one reserve in Saskatchewan, for example,
a large number of girls and women wanted to work in war industries in
Ontario, but only two of them actually managed to go to Kingston because their parents could afford to pay their fares. Some Native people
in Saskatchewan lacked the necessary funds to buy appropriate work
clothing after they had paid train fares and travelled to eastern Canada.[95] In such cases, the goals and prejudices of local agents and IAB bureaucrats could shape employment patterns of Native people. Thus, for
example, when two young women from Maniwaki, Quebec, expressed
an interest in war work, IAB superintendent of welfare and training,
R.A. Hoey, responded that their limited education best suited them to
work as domestics. A year later, when non-Native women – including
married women with children – were actively recruited and trained for
work in war industries, his response to inquiries from Native women in
Moose Factory was the same. Such views within the IAB prevented Native women from taking advantage of the war situation to obtain new

skills and higher wages.[96] Evidently, the bureaucrats were far more concerned with ensuring that their wards would not be dependent on relief, and with satisfying labour priorities, than with opening new opportunities for Native people. Many of them also believed that Native people were inherently suited only for menial tasks.

Although IAB officials believed that wage work in lumbering would 'look like heaven to Indians,' they had so little confidence in the abilities and industry of Native workers that they agreed only with great reluctance to pay the way of a small group from the Red Pheasant Reserve in Saskatchewan to Kapuskasing, Ontario, where the Spruce Falls Pulp and Paper Company was desperately short of workers. The white men who had worked there seasonally before the war had been lured to the south by better prospects.[97] The reluctance of IAB officials was based on an unsuccessful arrangement with an Ontario lumber company a few years earlier, when Native workers failed to remain on the job for the entire season. Instead of recognizing that labour turnover – whatever the workers' background – was a widespread problem in lumbering, the officials ascribed the failure of the earlier experiment to the character of 'Indians.'[98]

When the Spruce Falls company expressed great satisfaction with the workers from the Red Pheasant Reserve and sought many more Native workers, the IAB made the necessary arrangements. IAB officials still worried, however, that the men would not on their own initiative use their wages to support their families, who would continue to depend on relief from the IAB. Unless they 'are willing to assign 20 to 30 dollars a month to their families,' wrote one official, 'little benefit will accrue to the Department from this experiment.' Accordingly, the employer sent some of the men's wages directly to their families and, to ensure that the men stayed on the job, retained the remainder until the season's end. Only then was their trip home paid for and their remaining wages handed over to the Indian agent on their reserve.[99]

By contrast, the IAB was quite willing to pay the costs of sending Native labourers to the sugar beet fields of Manitoba, where harvesting was especially difficult because heavy soil on low-lying lands clung to beet roots. The Japanese Canadians who had been sent there earlier were unable to support themselves despite their hard labour.[100] Yet Superintendent Hoey believed that this was work to which 'the Indians ... could readily adapt themselves, and the experience gained would no doubt prove very valuable.' In fact, however, probably because Japanese Canadians worked in sugar beet fields, Native people were not used extensively in the fields until after the Second World War.[101] The IAB was also willing to recruit and pay the transportation costs of Native labourers from northern reserves to harvest other crops in the south. But although newspapers wrote in glowing terms about the contributions of Natives as agricultural labourers, even in this sector they encountered deep prejudices. Edna Jaques, reporting to the Writers' War Committee from Alberta, expressed views prevailing around Edmonton: 'You know as well as I do, how much work an *Indian* will do. In a pinch, he works about three hours and then you can't *find* him. Yet they are talking of sending Indians to help the farmers in the spring.'[102]

In some cases, the view of Native workers as shiftless and undependable may have been related to white perception of their preference for casual employment which could be combined with their own seasonal round of work.[103] In the Kenora district, for example, Native workers were willing to work as trackmen provided that they would be allowed to return to trapping, which provided better income, when it was in season. There was no great difference between their pattern of employment and that of farmers who took up other types of work in winter on condition that they would be able to return to farming in the spring. In the case of the trackmen, employers were so short of workers that they were willing to be flexible vis-à-vis their Native employees. In other sectors, the non-acquisitive attitude of Native people towards work continued to create problems. In some cases, they simply left their jobs once they earned a certain amount of money. Insensitive to cultural differences, employers and some officials of IAB ascribed this behaviour to inherent or racial attributes of Natives.

Towards the end of the war, the participation of Native workers in war production seemed to transform the perceptions of employers and IAB officials.[104] Some employers and nutrition experts recognized that malnutrition had at times been the cause of what appeared to be laziness and indolence among Native people.[105] Officials on the west coast of British Columbia discouraged Native men from enlisting 'because they were of far more value to the country to take the place of the Japanese in the fishing industry.'[106] The Indian agent in Williams Lake, in the interior of British Columbia, reported after the war that 90 per cent of the labour required for cattle shipped out of the Cariboo during the war was provided by Native people.[107] Such approbation was echoed in Ontario as well. Gifford Swartman, Indian agent from Sioux Lookout, reported that, according to local mine managers, only the labour of Native people had kept the mines from closing during the war. The war

'Alberta Cattle Production is essential for the war effort because European livestock resources are seriously reduced. This cowhand, rolling himself a smoke, is a typical cowboy of Indian descent.'
Library and Archives Canada, WR-2198. Photograph by Harry Rowed.

years also witnessed the development of better understanding of the tremendous variation in Native people's employment patterns, which depended in part on their access to wage labour. So deeply rooted was the view of Native workers' inferiority, however, that despite recognition of their important contribution to the war effort and of the serious constraints under which Native workers operated, IAB officials simply accepted that in the more competitive post-war labour market, the 'Indian' would be the 'first man to lose his job' and the 'last to get it,'[108] and that Native people would have to rely on trapping and handicrafts for their livelihood.

This examination of the Canadian labour market during the Second World War presents an apparent paradox: at a time of acute labour shortages, employers refused to hire, and English Canadian workers refused to work with, men and women of African, Asian, Native, and southern and eastern European origin. Specifically, these racialized workers were excluded from skilled and white-collar jobs. State officials colluded with such racist practices. They believed that accepting employers' and workers' racist preferences would prevent social unrest and disruption in war industries. Moreover, they found that the relegation of minority groups to menial work offered the important benefit of filling jobs left vacant by Canadians with wider options.

PART TWO

Discrimination Is Sabotage:
Minority Accommodation, Protest, and
Resistance

An African Canadian graduate of a Montreal commercial high school, Mrs. Chalmers, firmly believed that war-generated demand for office clerks offered a unique opportunity to overcome racist exclusion from white-collar jobs. Her conviction was so strong that she was willing to weather repeated rejections from a Montreal employer in her quest. She returned seven days in a row to one office which advertised a clerical position in a local paper; each time the employer informed her that the position had been filled. For six days she returned home only to discover that the advertisement was still in the paper. 'I decided to try a new policy,' she recalled. 'I decided that as long as he didn't say he was refusing me because of my colour, I'd answer that one ad. On the seventh day he gave up and hired me. He said he figured I must have something.'[1]

While Chalmers's persistence paid off, for Hidoko (Dick) Masuda racist barriers proved insurmountable. In 1943, as part of the government programme to relocate Japanese Canadians east of the Rocky Mountains, the young, Vancouver-born shipyard designer was supposed to travel to a lumber camp in Schreiber, Ontario. Claiming that he had had too much to drink, Masuda ended up in Montreal instead, where he approached a placement officer in search of war work. Instead of giving him a job, the officer notified the RCMP, and Masuda was tried for travelling without a permit. During the trial, he complained that he had been unable to obtain work in his trade, adding, 'the only job we can get is washing dishes.' The presiding judge was unsympathetic. Telling Masuda that he was fortunate not to be sent to the type of camps near Hong Kong where Canadians were interned by the Japanese, he sent him to an internment camp in northern Ontario.[2]

Although we will never know how many individuals from racialized minority groups took similar steps to overcome discrimination, how many succeeded and how many failed, an examination of the war years reveals not only the pervasiveness of discrimination against such groups in Canada, but also extensive resistance to discrimination. Even as charges of disloyalty and sabotage were being levelled against them from all directions, many minority group members steadfastly maintained that they were Canadians, entitled to the same treatment as other Canadians. As Constance Backhouse argues in Colour-Coded, while people subordinated by race understood the implications of racial discrimination all too well, they did not necessarily accept racist evaluations of their purported worth.[3] Indeed, we owe our knowledge of the extent of employment discrimination against minorities during the war to resistance by the victims of racist discrimination. In the course of fighting against it, minority group members collected and publicized evidence of discrimination and devised strategies and programmes for its elimination.

While they strove to demonstrate their loyalty to Canada by enlisting in the armed forces, purchasing war bonds, and supporting the Red Cross, minority group members also protested individually and collectively against their treatment as second-class citizens. The situation was complicated. On the one hand, criticism of the government and complaints about ill-treatment could easily be condemned as creating disunity during wartime. Some groups were particularly vulnerable to such charges, since their loyalties to Canada were in any event suspect. On the other hand, some racialized minorities recognized that a number of factors – the need for their labour, the ideological justifications for war, and the extended powers of the state in wartime – combined to create an exceptional opportunity for fighting discrimination. Instead of challenging discrimination by private employers, one by one, they could now direct their protest to representatives of the federal government. As a number of recent studies have shown, some minority activists believed that the state could have and should have intervened to end discrimination – in other words, they sought legal prohibition of employment discrimination. A parallel, more practical challenge to discrimination through the spread of industrial unions in Canada and state recognition of collective bargaining rights is less widely recognized. Like other Canadians, minority group members were planning for a post-war world. Ending discrimination occupied a central role in their plans.

The great differences in the history and circumstances of the diverse groups that faced discrimination necessarily influenced the type of integration that they envisioned. As we shall see, some of them deemed confining campaigns to protecting their own ethnic or racialized group to be most effective. At times they even chose to rely on transnational connections, especially links to their counterparts in the United States, to develop the most effective protest campaigns. Other groups concluded that intergroup collaboration would be a more effective way, indeed perhaps the only way, to combat prejudice and discrimination. These two approaches were not mutually exclusive. Minority groups thus laid the foundation for the intergroup relations movement that would become increasingly important in fighting prejudice and discrimination after the Second World War, both in the United States and in Canada.[4] In some groups, however, class and ideological divisions precluded collective action. Often only subgroups, generally the working-class and left-leaning elements, mounted active campaigns against discrimination.

2

Jews

We would like to bring to your attention an incident, which we encountered when applying for Help Wanted at the Unemployment and Selective Service, 174 Spadina Ave., an incident, which if neglected can lead to disastrous consequences for the Jewish people of Toronto. The young lady in charge, at the time, asked, 'do you prefer a Gentile or Jew'. And we received a telephone call from the board asking us the same question. We are very much concerned about this procedure. As it is contrary to the very principles for which our Jewish boys are giving their lives in this war. That is the principles of Democracy and for freedom against all forms of discrimination and intolerance.[1]

The writer of this excerpt, M. Wolfson, was the owner of Annabel's, a women's clothing manufacturer in Toronto. He was describing his experience with discrimination by state agencies, at the request of the Jewish Employment Service which was gathering such evidence in the autumn of 1942 as part of its campaign against racist employment discrimination. The letter's purpose and content provide a glimpse of the most coherent anti-discrimination campaign developed by Canadian minorities during the Second World War – that mounted by the Jews. Ironically, given that their purported 'unassimilability' was one of the main reasons behind Canada's refusal to admit all but a few Jewish refugees from Nazi Europe, what allowed Canadian Jews to mount such a programme was their relatively successful integration in Canada. By the 1940s many of them were English-speaking, and their ranks included disproportionate numbers of scholars and lawyers, who often undertook the necessary research and acted as spokespersons in the campaign against discrimination. To be sure, by 1939 there was a significant – albeit proportionally smaller – number of English-speaking, Canadian-educated women and men in other groups of eastern European descent as well, such as the Ukrainians. But what distinguished Canadian Jews was that their ranks also included the most highly unionized non-Anglo-Celtic workers in Canada, active in the unions of both of the two main organizational branches of the labour movement, the American Federation of Labor (AFL) and the Congress of Industrial Organizations (CIO). Within the Canadian left, which generally took a stand against discrimination, Jews were represented not only in the Communist Party, the mainspring of immigrant radicalism in the 1930s and 1940s, but also composed the largest and most outspoken ethnic minority within the Co-operative Commonwealth Federation. Both left-wing parties had to take Jewish interests into consideration, and fighting anti-Semitism – and prejudice and discrimination more generally – ranked high among these interests. Even candidates from the mainstream parties had to address such concerns. This was all the more so, given the concentration of Jews in working-class ridings such as Cartier in Montreal and Spadina in Toronto.

To cite the example of Montreal's Cartier riding, 55 per cent of the inhabitants were Jewish, 35 per cent French Canadian, and 10 per cent a variety of other nationalities. Three Jewish candidates ran in the 1943 federal by-election in the riding: Lazarus Phillips, a Liberal, closely connected to former member Peter Bercovitch, whose death while in office led to the by-election; Fred Rose for the Labour-Progressive (Communist) Party; and David Lewis for the CCF. The only French Canadian candidate, Paul Massé, represented the Bloc Populaire Canadien. Because of the historic links between French Canadian nationalism and anti-Semitism, his campaign intensified the sense of insecurity among Jewish voters. They viewed Massé as anti-Semitic and isolationist.[2] They voted for Fred Rose, who promised that 'his first act on being elected to parliament would be to introduce a Bill to the House making anti-Semitism a crime punishable by law.' In the 1944 federal elections, poet A.M. Klein, running for the CCF, attempted unsuccessfully to discredit Rose by pointing to his opposition to an anti-discrimination bill proposed in the House of Commons by CCF MP Angus MacInnis as evidence that he was insufficiently committed to fighting racism.[3]

In Toronto's Spadina riding, Joe Salsberg similarly attacked his adversary in the 1940 municipal elections for not standing up against anti-Semitism. The Canadian Jewish Congress (CJC), which had excluded Communists from membership as a result of the Nazi-Soviet Pact and the proscription of the CPC by Ottawa, actively campaigned against Salsberg and other CPC candidates. It organized a house-to-house canvass in the Jewish districts of Toronto and circulated anti-communist leaflets in English and Yiddish.[4]

Such clashes at election times signalled deep political and ideological divisions among Canadian Jews, as well as the partisan uses of the struggle against anti-Semitism. But Jews could sometimes subordinate divisions of class, and at times even of ideology, to their campaign against anti-Semitism.[5] The CJC's Committee on Economic Problems, for example, which included large employers, supported labour unions at a time when other minority group leaders were deeply suspicious of organized labour. This support was based less on ideological conviction than on a recognition of the role that labour unions played in countering discrimination. The committee decided to invite Jewish unionists from the Amalgamated Clothing Workers' Union and the International Ladies' Garment Workers' Union (ILGWU) to participate in plans to alleviate Jewish unemployment. First, committee members noted that one reason for the decline of employment for Jews in the needle trades was that non-union shops generally hired non-Jews – especially Italians and French Canadians. Hiring practices of unionized shops, by contrast, precluded racist discrimination; Mr Spivak, of the Amalgamated Clothing Workers' Union, explained to the Executive Committee on Economic Problems: 'Upon request of the shops, workers are sent out by the secretary of the union. No discrimination is practised in this instance, but workers are sent according to a list determined by a policy of seniority.'[6] Second, they were aware of the fact that some labour unions, not just in the garment industry, raised their voices against discrimination. Unions which brought together Jewish and gentile workers, moreover, could be used to gain the support of gentiles in the struggle against anti-Semitism.[7] The chairman of the committee, Gurston Allen, a lawyer and businessman, argued that the committee should therefore support labour unions.[8]

Organizational Base

By the outbreak of the Second World War, Canadian Jews were better organized than other minorities to fight discrimination. They had established an organization specifically for this purpose: the Joint Public Relations Committee of the Canadian Jewish Congress and B'nai B'rith (JPRC). The JPRC was founded in 1938, when the Public Relations Committee of the CJC and the Anti-Defamation League of B'nai B'rith joined together in response to the intensification of anti-Semitism in Canada and abroad. Within these Jewish organizations, 'public relations' stood for fighting anti-Semitism. The JPRC's role was to fight anti-Semitism not only in the field of employment, but on all fronts. Employment discrimination, however, was a central element in this campaign. Samuel Bronfman, head of CJC, captured the centrality of this concern in 1940 when he stated that the 'non-sectarian principle in employment is one pillar of democracy.'[9] Thus, alone among minority groups in Canada, the Jews entered the war with a special committee established to fight employment discrimination. The function of the CJC's Committee on Economic Problems was 'to enquire into the question of discrimination against the employment of individuals because of racial or religious prejudice, more particularly as it affects Jewish persons, and attempt to ameliorate the situation by certain concrete and specific action.'[10] Its members included two of the most accomplished specialists in labour law in the country, Bora Laskin and Jacob Finkelman, as well as social scientist Louis Rosenberg of the western division of the Canadian Jewish Congress in Winnipeg.[11]

By war's end, another organization, the Jewish Labour Committee (JLC), which would come to play a key role in subsequent anti-discrimination campaigns, also shifted its focus from trying to save Jews and socialists from Nazi Europe to fighting racism at home, particularly within the labour movement.[12] As its name suggests, the JLC comprised Jewish locals of such unions as the Amalgamated Clothing Workers of America, the ILGWU, the United Hat, Cap and Millinery Workers' International Union, the Bakers' Union, and the Pocketbook Makers Union, and of left-wing groups such as the Jewish section of the CCF, the Workmen's Circle (with socialist and anarchist members), and the Left Labour Zionists.

Studying the Causes and Nature of Employment Discrimination

Jewish activists focused specifically on employment discrimination even before the outbreak of war. They were motivated by mounting anxieties concerning the relationship between the rise of fascism and Nazism in Europe and North America, the intensification of anti-Semitism, and the impact of these political and ideological developments on the economic conditions of Jewish people. Their immediate economic concern was the high unemployment rate among Jews. Unemployment was high among all Canadians, of course, but Jewish community leaders in Canada and elsewhere believed that anti-Semitism exacerbated the unemployment problem for their co-religionists. The *achat chez nous* campaign in Quebec, which called on French Canadians to boycott Jewish businesses and led to discrimination against Jewish labour, was a particularly glaring example of the economic consequences of anti-Semitism.[13]

As they reflected on the problems of employment, Jewish activists identified a vicious circle: in Canada, as elsewhere, anti-Semitism had led Jews to be concentrated in a small number of occupations, an employment distribution that distinguished them from the surrounding population and in turn fuelled anti-Semitism. In western Canada, for example, disproportionate numbers of Jews were merchants or middlemen, whereas relatively few of them were engaged in agriculture.[14] As Louis Rosenberg explained on the eve of war, distributive occupational concentration spread anti-Semitism because nearly all western farmers had 'come into close contact with the Jewish cattle buyer, the Jewish trucker and the small Jewish buyer of eggs and other poultry products,' and it was 'comparatively easy to transfer the farmer's resentment against the economic system as a whole,' which gave him 'such low prices for his products, into resentment against the individual Jew and the entire Jewish community.' During the 1930s specifically, upwardly mobile Jews throughout Canada were concentrated in business and the liberal professions, domains of the country's economy that were 'the most venomously competitive.'[15] The majority of Jewish female high-school graduates studied stenography and typewriting, 'thus overcrowding the clerical field.' Canadian Jewish leaders knew through their connections with European Jewish communities that in such countries as Hungary Jewish occupational concentration had led to the imposition of Jewish quotas in such professions as law and medicine. They realized, however, that Jewish economic 'maldistribution' did not itself account for anti-Semitism. As committee chairman Gurston Allen pointed out, even if there had been three hundred thousand Jewish farmers in Germany, they would have been treated the same as Jewish doctors. But Allen believed that a more even occupational distribution would deprive anti-Semites of some of their ammunition.[16]

Some Jewish activists also feared that such liabilities would prompt young Jews seeking to make their way in Canadian society to abandon their faith and distinctive identity. The more conservative among them, moreover, feared that young people would be drawn to radicalism.

Such concerns reveal that for Jewish community leaders the quest for successful integration into Canadian society did not mean the abandonment of a distinctive Jewish identity, but equal opportunity for those who embraced it.[17]

Anti-Semitism was so pervasive, they observed, that even Jewish employers sometimes discriminated against Jews. Some Jewish employers defended their actions by explaining that they only turned away those Jewish applicants for jobs that required them to deal with the public, such as sales clerks and receptionists, because their 'Semitic' appearance might create a negative impression among prospective customers. Other Jewish employers shared the widespread negative stereotype of Jews as incapable of doing heavy work such as warehouse work, while yet others invoked the perceptions of Jews as inclined to join labour unions and create strife to explain their refusal to hire them.[18]

Committee members believed that showing the legitimacy of charges of discrimination was essential to a successful campaign against it. They gave serious thought, therefore, to the best means of uncovering and demonstrating practices of discrimination. In the process, they developed effective research strategies. For example, they argued that numerical representation in an occupation could not in itself indicate whether racist discrimination existed; data on the distribution of different groups within particular fields or places of employment was also necessary. In the insurance business, for instance, there were quite a few Jews, but almost all of them were in sales; there were almost no Jewish men and women in administration. But because of the rise of anti-Semitism and the outbreak of war, there was no time to employ the pioneering research strategies they developed to study anti-Semitic discrimination in general. The committee decided that its efforts would be guided by widespread views held within the community about discriminatory employers, both Jewish and gentile, private and public, and each employer would be investigated carefully and individually.

While employment was still scarce, the committee feared that a public campaign would not lead to new opportunities for unemployed Jews. They feared other minorities would see it as an attempt to obtain jobs for Jewish workers at their expense and would retaliate with their own particularistic campaigns.[19] Instead, they planned to proceed cautiously by approaching employers and requesting them to hire Jews. In the case of civic workers, they saw patronage at work. They recognized that in Toronto most of the patronage was handled by the Orange Order. Any publicity would bring to light discrimination against Roman Catholics rather than opening opportunities for Jewish workers. Instead, the committee decided to urge members of the Jewish community who had 'an entree with the heads of some of the departments,' to approach their contacts and 'say to them "will you give our boys and girls a break? Don't turn them down because they are Jewish."' Similarly, in the case of private employers known not to employ Jews, such as Laura Secord, the committee would request that applicants be considered on their merits, and not be turned away because they were Jews. Their approach was cautious and accommodationist.

Additional long-term solutions included training Jewish youth in occupations other than the needle trades. Committee members believed that Jewish carpenters, painters, and bricklayers had no access to training, possibly because of the exclusivism of craft unions. Consequently, gentile tradesmen believed that by taking on jobs in such trades, Jews lowered the standard of work and constituted unfair competition.[20] In any event, the committee believed that one way to take the wind out of the anti-Semites' sails was to encourage young Jews to train in newly emerging fields where they would face less competition, as machinists, automobile mechanics, refrigeration mechanics, or workers in the aviation industry.[21] The committee also looked to the federal government's Youth Training Programme as a way of providing young Jews with new skills. Few Jewish youth took advantage of this programme. The issue was complicated, however, for in many instances before applicants were taken on, they had to have the promise of jobs.[22] This problem persisted when the Youth Training Programme was transformed into the War Emergency Training Programme.

Even before the outbreak of the war, the executive of the Committee on Economic Problems considered legislation against discrimination. It learned from Professor Jacob Finkelman, an expert on labour law and chairman of the Committee on Social and Economic Research, that many American states had enacted laws against hiring discrimination.[23] The Committee on Economic Problems also considered the elimination of questions concerning religion on job application forms and a campaign against discriminatory job advertisements in newspapers.[24]

Gathering Evidence

These pre-war plans and campaigns set the stage for the wartime fight against employment discrimination by the CJC. At the beginning of the war these efforts remained behind the scenes. By 1940, for example, the youth division of the CJC was receiving advice from Professor Leonard Marsh about how to carry on vocational guidance work within the community.[25] On 14 March 1941, Minister of Labour Norman McLarty, in response to complaints from the JPRC and representatives of other racialized minorities, issued a circular to employers and secretaries of trade unions, urging them to refrain from discrimination against 'persons of foreign name or birth.' 'For the final outcome of the war to be successful against our common enemy,' the circular stated, 'we require the help of the various nationalities represented in our population regardless of creed or racial origin: we cannot hope to build up a truly national spirit if we have not the support of those who have given Canada the allegiance they formerly owed to the country of their birth.'[26] Because of the cautious, behind-the-scenes approach that still characterized the JPRC's work, Canadians were not aware that Jews played any part in this campaign.[27]

When the CJC continued to receive reports of discrimination against Jews in war industries, it decided in 1942 to 'depart from the established point of view of not criticizing the government.'[28] The organization decided to publicize both the incidence of discrimination and Jewish opposition to it.[29] The new tactic acquired greater urgency when government officials claimed that discriminatory treatment, such as employment advertisements specifying that 'only Anglo-Saxons' need apply, was exceptional.[30] Government plans to shift workers from nonessential to essential industries also intensified concerns within the Jewish community. Many of the Jews engaged in the retail sector, a substantial proportion of the community, would fall into the non-essential category. The committee wanted to make sure that they would not encounter discrimination in seeking new placements.[31]

Jewish activists believed that state involvement in such discrimination accentuated the need for protest. 'It was bad enough when in peace time, private employers advertising for workers asked for "Gentiles only" or "State race and religion,"' wrote one of them, 'but now that all "help wanted" ads must be cleared and approved by the UIC, it is intolerable that discrimination against applicants because of race or creed should be permitted to continue.'[32] Not only could protests against the government assume the high moral ground in their campaign, but they could avoid dealing with the widely held view that hiring employees was a matter of private business, a right of employers, in which the state was not entitled to intervene.

Solid evidence of racist employment discrimination would be necessary to convince the government to act more forcefully. When they received complaints about discrimination from Jews, state officials first referred the charges to the Department of Labour. When that department's investigation confirmed that employment discrimination had occurred, the JPRC proceeded to gather additional evidence.[33] Their task proved difficult at first: individuals were reluctant to come forward. The JPRC requested evidence through the pages of the Jewish press and by appealing to CJC members throughout the country. They required signed affidavits concerning employment discrimination in order to be able to go public.[34] The testimonies of Jewish employers, like that of M. Wolfson with which this chapter opened, constituted particularly strong evidence of state collusion with private employers in employment discrimination. But many prospective employees who had encountered discrimination also came forward to bolster the JPRC's campaign.

By the fall of 1942 Jewish activists believed they had obtained sufficient evidence to take their case to Ottawa. Two delegations met with Elliott Little, director of the National Selective Service Board, to protest discriminatory practices of war industries and local Selective Service agencies.[35] The first delegation, led by the ILGWU's H.D. Langer and accompanied by Percy Bengough, acting president of the Trades and Labour Congress, comprised AFL unions with a large proportion of Jewish members, such as the International Ladies' Garment Workers' Union, the Luggage and Handbag Workers' Union, and the Fur Workers' Union. Saul Hayes, executive director of the Canadian Jewish Congress and Professor Jacob Finkelman of the University of Toronto, both representing the JPRC, led the second delegation.[36]

The letters and affidavits gathered by the unions and the JPRC offer glimpses of how Jews of various classes saw their position in the workplace and in Canadian society more widely. Like M. Wolfson, many of them pointed to the contradiction between war aims and racist discrimination on the home front. They also asserted their loyalty to Canada and their sense of being Canadians. Jewish unionists emphasized that anti-Semitism and racism menaced labour institutions and threatened the labour movement's most fundamental rights.[37] The reliance on two separate Jewish delegations reflected the significance of class divisions within this minority group. The collaboration between the JPRC and labour activists in preparing the protests to Ottawa indicated the willingness and ability of Canadian Jews to transcend such differences in fighting against anti-Semitism, and racism more generally.

Long before the end of the war, Jewish activists began to worry about the possible effects of employment discrimination in the post-war period. To be sure, post-war planning preoccupied many other Canadians as well. Memories of the difficulties of reintegrating war veterans at the end of the First World War were still relatively fresh in the minds of many Canadians. Jews were additionally concerned, however, that anti-Semitism would force returning Jewish veterans into the work force in ways that would reinforce the anomalous employment structures that they were trying to eliminate.[38] Once they realized that they could do little against the murderous policies of the Nazis in Europe, Jewish leaders and activists directed their energies to helping Jewish survivors. In 1943 they created a subcommittee on post-war planning within the CJC's Committee on Social and Economic Research, in large measure to deal with the admission and absorption of Jewish refugees after the war.[39]

The new subcommittee's concerns provide a glimpse of the way Jewish activists understood 'race' and its impact on members of their group. Louis Rosenberg believed that the JPRC should campaign for the elimination of the classification of 'preferred' and 'non-preferred' races in Canada's immigration policy. He objected both to the racial theories on which that classification was based and to the fact that under this classification Jews ranked even below 'non-preferred' races, that is other groups of eastern and southern European origin, among those who would be admitted to Canada only by special permit.[40] Retaining such classifications could clearly be used to prevent Jewish refugees from gaining admission to Canada after the war.

In relation to racial classification for Jews living in Canada, Rosenberg advised the JPRC that merely eliminating questions about race from employment forms would not suffice to stop employment discrimination. He believed that the NSS was circumventing its own regulations against racist discrimination by asking job applicants to indicate their 'nationality,' even if they were naturalized Canadians. Rosenberg maintained that since the nationality of naturalized residents of Canada was 'Canadian,' to ask them to indicate an additional nationality was tantamount to asking for 'race' as defined by the Dominion Bureau of Statistics and could thus be used to perpetuate racist discrimination.[41] What is significant in this discussion of race is that colour is not mentioned. Despite the fact that anti-Semites did imply on occasion that Jews were not white, Jewish activists did not see classification by skin colour as a major problem. They were concerned with fighting against the notion of a hierarchy of races. Admittedly, their own placement in it provided much of the incentive to fight against that hierarchy. Most of them were also aware, however, that discriminatory practices based on racial rankings also injured other racialized minorities. When the NSS responded to the activists' complaint against the internal directive to NSS officials not to apply the prohibition against racist discrimination in cases 'of insurmountable obstacles in the way of the acceptance of the applicant' by saying that it affected only 'Negroes,' Rosenberg argued that even if that were the case the regulation was still of vital concern to Jews, 'since any official recognition and tolerance of racial discrimination must inevitably affect us [Jews].'[42]

Retraining, vocational guidance, and rehabilitation of veterans were additional reasons for the establishment of the subcommittee. According to Louis Rosenberg these tasks were especially important because the Canadian economy would develop in new directions following the war. He believed that heavy industry and construction were bound to become important. Because discrimination had forced Canadian Jews to rely on employment within the community, by their parents or relatives, they lacked the requisite skills to move into these new areas of employment. Anticipating such development and providing young Jews with the requisite training for these fields would be a way to counteract discrimination. Otherwise the excuse could be made that Jews were not being hired because they did not possess the necessary skills.[43]

Because Jewish activists believed that the problems which the Jews would face in the post-war world would not be 'solved automatically by the victory of the United Nations,'[44] the new subcommittee's mandate also included the protection of minority rights, outlawing anti-Semitism and making libel against a community a punishable offence.[45] The Committee on Economic Problems, aware of government planning for post-war reconstruction, wanted to establish links with relevant state bodies.

Campaigning for Anti-Discrimination Legislation

In preparation for the post-war world, the JPRC renewed and intensified its research on the introduction of anti-discrimination legislation in Canada.[46] Even the most committed proponents of such legislation were well aware of its limitations. Legislation would not eradicate prejudice and discrimination. They believed that 'a sense of toleration and mutual understanding' would be required for that. The legislation could, however, deal with the 'more open and offensive types of discrimination which imply contempt.'[47] Moreover, they believed that there was great moral value 'in having the law recognize that race hatred is contrary to the interests of the state.'[48]

To this end, the CJC's post-war reconstruction committee commissioned a study of the existing libel law in Canada. Committee members wondered if it would be possible to expand the powers of this law to encompass employment discrimination based on race, religion, and nationality. They obtained materials related to anti-discrimination legislation in New York and New Jersey through American Jewish organizations.[49] They also canvassed the opinions of Jewish legal experts and activists across Canada about the feasibility and likelihood of the introduction of such legislation. David A. Freeman, a Vancouver lawyer, informed them that the passage of such legislation in British Columbia was most unlikely, given that province's approval of discriminatory treatment of residents of Asian origin. Any proposed anti-discrimination legislation would threaten to outlaw the denial of franchise, restrictions to employment, and restrictive covenants widely accepted in the western province.[50] By contrast, Jewish CCF members believed that their party would be willing to propose such legislation in Manitoba and Saskatchewan.[51] In Quebec, however, a campaign in favour of anti-discrimination legislation was certain to meet 'negative results,' given the 'strong anti-Semitic atmosphere in the province.'[52]

In 1943, Ontario seemed to offer the most promising field for the passage of such legislation. A private member's bill, introduced by J.J. Glass and drafted with help from the CJC, proposed to make illegal 'the use of signs on public places which restrict access to people deemed to belong to a given race or to adhere to certain religious beliefs.' It also sought 'to prohibit the right of prospective employers when advertising for a worker to announce that applications will only be considered if they come from persons of a certain race or creed.' The bill's proponents offered a number of justifications for such legislation. They pointed to the war aims of the United Nations, arguing that Canadians could not 'consistently criticize Hitler and his minions for their murderous attacks on the Jews and other groups in Nazi-controlled Europe' if Canadians condoned 'offensive discrimination' in their own country. They added that returning Jewish war veterans willing to sacrifice their lives overseas in the Canadian armed forces should never be confronted with racist discrimination at home. Importantly, Jewish advocates of anti-discrimination legislation in Ontario recognized the rights of other

'J.B. Salsberg giving a political speech, ca. 1942.'
Ontario Jewish Archives, accession 2004-5-28.

racialized minority groups; they reported: 'while the Jews have a pecu-
liar interest in the elimination of all irritating forms of discrimination,
other groups in Canada, and many belonging to "new Canadians" de-
serve similar protection.' They believed that the future integrity of the
British Commonwealth depended on assurances of fair play 'for all the
ethnic elements' which made up 'the population of His Majesty's subjects.'[53] Unfortunately, the members of the legislature and the public at
large reacted with indifference.[54] The private member's bill, therefore,
had no chance of being adopted.

The following year, when the Conservative government of Ontario
Premier George Drew did introduce the Racial Discrimination Act,
which prohibited the publication or display of discriminatory signs,
symbols, emblems, or other representation indicating discrimination or
the intention to discriminate, both the CJC and Communist MPP Joe
Salsberg took credit for this development. Representatives of the CJC
noted that they met with the premier, submitted 'quite far-reaching
drafts upon which the Government based the actual bill,' convinced the
CCF to hold off on its own proposals for anti-discrimination legislation,
and prevailed upon newspapers opposed to such legislation not to discuss their reservations until after the bill's passage.[55] In an interview
with historian James Walker, Salsberg claimed that he was able to pressure the premier into advancing the bill because the minority Conservative government was vulnerable in the legislature.[56] Unlike the CJC,
Salsberg sought publicity for his initiative, since he knew that successful
action in this area would increase the standing of the Labour-Progressive Party (LPP) among Jews and other minorities. Perhaps that is why
his role in the introduction of Canada's first anti-discrimination bill is
better known than the CJC's. The CJC's support, despite Salsberg's public promotion of the bill, illustrates the willingness of Jewish activists to
disregard ideological differences in fighting discrimination. Although
the passage of this bill marked an important step in the legal prohibition
of discrimination, the legislation disappointed activists because it did
not contain the provisions against employment discrimination which
had been in the original draft. The advocates of anti-discrimination
legislation were also concerned about the vehement Protestant protest
against the bill, led by Toronto alderman Leslie Saunders, editor of *Protestant Action*, and Reverend T.T. Shields, Baptist minister and president
of the anti-Catholic Canadian Protestant League.[57]

The CJC also supported two unsuccessful attempts to pass anti-
discrimination bills in Manitoba and in Ottawa. In 1942, H.M. Caiser-

man sent information about American anti-discrimination legislation
to MP Peter Bercovitch, suggesting he approach the government 'for
similar legislation in Canada.'[58] In 1944, the CCF introduced an anti-
discrimination bill in the Manitoba legislature. The proposed 'Act to
Prevent Discrimination because of Ethnic Origin or Adherence or non-
Adherence to a Religious Belief' resembled the text of the Glass Bill,
but also included a section prohibiting employers from requesting information concerning ethnic origin or religious belief from employees
or applicants.[59]

Transcending Sectarian and Ethnic Boundaries

The conclusion that Jewish activists drew from the very modest success
of their legislative campaigns was that much more preparation was
required.[60] This groundwork would consist of education and stronger
links with potentially sympathetic organizations in the wider community such as churches, labour organizations, businesses, and women's
organizations. The benefits of these campaigns would extend to all
other racialized minorities, for Jewish activists held that while Jews
had a particular interest in this type of legislation, all minority groups
deserved legal protection. The scope of the CJC's Committee on Social
and Economic Research extended to the study of prejudice and discrimination in general, encompassing discrimination against 'Catholics, Negroes, Chinese, Japanese and Italians.'[61]

The effort to transcend sectarian boundaries, however, preceded the
Second World War. Taking their cue from American religious leaders,
in 1934 Canadian Jews and Protestants, under the leadership of Rabbi
M.N. Eisendrath and Reverend Edwin Silcox of the United Church, established the Committee on Jewish-Gentile Relationships in Toronto.
Modelled after the American National Conference of Christians and
Jews, the committee invited Christian and Jewish leaders to participate
in seminars to improve relations between the two groups. It also distributed a series of pamphlets intended to dispel myths about the Jews
and to fight anti-Semitism.[62] In 1940 the committee was revitalized as
the Canadian Conference of Christians and Jews under the directorship
of Reverend Silcox. The conference's main goal was to foster harmonious relations among Canada's different religious denominations.[63] Its
publication, *Fellowship*, appeared every six weeks, and copies were sent
to thousands of clerics and influential laypersons. Among other actions
to fight discrimination, it publicized campaigns for the introduction of

anti-discrimination bills during the war.[64] Most of the funding for the conference came from the CJC.[65]

Collaboration with non-Jews extended to secular organizations as well. The cordial relations between the CJC and organized labour in Canada meant, for example, that unions provided another important avenue for fighting against anti-Semitism specifically and 'race hatred' more generally. The labour subcommittee of the CJC's central region distributed educational material to unions, much of it obtained from American Jewish organizations. Jewish war veterans initiated resolutions against discrimination at the conventions of the Canadian Legion.[66] Jewish activists such as Ben Lappin and Ben Kayfetz took part in meetings both of religious and secular voluntary associations sympathetic to the Jews, such as the Fellowship for a Christian Social Order, the Student Christian Movement, the YMCA, the YWCA, the Workers' Educational Association, the Canadian Association for Adult Education, and the Canadian Institute of International Affairs, and supplied such bodies with anti-racist literature.[67]

Aware of the collaboration between American Jewish agencies and academia to study the origins of prejudice and to develop strategies to oppose it, the CJC sent JPRC member Manfred Saalheimer to New York in 1944 to study this research as well as prospects for social action. Saalheimer spoke to such leading social scientists in this field as Max Horkheimer, director of the Institute of Social Research at Columbia University and research consultant in domestic defence for the American Jewish Committee; Kurt Lewin, professor of psychology, chief consultant of the Commission on Community Inter-Relations, and director of the Research Centre for Group Dynamics at MIT; Dr H.H. Giles, director of the Bureau of Inter-Cultural Education; M.A. Davis, professor of sociology at Yale University and a member of the National Refugee Service Committee for the Study of Recent Immigration from Europe. These academics, with funding from American Jewish organizations, were conducting research on anti-Semitism. Some of these scholars, Kurt Lewin notable among them, became advocates of 'action research programs.' These programmes looked for the roots of anti-Semitism rather than its manifestations. They also studied the forces that exacerbated or mitigated anti-Semitism.[68] These scholars and activists advised Saalheimer that the impersonal, mass appeals against anti-Semitism through the press, radio, pamphlets, and the like had not proven very effective. Instead, they advocated fighting prejudice through more intimate groups such as labour, business, women's, and other voluntary organizations. Since the American scholars believed that the roots of prejudice in general, and anti-Semitism in particular, were psychological, they concluded that efforts to fight against it should address the emotions rather than the intellect.[69] Saalheimer and Horkheimer agreed to apply the new approach in Canada by examining the impact of American cultural anthropologist Hortense Powdermaker's *Probing Our Prejudices* on several YMCA and YWCA clubs in Montreal. Saalheimer's support for the American approach and the subsequent adoption of this approach by the CJC marked a conservative turn, or a depoliticization, in the Jewish community's anti-discrimination campaign. Some of the activists accepted Horkheimer's conclusion that although anti-Semitism 'may to a good deal have its root in economic conditions,' they should 'concentrate on its psychological roots' as they could not 'change the economic structure anyway.' They began to view anti-Semitism as the product of individual psychology rather than social and economic forces.[70]

Jewish activists introduced Canadian organizations to innovative American anti-discrimination programmes and publications. One of the most interesting of these was the Springfield Plan, initiated and funded by the American National Conference of Christians and Jews. Designed by a committee of anthropologists, sociologists, social psychologists, and other social scientists and educators, the plan was introduced in Springfield, Massachusetts, schools in 1939. The Springfield Plan provided students with citizenship education while fighting racial prejudice. Children were taught about the contribution of minority groups to their community, and the music and arts of different groups. They celebrated holidays such as Christmas and Hanukkah together. The plan not only revised school curricula to foster appreciation of ethnocultural diversity and fight prejudice, but it required hiring teachers who would represent the multi-ethnic composition of the population of Springfield. The goal was to educate through experience. Pupils had a measure of control over school life through collaborating with teacher and parent committees. The schools also attempted to ensure equal access to employment for their pupils. Springfield schools refused to disclose the racial, ethnic, religious, and national background of pupils applying for jobs. Employers, the educators reasoned, would thus be unable to discriminate in hiring.[71] The CJC first discussed plans for 'intercultural education' with Ontario's Deputy Minister of Education as early as 1940, but it continued to publicize the Springfield Plan specifically throughout the war. The plan was introduced after the war in Teck Township, Kirkland Lake, and Welland.[72]

Canadian Jews assumed a leading role in fighting employment discrimination during the Second World War for three main reasons. First, their
ranks included not only English-speaking, educated professionals, but
also a large number of organized workers, social democrats, and communists, all of whom were willing and able to lead such a fight, even
to the point of overcoming class and ideological divisions. Second, the
JPRC, established in 1938 specifically for fighting discrimination, was
joined by the end of the war by the Jewish Labour Committee (JLC), to
provide their anti-discrimination campaign with a solid organizational
base. Third, Jewish activists in Canada received guidance and support
from American Jewish organizations with greater resources and more
developed anti-discrimination organizations and strategies.

Canadian Jews played a key role both in convincing the NSS to denounce employment discrimination and in shaping the strategies of
campaigns to publicize the prevalence of racist discrimination and to
prohibit such discrimination by law. Their approach was adopted and
refined by human rights activists in the post-war period. It is worth
noting, however, that while Canadian Jewish activists adopted many of
the ideas and strategies of their American counterparts, the links of the
Canadian Jews to the CCF and to social democrats within the labour
movement contributed to growing differences between the Canadian
and American campaigns. During the war, the JPRC and the JLC both
strengthened their connections to organized labour, supplying unions
with educational materials about racism and discrimination and gaining the unions' backing for campaigns to fight discrimination. After
1947, the CJC ceded this field to the JLC and helped to fund its programmes. Jewish membership and influence in the CCF, with which
the JLC had close connections, was crucial to safeguarding the labour
orientation of the Canadian anti-racist movement. As the Cold War en-
gulfed Canada, communists who had been active in the fight against
discrimination lost their influence. The JLC, itself strongly anti-communist, but with close ties to social democratic unionists, was able to
prevent its anti-discrimination campaigns from following the new orientation of American Jewish human rights activists, namely, focusing
primarily on the psychological roots of racism at the cost of neglecting
the social and economic manifestations of racist discrimination.[73]

3

Other Racialized Citizens

African Canadians

The African Canadian wartime campaign against discrimination resembled that of Jewish activists in many ways. They too seized the opportunity of the state's involvement in the labour market to direct attention to racist discrimination and to urge state officials to stop it. They too advocated legislation against discrimination. Because they were fewer in number, however, and no national organization united them, the African Canadian struggle against discrimination was decentralized. Churches, community organizations, and labour unions in big cities such as Montreal and Toronto, but also in small towns in southwestern Ontario with high concentrations of people of African descent, protested on their own initiative against discrimination and developed strategies to resist it. Like Canadian Jews, they too looked to organizations in the United States for inspiration and guidance in their struggles. Because of their small number, however, African Canadians were not at the centre of discussions and campaigns on state-minority relations in Canada, nor could they wield anything like the kind of pressure employed by African Americans to force their government to take steps against employment discrimination. The group's small size, especially as compared with the number of African Americans, is an important reason that colour as the basis of racial classification and discrimination was much less visible in Canada than in the United States.

In the absence of nation-wide African Canadian organizations, African Canadian churches played an important role in anti-discrimination campaigns. In 1944, a deputation composed of Toronto's African Canadian elite, including two physicians and a representative of the sleeping car porters, and headed by Reverend W.C. Perry, pastor of the Grant African Methodist Episcopal Church on Soho Street, delivered a petition signed at the 59th Conference of the Colored Congregations in Ontario and Quebec to the Ontario provincial legislature. The petition expressed 'grave concern' over the 'denial of the fundamental rights of Negro citizens through discrimination in the field of employment,' and also asked for legal protection against discrimination based on race, colour, or creed, and 'against any person resident in Canada, with reference to religion, education, employment, housing,' and for 'the right to hold any rank in the armed forces of Canada or its government service.'[1]

Individual African Canadians also drew on religious precepts to protest against racism. In a letter to Prime Minister King, Philip Shadd from Fletcher, a small town near Windsor, invoked the teachings of Christ, whom he described as 'the founder of democracy,' to criticize government policy: 'We were told by the founder of democracy – Christ Jesus – to first cast out the beam from our own eye, then we can see clearly to cast the mote out of our brother's eye.' Shadd called upon the government to prohibit 'the colour line,' pointing to the hypocrisy of tolerating racism at home while African Canadians were shedding their blood for Canada and democracy abroad.[2]

Not surprisingly, railway porters played an important role in the campaign against discrimination. Students of African Canadian history have explained that the porters, who were prevented from taking most other railroad jobs by racism, nevertheless enjoyed high status in their communities. Their exclusion from so many jobs in the wider economy meant that the job of railway porters became one of the most secure jobs for African Canadian men.[3] During the war, a campaign was undertaken to organize the Canadian Pacific Railway's (CPR's) Black porters by no less a figure than African American activist A. Philip Randolph. President of the Brotherhood of Sleeping Car Porters (BSCP), Randolph evoked tremendous admiration within and beyond Black communities in North America when he forced President Roosevelt to create the Fair Employment Practices Committee to end racist discrimination in American war industries by threatening to march on Washington at the head of millions of African Americans. During his wartime visits to Canada, Randolph warned that 'the people must not relax their efforts to protect the rights of labor and minority groups at home,' lest the war be won in Europe but lost 'in Canada and the U.S.A.'[4] By 1942 he convinced the CPR porters to join the BSCP. A year later the union won recognition from the railway company.[5]

Porters employed by the publicly owned Canadian National Railway (CNR) were already unionized by this time. They belonged to Division 175, the Road Roamers, of the Canadian Brotherhood of Railway Employees (CBRE). The division originated in 1917 as an independent union, the Order of Sleeping Car Porters, because the constitution of the CBRE, which represented other railway workers, restricted membership to white employees. CBRE president A.R. Mosher suggested in 1918 that African Canadian porters should join his union as the Canadian Brotherhood of Colored Railway Employees. John Arthur Robinson, the president of the Order of Sleeping Car Porters' union, declined this invitation, expressing his organization's early anti-racist stand: 'regardless of the fact that your organization has a "color" line in your constitution it was not our intention to have a "color" line in the Order of Sleeping Car Porters.'[6] In 1927, after the CBRE eliminated the 'colour line' from its constitution, the African Canadian railway workers' local became part of that union. Black workers, however, continued to face discrimination because in the collective agreements between the union and the CNR, seniority and promotion remained confined to the group in which employees were hired.[7] On most lines, they could work only as porters. Only the Toronto district hired them as third cooks as well, but they were still barred from all other positions in the dining cars and from becoming conductors in sleeping cars. Even as Mosher was declaring publicly that he believed the labour movement to be the most potent instrument for overcoming the economic, racial, and political differences that divided the people of Canada,[8] his union was instrumental in perpetuating the CNR's racist employment practices.[9] The contradiction between such discriminatory practices and the stated aims of the allied powers during the Second World War, as well as Randolph's successful campaign among CPR porters, spurred CNR porters to fight against discrimination. They believed that ending such discriminatory practices by the publicly owned company would set an example for private enterprises that also discriminated against African Canadians.[10] CNR porters did not hesitate to threaten that unless the CBRE took action on their behalf, they would leave the union, which belonged to the small, nationalist All-Canadian Congress of Labour, and join the American Federation of Labor–affiliated BSCP.[11] J.A. Robinson warned Mosher to recognize that, owing to its heterogeneous composition and non-racist attitudes, the international union was a more suitable agent for African Canadian porters than the national one.[12]

Competition from the BSCP forced white union officials to pay attention to the demands of their 'coloured' members. The September1942 convention of the Brotherhood of Railway Employees and Other Transport Workers condemned racial discrimination.[13] CBRE officials also threatened the CNR management that unless they hired some African Canadians to work as third cooks in their dining cars, they would report them to the Ministry of Labour.[14] Despite these efforts, equality for Black workers was not attained until more than a decade following the war, in the wake of new, post-war, federal anti-discrimination legislation.

Communists of African descent also promoted unions within African Canadian communities. Addressing a number of African Canadian organizations and other minority groups in Toronto on May Day, 1943, African American poet Langston Hughes described the 'progressive labor movement,' by which he apparently meant the Congress of Industrial Organizations, as 'the most promising avenue for Negroes for full collaboration with their fellows in building real unity.' He pointed out that Black people were primarily poor and working class, and that their 'destiny was interwoven with the destinies of the workers everywhere.'[15]

Protest against employment discrimination was not confined to unions and radical parties. African Canadian community organizations also challenged employment discrimination. In Montreal, where Black women could not obtain jobs in war industries, the executive director of the Negro Community Centre convinced the local head of the NSS to test the women's abilities to perform such jobs. Although the women attained perfect scores on the test, the NSS official still refused to assign them to manufacturing jobs. In frustration, African Canadian activists held a mass meeting and selected a deputation to Ottawa to demand that qualified African Canadians be hired by war industries. Only then did NSS officials agree to hire African Canadian women.[16]

Montreal's African Canadians established a chapter of the National Association for the Advancement of Coloured People (NAACP) in 1943 on the occasion of a meeting called to protest against a racist article in the publication of Canadian Car Munitions. The main goal of this organization was to encourage people of colour to get higher education to equip themselves for a variety of jobs. Special efforts were necessary to promote higher education within the community because 'before the war coloured people would say "what's the use of spending time and money getting an education, it won't lead anywhere."'[17]

Among the most eloquent defenders of African Canadian rights were members of the Amherstburg Community Club, a Christian youth organization in the small Ontario town which had drawn a substantial number of Black migrants from the United States a century earlier because of its proximity to Detroit and the Canadian border. A letter seeking the support of the local MP, Murray Clark, from the club's president, Alvin McCurdy, gave expression to the African Canadian view of rights and citizenship:

> We want every right and privilege to which our citizenship entitles us, no more, no less. Segregation and discrimination nullify our citizenship and they must be abolished for the sake of democracy itself ... In failing to recognize the faculties of the colored man and woman at this time and crisis, our country limits its own destiny; in denying us jobs, our country denies itself increased production; in promoting segregation the country destroys national unity.

McCurdy pointed to the incongruity of the conscription of African Canadians to defend democratic rights abroad even as they were being denied equal rights at home. Without such rights, he explained, 'we fight our country's battles as slaves of old and not as free men.' An end to employment discrimination topped the list of reforms sought by McCurdy and his club. They wanted all industry involved in the war effort to 'treat all labor alike, regardless of race, color, or creed, religion or national origin, in hiring and upgrading and training of men and women.' McCurdy believed that the introduction of a bill of rights was the best way to end discriminatory practices.[18] While calling for legislation, the club's president also protested to the NSS against southern Ontario employers who refused to hire African Canadians and against government officials who colluded in such practices.[19]

Members of Amherstburg Community Club clearly saw the UAW as an ally since they sent a motion calling for anti-discrimination legislation to Local 200 of the union in Windsor. And their trust was not misplaced. The local endorsed the motion in its publication, *Ford Facts*, and sent it on to the union's district council and the local MPP, explaining that vested interests had too long used racism as a weapon to divide workers, and calling upon all interested lodges and clubs to take up the fight against discrimination and make the Atlantic Charter 'a living document.'[20]

Like Jews, African Canadians supported efforts by other minorities to fight against discrimination. A group of young African Canadian men in Toronto, for example, established the Anti-Discriminatory Committee in 1943, which collaborated with the Labor Youth Federation in campaigning among labour unions to support J.J. Glass's anti-discrimination bill in the Ontario legislature.[21]

One of the chief concerns of the 1944 conference of the Joint Council of Negro Youth in Toronto was the denial of economic opportunity:

> Despite the fact that the Negro in Canada has had to face the question of racial discrimination and prejudice in a different and more subtle form than in the United States, the result of this practice has been the same. Discriminatory practices in society invariably result in the lowering of the economic standards of the people against whom these practices are directed, as its effects are felt in employment, housing, wage levels, etc. and more generally in education and culture, which affect the ability to function as useful and contributing members of society.

The conference concluded that the 'Negro' had had a central role in fighting discrimination, but not alone. The most effective strategy involved cooperation with 'his allies,' that is, other minority peoples and 'all who fight for the full extension of democracy to all sectors of society.' After hearing MPP Joe Salsberg speak about his anti-discrimination bill, the meeting resolved that one of its first tasks must be to prepare a brief concerning cases of discrimination against 'Negroes,' to be publicized and presented to the Canadian Youth Commission. They also resolved to work for broader unity among minority groups and to fight against anti-Semitism.

Plans were wide-ranging. They included the establishment of interracial committees which would include, among others, NSS officers. But the conference placed emphasis on unions:

> Trade Unions have in the past and can in the future make an aggressive move towards the breaking down of racial discrimination. Seeing that Negroes are employed in all industries that they are capable of handling, bringing pressure to bear on management, which it was agreed had the right either to permit or prohibit employment of Negroes, would insure the employment of Negroes. Lay-offs on a seniority basis was also agreed to be a step trade unions have taken against discriminatory practices, such as the Negro being the last hired and the first fired.[22]

The UAW, CPR employees, the United Steel Workers of America, and the LPP were represented at the conference. As in the case of the Jews, however, the labour and left-wing orientation of the group did not preclude collaboration with other segments of the community. The meeting itself was held in a Baptist church, and the young participants, who included members of various church groups, envisioned an important role for religion in their struggle. 'Religion contains the essence of democracy,' they found, 'in that it considers all men equal,' adding that 'religion is a compelling driving force that makes for the betterment of mankind, and combats tendencies toward defeatism.'[23]

'Peripheral' Europeans

Eastern and southern Europeans asserted their rights as citizens by protesting against discrimination. The value of their labour for Canada, they maintained, entitled them to equal rights. Adopting a white settler colonist perspective of nation-building, Ukrainians, the largest of these groups, pointed to their role in opening up the Canadian West. In November 1940, Alberta MLA William Tomyn, for example, spoke at a Ukrainian teachers' convention in Mundare of the hardy Ukrainian pioneers whose sweat and blood moistened Canada's 'rich land.' 'The great wheat fields of Western Canada,' he added, 'are so many written pages of the great book of wonders of the early Ukrainian settlers. They are the unfailing testimony of their hardships, their toils, their enduring courage and amazing service to Canada.'[24] These immigrants were acutely conscious of performing the least desirable jobs in Canada: 'For a time the bulk of Ukrainians formed a pick and shovel caste, claiming exclusive possession of the poorest and least honourable occupations.' But they insisted that no inherent characteristics doomed them 'forever to serve at the tail end of the wheel-barrow.'[25]

Immigrants from Hungary pointed to the deep injustice of being relegated to an inferior status despite their contributions to building Canada. Rozsa Páll Kovács, poet and wife of Hungarian Presbyterian minister Jenő Molnár, saw in the classification of Hungarian immigrants as 'non-preferred' an expression of their rejection by their new homeland. In a poem entitled 'Non-Preferred,' she wrote:

We are not wanted.
But the mine-shaft gapes for us.
Magyar muscles strain to the thud of the pick ...

'Drumheller, Alberta. Steve Pinter, born in Budapest, combines timbering with
actual mining on the face, 1943.'
Library and Archives Canada, WR-2604. Photograph by Harry Rowed.

> And there Satan lurks as we seek the vein,
> Battering, cleaving, forcing open
> In naked toil, in everlasting night,
> The gates of infinite treasure.
> All this for thee, young country.
> In vain, reproachfully and coldly,
> Thou turnest away thy face.[26]

An anonymous Croatian poet from the gold-mining region of northern
Ontario also protested against the bleakness and danger of immigrant
miners' work through poetry:

Like worms through tunnels they
   crawl,
And heavy rocks pull up to the daily sun,
During their life they dig their
   grave,
Passing their entire life in
   darkness.[27]

Unlike the Jews and African Canadians who celebrated the growth of the labour movement during the war years as a sure way of counteracting employment discrimination, minorities of European origin responded to the inroads that unions, especially industrial unions, made among immigrant workers in diverging, even conflicting ways.

Despite their awareness of prejudice and discrimination, Ukrainian Canadian middle-class leaders who had been successful in Canada (professionals, small-business owners, and prosperous farmers) ascribed racism, by and large, to a minority of Canadians, and continued to believe in the inevitable rewards of honest labour and the possibilities of upward mobility. They accepted the status quo and believed that Ukrainian Canadians should be grateful to their adoptive land for giving them freedom of worship and 'a right to preserve their own customs, and culture – language and song.' Consequently, 'much progress' was made by Ukrainian Canadians 'economically, culturally and religiously.'[28] Some of them blamed the inequality between the 'English' and the Ukrainians on 'low standard of living, superstition and ignorance' of the latter, traits which they believed had to be 'eradicated at all costs.'[29] They saw the diversity of occupations among Ukrainian Canadians as evidence that they were not inferior to other Canadians, and that Canada offered them a great many opportunities. 'As compared to their immigrant fathers the proportion of laborers among the sons of the Ukrainians is halved, while that of the professional men is doubled.'[30] Further evidence of 'swift climbers' was the large number of second-generation Ukrainian teachers in Canada. Such leaders emphasized the loyalty of Canadians of Ukrainian descent, not the discrimination they faced. Others, such as Anthony Hlynka, Social Credit MP from Alberta, lamented that jobs in the RCMP and in the civil service were limited to those of 'British racial origin.' Hlynka, moreover, characterized as 'Hitlerian' the statement of a Saskatchewan relief officer to the effect that 'there should be two scale[s] of relief, one for Central Europeans and one for "white people,"' but quickly added that the Liberal government was attempting to eradicate such attitudes and policies.[31] He did not find it necessary to assert the 'whiteness' of central Europeans vis-à-vis any other group. The alternative he presented was of the government treating all groups of citizens equally. Even he, however, displayed little awareness of the widespread discrimination against group members in war industries. Since most members of the Ukrainian Canadian elite believed that their fellows were making good headway in Canada, they could focus their attention on developments abroad. Their primary goal in dealing with Ottawa was to gain support for the establishment of an independent Ukraine in Europe.[32]

Wasyl Buryanik, Saskatchewan leader of the Ukrainian Self-Reliance League, a lay organization of the Ukrainian Orthodox Church, explained that one of the reasons that Ukrainians voted 'no' in the plebiscite to release Prime Minister King from his promise not to introduce conscription was to protest against widespread discrimination by Winnipeg employers who refused to hire Ukrainian 'boys and girls ... on account of their names.'[33] An advisor to Prime Minister King believed that Ukrainian Canadians were shifting their loyalties from the Liberals to the CCF because of employment discrimination. On the occasion of the Liberal Party conference on 29 September 1943, the advisor cited an editorial from *Ukrainian Voice*, the organ of the Ukrainian Self-Reliance League, which suggested that Ukrainian Canadians would be better off supporting the CCF because the Liberal and Conservative parties discriminated against them. The editorial stated: 'Every government, provincial or dominion, has at its disposal a number of Government positions. And if such a government is not allowing such positions to the Citizens of Ukrainian descent but always gives priority to citizens of the English, French or Scotch descent, then the Ukrainians are quite justified to consider themselves aggrieved, slighted.' The editorial's claim that the CCF treated Ukrainians with less prejudice than the Liberals was meant to pressure the Liberal Party to give more consideration to Ukrainians. The prime minister's advisor added that this editorial accurately reflected the reason why people of central European origin in western Canada were turning from the Liberal Party to the CCF.[34]

Left-wing Ukrainians belonging to or sympathetic to the Communist Party paid more attention to prejudice and discrimination. In 1942, *Ukrains'ke zhyttia*, a pro-communist newspaper, denounced the refusal of 'petty bosses and foremen' to employ workers with names ending in 'sky', 'uk,' and 'enko' as a form of racist discrimination the 'fascists use to disunite people and workers allied to the war effort.'[35] Two years later it described Ontario's anti-discrimination bill as a 'move in the right direction,' but criticized its failure to cover cases of racial and religious discrimination in employment.[36] This commitment to fighting employment discrimination seemed to appeal to many working-class people of Ukrainian descent.

J.J. Billoki, for example, the Ontario-born son of Galician immigrant parents, became a union activist in response to discrimination. In 1939, he went to work at the Falconbridge smelter in Sudbury as a furnace feeder, alongside other people of eastern European descent. The conditions that he found at the smelter appalled him: he and his co-workers were breathing in the black dust and red hot ashes that flew around the furnace. Billoki approached supervisor Charlie Taylor to ask for ventilation and higher wages for the furnace feeders. He justified his request by pointing out that the jobs were 'really hard and important,' explaining that the eastern Europeans had come from the Coniston smelter and built Falconbridge. Taylor responded with contempt, turning to another supervisor to say that if the men did not like their treatment at Falconbridge, they should get rid of them. To Billoki he said: 'Well, Christ mate, we can't get a white man to work on that job.' Outraged, Billoki 'put Taylor in his place.' Billoki recalled: 'I said "Charlie my dad came here in 1909, to this country, and I know that you came in here in 1929, and I don't know what colour you are calling my dad," but I said that "he is every bit as white a man or better than you are."' He added that he would go to the floor and tell the men that he tried to get them a 5-cent increase and that a disdainful Taylor responded that a 'white man' would not stay on that job. Billoki credited such discrimination for the 'mushrooming' of the union movement at Falconbridge. The men voted to join the International Union of Mine, Mill and Smelter Workers and Billoki became the international 'rep' for the union.[37]

Ann Hunka recalled how readily minority workers at the Electro Metals plant in Welland signed cards to join the United Electrical, Radio and Machine Workers' Union when she approached them in December 1942.[38] Seven years earlier, Hunka's husband William had been fired from his job at the local Page-Hersey steel pipe plant for his role in organizing an unaffiliated union whose demands included union membership irrespective of 'trade, nationality, race, creed or political opinions' and the right of each union member to 'express his opinion in his native language.'[39] The desire to ensure job security for radical minority workers was thus understandably decisive in convincing the shy and retiring Hunka to take a leading role in organizing the United

Electrical Workers' local. Significantly, despite or perhaps because of her experience as a worker at the local Empire Cotton Mills before the war, Hunka did not consider the role the United Electrical Workers might play in improving the position of women in the workplace. She recalled that she and other women workers in war industries, anxiously awaiting the return of enlisted husbands and other male relatives from overseas, were willing to give up their jobs to them, and hoping to withdraw from the workforce altogether.[40]

Records of wartime industrial strikes confirm that many workers of Ukrainian descent, women and men alike, saw support for the labour movement as their best guarantee for fair treatment in Canada. During a 1941 strike at the Campbell's Soup Company in New Toronto in support of the Packinghouse Workers' Organizing Committee, for example, women workers of Ukrainian descent who lived near the factory and worked for Campbell's during the 'tomato season,' were the most resolute strikers.[41] They faced determined opposition from Premier Hepburn, who denounced the strikers and paid to bring busloads of tomato growers from Essex and Kent counties to process their own produce. Although the strike was peaceful, he also sent in the Ontario Provincial Police. In the meantime, company representatives visited the homes of workers to urge them to return to work. However, only a fraction of the workers did so. The rest stayed away until the company agreed to raise wages and recognize the principle of seniority. Recognition for the Packinghouse Workers' Organizing Committee as their representative was the only goal that the strikers failed to accomplish.[42]

Like Ukrainian Canadians, Canadians of Hungarian descent also held competing visions of integration into Canadian society. Members of the Hungarian Canadian elite distrusted the CIO and feared the popularity of industrial unions among minority workers. Béla Eisner, an employee of Sun Life Insurance Company in Montreal, for instance, who was given leave with pay for three months to travel to Hungarian communities throughout Canada and to report about conditions within them to the Nationalities Branch of the DNWS, identified prejudice and employment discrimination as major sources of discontent among workers of Hungarian origin.[43] Perceived as inferior 'foreigners,' they never obtained the 'good,' 'softer' jobs, and they were seldom promoted because Anglo-Canadians did not want to work under 'foreigners.' Eisner believed that Hungarian immigrant workers and their children distrusted the Canadian government, both because it had done nothing to protect them from losing their jobs at the end of the First World

War and because it did nothing to protect them when their difficult jobs damaged their health or when their employers dismissed them. He warned that all these grievances led them to support the CIO.[44]

The *Kanadai Magyar Ujság* (Canadian Hungarian News) provides an example of how socially conservative Hungarian Canadians envisioned ideal labour relations in their new home. Commenting on 'Canadians All,' a government sponsored radio programme that introduced the contributions made by different minorities to Canadian society, the paper editorialized that such programmes served the great goal of Canadian unity, not just by familiarizing different groups with one another, but also by helping 'the development of Christian relations among workers and their employers and thus advancing social and world peace, the triumph of Christ's love.'[45] The newspaper, which had received subsidies from the right-wing Hungarian government of Admiral Nicholas Horthy until the outbreak of the Second World War, acknowledged that most group members were workers and peasants whose major contribution to Canada was their toil. Gusztáv Nemes, the paper's editor, wrote in a 1943 English-language editorial:

> We are so proud of those simple workmen, and those nameless Canadian pioneers of Magyar origin, who amid thousands of privations helped to form Canada into what it is today. We are proud of the Canadian-Hungarians who built roads, railroads and canals, worked in factories, on farms and in public utilities; and who frequently for low wages and perhaps only seasonally employed, did their best and contributed in the building of the country. We are proud of those who work in offices, those engaged in fine arts, music, painting, architecture, pleasing everybody and furthering the cultural development of our Canada.[46]

Its accommodationist stance led the *Ujság* to report that the CCF and labour unions were making considerable headway during the war. But by protesting that material gain rather than idealism motivated those few Hungarian Canadians who were active in radical circles, the paper revealed anxiety that radicalism would discredit the group as a whole in Canadian eyes.[47] The paper acknowledged that immigrants encountered prejudice in Canada, but it downplayed the seriousness of biases which, it asserted, only a minority of Canadians embraced.[48] It declared that in a democratic, united Canada there would be no place for expressions such as '"foreigners," "second class citizens," "chosen people," "white men," or even "bohunk."'[49] It was up to Canadians of 'non-

Anglo-Saxon descent' to convince, even educate, Anglo-Saxon groups to accept minorities 'in full equality in heart and mind.'[50] Similarly, it was up to members of historically disadvantaged groups to improve their position in Canadian society by obtaining an education or skill.[51]

Despite the Hungarian elite's anti-radicalism and antipathy toward the CIO in particular, however, many Hungarian workers enthusiastically supported new industrial unions. In a letter to the *Kanadai Magyar Munkás* (Hungarian Canadian Worker), the Hungarian-language communist paper, István Juhász, a miner from Nacmine, Alberta, argued, for example, that Hungarian workers earned the right to equal access to employment and to living wages because they had contributed to building Canada with their labour. He believed that the only way they could attain equality, given nativist attitudes, was through the miners' union.[52] In another letter to the *Munkás*, Hungarian worker 'J.J.' criticized 'foreign' workers who responded to anti-foreign hysteria by working harder than native-born workers. Such behaviour simply reinforced the treatment of immigrant workers as second-class citizens, aided exploitation, and ultimately alienated Canadian workers. He urged Hungarian workers to join labour organizations and insist on their rights. An editorial in the same paper denounced the mass hysteria against 'foreigners.' 'Hungarians and other immigrants are not foreigners,' it stated, 'they are Canadians ... Through their labour and through the basic principles of democracy and culture, they have won the right to feel just as much at home here and to be treated exactly the same as any other nationality among this big country's eleven million inhabitants.'[53]

Although the Communist Party was the strongest advocate of industrial unions among immigrant workers of Hungarian origin, as among other groups from the 'peripheries' of Europe, support for such unions was not limited to communists. Minority workers believed that membership in unions would end their vulnerability in the labour market. 'We knew that it [the union] would be good ... They won't be able to just let people go,' recalled a Hungarian worker from Welland who was otherwise not politically radical. His daughter elaborated: 'The biggest problem was that it was mostly "English" in higher positions and if they didn't like someone's face or something like that, they simply kicked him out. So people joined together to put a stop to this. Now they had a defender, that's why they signed up ... Now people could speak up if they didn't like something. Before if you said something the next day you noticed that you had no punch card. You could go home.'[54] A

Windsor worker noted the benefits immigrants derived from unions by describing the corrupt practices of foremen before unionization: 'when there was no "uni" [union] or nothing. We got the "peda" [payday] and when we headed home the "boss" was standing in front of the hotel, waiting. We had to buy him drinks until midnight. He didn't pay.'[55]

Communist leadership was responsible for the strongest protest against discrimination and most committed support for unionization among Polish Canadians as well. During the 1941–2 Kirkland Lake gold miners' strike, the Polish Canadian communist newspaper *Głos Pracy* (Voice of Labour), reporting on the exploitation of Slavic miners, cited a Polish miner from Timmins who said: 'our Slavs are kept in the mines simply because they are productive. They do the heaviest work, have the worst and most dangerous contracts.' The paper noted organizing drives and all CIO-led wartime strikes, pointing out whenever a large number of Polish workers participated in them.[56] On its own account and on behalf of other CIO unions, such as the Toronto locals of the United Electrical, Radio and Machine Workers and the United Shoe Workers' Union, the Communist-led Polish People's Association offered financial and organizational support to striking workers at two rubber factories in Kitchener in 1939. The strikers sought recognition of the United Rubber Workers (a CIO union). They also demanded increased wages, arguing that because of speed ups they were working harder and producing more, but that this was not reflected in higher wages.[57]

Związkowiec (The Alliancer), described by the Wartime Information Board's foreign-language press survey as 'mildly socialistic,'[58] was also sympathetic to organized labour. In 1939 it published a letter from an Oshawa worker applauding the failure of efforts of Ontario Malleable Iron Company to dissuade Polish workers from supporting the Steel Workers Organizing Committee in a strike for union recognition. The company apparently hired a Polish spy, who warned that the strike was led by communists and that it would make England unhappy and thus have serious repercussions for the fate of Poland.[59] Adam Borsk, the Polish-speaking son of Polish immigrants, was successful in recruiting large numbers of workers of Polish descent in the meat-packing industry for the pro-CCF Packinghouse Workers' Organizing Committee.[60] Peter Taraska, an anti-communist member of the Winnipeg School Board and general secretary of the Polish Relief Fund, charged by officials in Ottawa's Nationalities Branch to inform them about developments in Polish Canadian communities and the mood among Polish

Canadians, reported that when he visited Sault Ste Marie in 1942, 'a strike called by the CIO was in full swing.' The Poles to whom he spoke there were 'quite proud to be out on strike.' Taraska also believed that the Poles employed in lumber camps around the Lakehead region were decidedly left-leaning.[61]

The case of Tony Gervasio, an Italian Canadian worker at Stelco in Hamilton, sheds light on the appeal of industrial unions to workers of Italian descent. In 1939 he had been appointed foreman because he was such an asset to the steel company's baseball team. A week after Italy entered the war in 1940, the 'Mounties' appeared at the plant and arrested two hundred Italians who belonged to 'an Italian cultural club that was run by fascists.' Gervasio and all other Italian Canadians who had managed to work their way up to skilled jobs were demoted to labourers' positions. He did not find the claims that they constituted security risks credible, saying 'If they were saboteurs, why would they let them stay in the plant? This was an excuse to get them off the good jobs.' Consequently he became a union organizer. 'I thought it would be a matter of security, that the company couldn't say: "Okay, you're out."'[62]

Although the part they played has received little attention from historians, perhaps the best illustration of the intensity of protest against employment discrimination by workers of eastern and southern European descent, and of the broader implications of this protest for the Canadian labour movement, was their role in the gold miners' strike of 1941–2, in Kirkland Lake. The strike was fought to obtain recognition from mine operators for the International Union of Mine, Mill and Smelter Workers (Mine-Mill) as the miners' bargaining agent. Miners abided by the government's regulation to submit to conciliation in this dispute, while mine operators refused to meet with the conciliation board. The board unanimously recommended recognition of Local 240 of Mine-Mill, but the employers refused to recognize the union. The government, which had earlier passed a regulation recognizing workers' right to bargain with employers through trade unions or other representatives of their choice, did nothing to force gold-mine operators to bargain with Mine-Mill. Convinced of the inadequacy of federal labour policy and of the pro-employers stance of King's Liberal government by the failure to enforce the conciliation board's decision, the labour movement threw its full support behind the strikers. But the entry of the United States into the war in December 1941 and the substitution of the Lend-Lease programme for gold transfers to finance war

'Coal mining, Mitchell, BC. Each night before going on shift, miners check their bulletin boards for further union notices, government orders, or income tax changes. They are Charlie Koska, a Czech of 64 years, and Albert Ciamolini, an Italian who has been in Canadian coal mining since 1903, and who has two sons working in the same mine.'
Library and Archives Canada, WR-2710. Photograph by Harry Rowed.

production undermined the striking miners' strength. The declining demand for gold meant that neither mine operators nor the government saw great urgency in ending the strike, and after roughly two long, cold winter months the strike collapsed. Despite its defeat, however, the strike marked a turning point in labour relations in Canada. It convinced organized labour that legislative support was required to protect workers' rights. 'Remember Kirkland Lake' became the rallying cry for strengthening the labour movement and for supporting the pro-labour CCF in elections.[63]

What was the role of 'foreign' workers in the Kirkland Lake strike? Police reports from the gold-mining region suggested that the majority of Anglo-Canadian miners went back to work before the strike's end, while the majority of 'foreigners' stayed out.[64] Given the nativist belief that 'foreign' workers were radical, one might be tempted to dismiss such reports as an attempt to break worker unity by fomenting ethnic divisions. But labour organizers confirmed that the most radical and committed of the strikers and their supporters were immigrants, among them many women. Bob Miner, a CIO organizer then active in Kirkland Lake, recalled that during the long strike 'Yugoslavs' stopped members of their ethnic group from relying on relief from the union. '"Leave that for the goddamned Englishmen," they argued, "they might go to work if they don't get strike relief."'[65] While not all immigrants approved of the strike, CIO supporters were sufficiently numerous to exert pressure on strike breakers from their own ethnic groups. A woman who ran a boarding house, for example, was threatened that if she continued to admit scabs, she would soon have no tenants at all. The wives and daughters of strikers and other female sympathizers joined them on the picket line. Militant Yugoslav women among them threw paprika in the eyes of strike breakers, sending a number of them to hospital.[66]

Unfortunately, we have no detailed first-hand testimony explaining the strikers' motives. A report from the Kirkland Lake police department to the commissioner of police for Ontario, however, which blamed 'foreigners' for labour trouble in the gold mines, inadvertently revealed both their grievances and the hostility they faced from some of their English Canadian neighbours. During the Great Depression, the report stated, 'it was quite impossible to obtain work unless you had the proper contacts and could either put $150.00 up for a job or sign away so much of your pay until paid up.' Instead of seeing that desperation led immigrant workers to succumb to this practice, the report blamed them for the prevalence of this 'vile method.' 'The Canadian citizen would

not stand for such methods,' it claimed, and added that 'shift bosses ...
were quite frequently seen at the houses of foreign employees who fed
them liquor free and allowed them to use their houses for immoral purposes.'[67] Although records of the mining company suggest that only
one third of its employees were foreign-born (and that figure may have
included those born in Britain),[68] the report claimed that 'it was quite
common knowledge at the Teck-Hughes [mine] that unless you were
a foreigner you could not obtain a job.'[69] According to the local police,
'those very foreigners who had paid for their jobs in the first place,'
were responsible for sowing the 'seeds of social unrest' and introducing
communism among the miners. They were aided by 'a small band of
English speaking miners,' because 'white' employees were angry about
the 'large foreign element' in the mines.[70]

Colin Clarke, an English Canadian resident of Kirkland Lake, believed that 'foreigners' continued the strike even after many of their
English Canadian counterparts returned to work due to their conviction that only the union would have provided them with some security. They mistrusted both their English Canadian neighbours and the
law. Clarke believed such mistrust to be well founded. Despite the
fact that immigrants were 'brought to Canada by the boatload to do
... common labor and colonize ... areas,' as soon as Italy entered the
war in 1940, local residents suggested boycotting 'alien labour.' When
the mine operators refused union recognition, although the majority of
workers supported unionization, the government did nothing to force
the employers to respect the law.[71] The behaviour of strikers who were
not rehired after the strike provides additional evidence of their strong
commitment to labour unions. Many of them migrated south, found
employment in war industries, and became key activists in support of
the CIO.[72]

People of Colour and Minorities of European Descent

In what may be the only systematic exploration of the relationship between race, identity, and colour among a group of eastern European
descent in both Canada and the United States, Vic Satzewich suggests
that the creation and assertion of a national identity by Ukrainians may
account for the failure of group members to seek inclusion in the white
race. Stateless in Europe, most Ukrainian peasant and working-class
immigrants to Canada during the late nineteenth and early twentieth
centuries identified themselves as belonging to a particular village or

region rather than as Ukrainians. The development of a Ukrainian national identity in North America was initiated by the group's educated, mostly clerical, elite. Although they were perceived as non-white in North America, they were so focused on gaining national recognition based on European loyalties and statehood in Europe that they were not much interested in their placement within the racial hierarchies of their new homelands.[73] But the formation of ethnic identity and the quest for inclusion in the white race were not necessarily mutually exclusive. In the United States, where workers of European descent feared competition from the integration of African Americans in the workplace and a drop in the value of their homes from the integration of neighbourhoods, Ukrainian Americans appear to have assigned importance to their 'whiteness' as well as to their ethnic identity.[74] That whiteness played a less significant role in the formation of Ukrainian Canadian identities was more likely the result of distinctly Canadian circumstances than of concerns relating to ethnic identity and statehood in Europe.

Canadians of eastern European origin, whatever their class background, did assert their whiteness when colour was the basis for discrimination and prejudice against them. To continue with the example of people of Ukrainian origin, when Ukrainian Canadian MP Hlynka protested vehemently in the House of Commons against the Saskatoon relief officer who wanted to introduce separate scales of relief for 'central Europeans' and for 'white people,' as we have seen, he did not find it necessary to assert the 'whiteness' of central Europeans to subordinate any other group. He proposed that the government simply treat all groups of citizens equally. J.J. Billoki's recollections of the racist denial of 'white' status to workers of eastern European origin offer another good illustration of the distinctive features of the association between colour and race in wartime Canada. When, in response to Billoki's complaint about the appalling working conditions of eastern European furnace feeders at the Falconbridge smelter, his English Canadian supervisor exclaimed that no 'white man' would be willing to perform their job, the comment was clearly meant and understood as derogating. To assert his own dignity, and by extension that of his co-workers, Billoki claimed to be every bit as white as the supervisor. Unlike men and women of similar background in the United States, however, who sought to gain acceptance as whites by distinguishing themselves from African Americans, Billoki's claim to whiteness was not made in order to distance people of eastern European descent from allegedly inferior 'coloured' groups in the workplace or community. That the equation between whiteness and rights did not require any explicit statement about the inferiority of people of colour was less a reflection of greater tolerance among Ukrainian Canadians compared to Ukrainian Americans than a consequence of the different make-up of the populations of the two neighbouring countries. In all likelihood there were few or no people of colour at Falconbridge or in Sudbury during the Second World War. Consequently, workers of 'peripheral' European origin were the most marginalized 'others' in the workplace, and probably also in the community. The reason for their enthusiastic support for Mine-Mill was, as Billoki's recollections imply, the promise of equality and an end to racist discrimination.

Hungarian Canadian Béla Eisner believed that Hungarian Canadian workers would be thrust into the ranks of the CIO by the racist insults hurled against them. Among these insults none was more humiliating, according to Eisner, than that Hungarian Canadian men were 'not considered to be "white men."' Like Ukrainian Canadians, however, when they asserted their whiteness, Hungarian Canadians did not do so as a way of distancing themselves from and asserting the inferiority of people of colour. Indeed, when they were labelled 'foreigners,' a more common form of derision in Canada than the denial of whiteness, they frequently responded that English Canadians (or French Canadians) were foreigners too. The only true Canadians were the 'Indians.'[75]

Such responses illustrate not that minorities of European origin were more tolerant in Canada than in the United States, but rather that in the absence of the kind of black-white polarization that prevailed south of the border, these groups did not see colour as the main criterion for incorporation into Canadian society.

Intergroup Collaboration

Perhaps because they did not view racist prejudice and discrimination as serious obstacles to the progress of their respective groups in Canada, the elites of eastern European groups were less committed to interethnic collaboration than Jewish leaders were. Indeed, the only formal programme of such collaboration during the war, the Canadian Unity Council, was established in 1941 in Winnipeg at the initiative of Jack Steinberg, the president of the Winnipeg lodge of B'nai B'rith and the executive director of the western division of the CJC. It included members of the elites of twenty-two ethnic groups in the city. It also invited participation by Winnipeggers of English, Irish, Scottish, and Welsh origin and included representatives from the Winnipeg Rotary Club, the YMCA and the Young Men's Board of Trade. Robert Fletcher, of the Winnipeg St. George's Society and former deputy minister of education of Manitoba, was elected as the council's first chairman.[76] Its vice-president was B.B. Dubienski, from the Polish community, and its corresponding secretary was local Jewish activist and educator Louis Rosenberg. The Unity Council's goals were to create 'among the Canadian people a greater unity and mutual understanding, resulting from a common citizenship, a common belief in democracy and the ideals of liberty, and the placing of the common good before the interests of any group, whatever their national or racial origins, as equal partners in Canadian society.' The elimination of intolerance and discrimination based on descent, race, creed, or country of birth was identified as a major step toward the building of Canadian unity. The main activities of the council, whose members met once a month, consisted of familiarizing one another and the public with the culture and customs of their respective groups, through lectures and exhibits of handicrafts, and preparing immigrants for naturalization.[77] In other words, members placed their faith in the ability of education gradually to overcome prejudice and discrimination.

The impact of the Unity Council's programme is difficult to judge. It did apparently disseminate articles published across the border by the Common Council for American Unity. The Common Council, established in 1940 to foster harmonious relationships among American mainstream and minority groups, had an extensive network of connections to foreign-language newspapers and published articles from leading American intellectuals.[78] The Hungarian-language *Ujság*, for example, carried anti-racist articles originally written for the Common Council's publication, *Common Ground*, by anthropologist Margaret Mead. On the occasion of Labour Day the Hungarian-language newspaper also published an article strongly supportive of labour unions. It reproduced these articles, which focused on topics that it did not otherwise cover and were written in a tone at odds with its general approach, without any comment or explanation.[79]

Although people of African, and southern and eastern European descent, like Jews, had the right to vote in Canada, their reactions to employment discrimination were markedly different. African Canadians, far fewer in number than 'peripheral' Europeans and facing more intense discrimination, joined forces regardless of class or ideological orientation in anti-discrimination campaigns. Like Canadian Jews they recognized that the contradiction between Canada's declared war aims to fight for democracy and toleration and its treatment of minority workers on the home front offered a unique opportunity to challenge racist employment discrimination. Again like Canadian Jews, African Canadians drew on the resources and example of their American counterparts and entered into alliances with other racialized minorities to build their anti-discrimination campaigns.

Canadians of southern and especially eastern European descent were more numerous, but more divided than African Canadians. While not unaware of employment discrimination, those among them who had gained access to the sources of power in Canadian society through education, economic success, or both, generally advocated a patient, accommodationist approach to the integration of minorities in Canadian society. Others, mostly working-class Canadians of eastern European descent, believed that the organization of labour and a re-organization of Canadian society along social democratic or communist lines would provide the most effective routes for attaining equality. For them, membership in labour unions and left-wing organizations afforded interaction with people of diverse backgrounds. As we shall see, the labour movement's plans and actions to fight racism were motivated primarily by the need to gain the support of minority workers for its wartime organizing drives, while the CPC's programme to build working-class internationalism emphasized class consciousness over the particularistic concerns of minorities who suffered from discrimination. The involvement of minority workers in these campaigns nevertheless reinforced ongoing commitment to fighting prejudice and discrimination. Because their role has not received adequate attention, one of the most significant labour victories in the post-war settlement is frequently overshadowed in historical accounts.

4

The Disenfranchised

Canadians of Asian Descent

When white Vancouver Island miners belonging to the United Mine Workers of America went out on strike at the Dunsmuir Mines in Union Bay in August 1942, their co-workers of Chinese descent, who were not members of the union, also went on strike. White miners were protesting against receiving lower wages than unskilled workers in war industries; Chinese workers were protesting against being paid less than white miners at the Dunsmuir Mines. The Chinese washermen, dumpers, and trimmers, whose work was essential for supplying coal to ships on the Pacific coast, used the government's wartime role in adjudicating disputes over wages to accomplish their goal. They stayed out even after the unionized miners returned to work, agreeing to resume working only when the National War Labour Board promised to approve an increase in their wages which brought them into line with those of white miners.[1]

Like these miners, disenfranchised people of colour, Canadians of Chinese, Japanese, and East Asian descent, and Native Canadians recognized that Canada's declared war aims and its campaigns for wartime unity presented them with opportunities to protest against discrimination. Understandably, these groups fought wartime campaigns first and foremost to obtain the franchise and, in the case of the Chinese especially, to end exclusion from Canada, and scholars have consequently paid the greatest attention to these quests. Each of these groups also perceived, however, that growing labour shortages during the war enhanced their chances of ending discrimination in employment. Despite the racial exclusivism of some trade unions, generally speaking these minority workers came to see labour unions as effective agencies in their quest for fair employment practices.

Prior to the Second World War, Chinese Canadian communities were as divided ideologically as many groups of European origin were. Chinese merchants and Freemasons advocated accommodation to Canadian society, whereas such working-class organizations as the Chinese Workers' Protective Association (established in 1923) were left-leaning and connected to the Communist Party.[2] They favoured a radical reorganization of Canadian society. During the 1930s and 1940s, however, Chinese Canadians of different classes and ideological leanings united in response to Japan's attack on China. Although the main goals of their activism in Canada were to obtain the franchise and to open Canada's gates to immigrants from China, they also protested against employment discrimination. Indeed, protest letters from Chinese Canadians erroneously called up for military training reveal that they saw the concentration of so many members of their group in low-paying, unskilled jobs as a key manifestation of anti-Chinese discrimination in Canada. Most of the Chinese in Canada 'are old and weak,' wrote Charles Woofay of Kingston.'Their occupation is that of a laborer. They have no military training. Prior to being admitted into Canada each had to pay an exorbitant sum of $500 as head tax ... for the privilege to obtain a job at hard labor. Now that Canada is in the war, she finds herself lacking in manpower. She is desirous of drafting this insignificantly small number of Chinese into the army.'[3]

Chinese workers recognized that labour shortages enhanced their ability to demand better wages and working conditions. Excluded from most trade unions at the war's outset, they began to organize members of their own group. In 1942 they established the Chinese Trade Workers' Association, which consisted of shipbuilding workers, agricultural workers, and grocery workers.[4] A year later, however, Chinese and 'East Indian' sawmill workers in Youbou, BC, appealed to the International Woodworkers of America (IWA) for assistance in obtaining equal pay to other workers, and the union responded by calling upon the regional war labour board to apply the principle of equal pay for equal work.[5] Yet not all disenfranchised workers in the lumber industry appeared to trust that the IWA would stand up for them. In July 1943, roughly fifteen hundred Chinese Canadian shingle workers and about the same number employed as shipbuilders – none of whom were affiliated with trade unions – declared their intention to strike for pension benefits for their wives and children that white workers in these two industries had already secured. They demanded to be treated like other workers. This time, three unions (the UAW, the Union of Shipbuilding Workers, and the IWA) interceded and averted the strike. These CIO unions declared that workers should not be divided along racial and ethnic lines and promised to resolve the grievances of Chinese Canadian workers through their unions.[6]

This initiative on the part of the CIO unions marked the beginning of an organizing drive among minority workers in British Columbia. In the summer of 1944, the IWA hired Roy Mah, a twenty-two-year-old Chinese Canadian university student, to organize Chinese Canadian lumber workers. Born in Edmonton, Mah spoke fluent English and Chinese. The University of British Columbia (UBC) student was also secretary of the Chinese Youth Association of Victoria. He became familiar with the lives of working-class Chinese Canadians during the summers, when he worked in sawmills, restaurants, and coastal CPR boats.[7] The Fish Cannery, Reduction Plant and Allied Workers' Union hired Chan Kwan in the same year to organize Chinese Canadian shore workers in the BC fishing industry. Kwan had been active in left-wing protests and strikes during the Great Depression. Following the outbreak of war, he found employment in a Vancouver shipyard, where he became a shop steward in the Dock and Shipyard Workers' Union.[8] The immediate success of the two organizers suggests that Chinese Canadian workers believed that the international unions would best serve their interests, despite their less-than-stellar record. Possibly because of language difficulties, Mah established Chinese sub-locals of the IWA. He also wrote the monthly Chinese language edition of the *B.C. Lumberman*, the IWA's newspaper. Roughly two thousand Chinese Canadian lumber workers responded to Mah's efforts with enthusiasm. Twelve hundred of them joined the union almost immediately. During Kwan's first month as organizer, two hundred Chinese workers who had never before held union cards joined the Fish Cannery, Reduction Plant and Allied Workers' Union.[9] Chinese Canadians, at least one of them with a background of union activism in China, were also active in Ontario. The presence of such men may help to explain why the UAW in Windsor, for example, objected to the fact that Chinese Canadians were sent to work in restaurants and laundries.[10]

Middle-class Chinese Canadians, like their Jewish counterparts, approved of group members joining such trade unions. They believed that membership in the labour movement would allow Chinese Canadian workers to overcome employment discrimination.[11]

'War Equipment for China – Small Arms Ltd., Long Branch, Ontario, April 1944. Agnes Wong, who comes from Whitecourt, Alta., assembles a sten gun for China. These stens are extraordinarily simple in construction and are one of the deadliest small arms in use.'
Library and Archives Canada, Ronny Jaques, National Film Board of Canada, PA-108043

As their joint campaign with Chinese Canadian lumber workers in Youbou suggests, during the war years, Sikh lumber workers also saw the IWA as an agency for attaining equal treatment in the workplace. Darshan Singh Sangha was in charge of IWA organizing among them. The Punjabi-born activist came to Canada in 1938 with the intention of studying at UBC. Having become active in the Labour-Progressive Party, however, he left university and went to work in logging and joined the IWA. He rose to the position of district trustee of the union and became the LPP's director of education in Victoria.[12]

Meanwhile, Sikh Canadians continued their campaign, begun decades before the war, to obtain the franchise. They also spoke out against racist description of their group. In 1944, for example, when BC Minister of Labour George S. Pearson resisted granting 'East Indians' full citizenship rights on the grounds that Sikhs, Chinese, and Japanese were 'unreliable, dishonest and deceitful,' the Vancouver Sikh community sent a delegation to Victoria to demand an apology.[13]

Despite the state restrictions against them, Japanese Canadians also protested against discrimination. Like other disenfranchised groups of Asian descent, they objected to the denial of citizenship to them long before war's outbreak.[14] Indeed, the demand for the vote was the first action of the Japanese Canadian Citizens' League (JCCL). The group was organized in 1936 in Vancouver, primarily by Canadian-born (Nisei) students of Japanese origin. Its main goal was to publicize the aims of Nisei by sending delegates to various congresses of youth groups. Shinobu Higashi explained the JCCL's views to the Student Christian Movement through the movement's publication, *The Canadian Student*. Discrimination against Japanese Canadians rested 'on racial differences – a criterion hateful to all thinking people,' he wrote, 'since it connotes race inferiority and superiority as the case may be.' Higashi protested that the members of his group 'are an integral part of Canada, for by training, by birth, and by law, they are Canadian.'[15] The leading role played by these highly educated youths is not surprising, since as we saw they faced even greater obstacles than young, Canadian-educated Jews and others of eastern European descent. But because they opposed community domination by their immigrant elders, the group did not have widely based support in the Japanese Canadian community before the war. Their message of resistance became more appealing following the relocation of all Japanese Canadians.

The same educated, young Nisei established the English-language newspaper *New Canadian* in 1938. Tommy Shoyama, one of the leaders of the JCCL, was a UBC commerce graduate who had failed to find an articling position necessary to qualify as a chartered accountant. He and his friends hoped to use the English-language newspaper to fight 'the discrimination and handicaps under which people of Japanese ancestry laboured' in BC. The paper became even more important once war broke out and unleashed a 'virulent political campaign against the Japanese community.' 'We used the editorial columns essentially

'Niwatsukino family working in Turin, Alberta, 1942.'

University of British Columbia Library, Rare Books and Special Collections, Japanese Canadian Photograph Collection, JCPC 25.090.

to continue to protest and to call for "British fair-play", civil rights,'
Shoyama recalled.[16]

Since their labour was important in the booming wartime economy,
withholding it was one of the chief means of resistance available to
Japanese Canadians. During the evacuation from the British Columbia
coast, Nisei opposed the government's practice of separating families
by sending married men to road camps. They responded by organizing sit-down strikes and succeeded in forcing the government to allow
married men to rejoin their families in the interior and to send single
men to lumber camps in Ontario.[17] But separation from families was
not the only reason for the strikes. A strike in New Denver, for instance,
was directed against poor working conditions and pay. Japanese Canadian workers were also unhappy about the way they were treated
by the supervisors of the camp.[18] As Kinzie Tanaka, the former vice-
president of the JCCL,[19] explained to the BCSC, Japanese Canadians
everywhere would be much more motivated to work if they gained
access to supervisory jobs as foremen and timekeepers; skilled jobs as
chainmen and rodmen; and white-collar jobs for women as stenograph-
ers and nurses.[20]

Although some Japanese Canadians, desperate to keep their families together, agreed to move to southern Alberta to undertake back-
breaking stoop work in the beet fields, they were not willing to accept
discriminatory treatment from Alberta sugar beet growers. The growers had called for Japanese labour at least partly because labourers of
European descent, primarily Hungarians, had organized a union (the
Alberta Beet Workers' Union) and were using labour shortages to demand higher wages and better working conditions.[21] The growers
attempted to limit the ability of Japanese Canadian labourers to bargain for higher wages by tying them to a single employer. They also
required Japanese Canadians to produce more beets than other workers to obtain bonuses. But workers of Hungarian and Japanese descent
thwarted the growers' plans by joining forces.[22] A provincial official
described their actions as 'exploiting the farmers and holding them up
for money,' but admitted that the southern Alberta sugar beet farmers
'looked upon the Japanese as war slave labour with which they could
do anything.'[23] Organized protest improved the working conditions of
Japanese Canadian beet workers.[24]

When the government attempted to disperse Japanese Canadians
east of the Rocky Mountains by subjecting them to NSS regulations
empowering the state to place workers in essential industries, Nisei

who otherwise favoured dispersal, such as the *New Canadian* staff, recognized an opportunity to draw attention to the discrimination they faced. An editorial in the paper declared that the regulations could not apply to Japanese Canadians who were subject to a special order which prohibited their employment in British Columbia.[25] Nisei in British Columbia reasoned that

> it cannot be argued that applying the regulations to the towns is merely treating Japanese-born Canadian citizens like everyone else. No one can argue that as long as there exist such invidious distinctions against Japanese Canadians as the curtailment of liberty of travel or the right to make a home at will, the bans on the use and possession of radios and cameras, the prohibition of hunting, fishing or trapping, the withholding of workmen's compensation benefits, the necessity of special permits for the lease or purchase of agricultural land, the denial of a fair ration of liquor or the undemocratic exclusion from the right to vote.[26]

Attributing the protest to the brilliant legal minds among the Nisei, officials were forced to concede that compulsory employment under NSS regulations could not be imposed on Japanese Canadians.[27] Arthur MacNamara, federal deputy minister of labour, offered what he described as a 'Bill of Rights' to Japanese Canadians willing to relocate east for farm work: a guarantee of wages equal to prevailing rates in Ontario and Quebec, and the possibility of returning to British Columbia if no suitable employment was obtained for them at the end of the season.

Nisei in eastern Canada saw labour unions as key agencies for helping racialized minorities. Aware of contradictory attitudes towards them within labour organizations in different parts of the country, Japanese Canadian bush workers in Port Arthur, Ontario, blamed the ignorance of union officials on the lack of attention in the labour press to the difficulties of Japanese Canadians. To obtain favourable coverage for their group, they met with officials from communist-affiliated unions at the home of one of the union members and agreed to support the *Canadian Tribune* financially. Although they recognized that the communist newspaper did not enjoy unanimous support in labour circles, these Nisei believed that even those who disagreed with its politics read the paper.[28]

Choosing to focus on the benefits that racialized workers gained from joining the Canadian labour movement, an editorial in the *New*

Canadian announced proudly that the Port Arthur Lumber and Sawmill Workers' Union Local 2786 had become a subscriber to the publication because a number of Japanese Canadian workers had joined the local. The editorial attempted to convince Japanese Canadians that although membership in unions had not prevented their evacuation from the coast, unions were 'democracy at work' and democracy would work for them as Canadian workers. For these Nisei, as for the other minorities in wartime Canada, a key principle of democracy was that it drew no distinction 'as to race, color or creed.' By joining the Pulp, Sulphite and Paper Mill Workers' Union local in Ocean Falls, BC, in 1937, for example, Japanese Canadians had not only improved their wages and working conditions, but had also broadened their contacts with 'fellow occidental workers.'[29] The editorial neglected to mention that the union did not eliminate, but merely reduced, the wage differential between Japanese and white workers. Despite union membership, Japanese Canadians continued to earn about three quarters of the wages earned by white workers.[30] Membership in the Camp and Mill Workers' Federal Labour Union, however, did lead to the affiliation of Japanese Canadian mill workers with the Vancouver, New Westminster and District Trade and Labor Council and with the Trades and Labour Congress of Canada. The Vancouver Trade and Labor Council subsequently supported broadening the franchise to Canadian citizens of Japanese origin, and the labour movement eliminated from union constitutions provisions excluding 'all those who could not assimilate with Canadian society.'[31]

The bush workers in Port Arthur were not the only Japanese Canadians who joined unions in central Canada. At the Federal Steel Company in London, Ontario, for example, several Japanese Canadians were active in organizing a United Steel Workers local, and when it was established, members elected Japanese Canadians to the positions of president, secretary, and executive board member.[32] The *New Canadian* deemed the entry of Japanese Canadian workers into trade unions 'one of the most important advances' they could make 'in truly becoming a part of Canadian society.'[33]

Despite its acceptance of the expulsion of Japanese Canadians from coastal British Columbia, support for the CCF was strong among Nisei. Nisei remembered that alone among Canada's and British Columbia's political parties, the CCF defended Japanese Canadian rights. For example, vacillating through the 1930s, the CCF finally endorsed Asian enfranchisement in 1939.[34] When in 1944 the CCF attained power in

Saskatchewan, that province alone appointed Japanese Canadians to responsible positions in the provincial civil service. CCF politicians also spoke up for Japanese Canadians in provincial legislatures and in Ottawa, wrote sympathetic articles about them, and maintained cordial relations with Japanese Canadian associations, especially labour unions.[35] Many years after the Second World War, when he was an influential civil servant in Ottawa, Tommy Shoyama explained that the CCF appealed to him because before and during the war 'the only people who offered any sort of sense of defence or concern for the Japanese minority were in fact the CCF members of the legislature – the two Winches in particular, and of course in Ottawa, Angus MacInnis – they were outstandingly courageous given the political temper of the times.'[36] The social democratic party's record was sufficiently well known among Japanese Canadians that they turned to its members when they sought allies against discrimination. In the spring of 1939, when the Vancouver Hotel dismissed its Japanese Canadian bellboys and valets, for example, they turned to MP Angus MacInnis for help.[37] Unfortunately, MacInnis's intercession could not save their jobs.

Like other racialized minorities, Japanese Canadians followed developments in the United States and drew inspiration from the activities and accomplishments of Japanese Americans. In its pro-union campaign, for example, the *New Canadian* reprinted the explanation of the Japanese American *Pacific Citizen* that the CIO's success and vigour were due to 'two bold decisions to unionize labor by industries, rather than by crafts, and the decision to include all workingmen, regardless of race, color or creed, within its membership.'[38] According to a secret report by the RCMP intelligence section, Japanese Canadians in the interior of BC were organizing civil liberties unions 'with a view to studying current Nisei problems.' They were apparently motivated by the United States appeals court decision that persons born in the United States, whether of Japanese or any other racial origin, were American.[39]

Native Canadians

Native Canadians from Nova Scotia to British Columbia first raised their voices in protest during the Second World War upon receipt of notices for compulsory training for home defence.[40] By 1943, when conscription became a possibility, their protests reached a crescendo. Native Canadian activists defied the Department of Indian Affairs's prohibition of Native political organizing. They established the Canadian section of the North American Indian Brotherhood (NAIB) under the leadership of Jules Sioui, from the Huron village of Lorette in Quebec, Andrew Paull, from the Squamish band of British Columbia, and Cree Chief John Tootoosis, from the Poundmaker reserve in Saskatchewan.[41] The NAIB quickly organized a convention in 1943, and held another in 1944. Petitions and letters from individuals and bands challenged Ottawa's right to mobilize Native men on the grounds that treaties with the British Crown guaranteed their autonomy. Jules Sioui argued, for example, that since Native Canadians had not surrendered their sovereignty, their members were not British subjects or citizens.[42] The Six Nations Council objected to compulsory military training on the grounds that 'the Indian has no voice in the government of Canada.' Its members pointed to the contradiction between the 'democratic freedom' for which the current war was purportedly being fought and the denial of the franchise to Native people.[43] Additional forms of discrimination against Native people also provided grounds for protest. For example, Robert George of Ravenswood, Ontario, argued that Natives should not be liable for compulsory training, both because they had signed treaties with the Crown and because of prejudice and discrimination. 'Since the government has made the Indians their wards we have been classed as the lowest of human beings in this country,' he wrote in 1941 to F.C. Davis, associate deputy minister of national war services.[44]

The same logic informed resistance to NSS regulations concerning work on the home front. But while protest against conscription focused on political rights, protest against employment discrimination also touched on social and economic rights of Native people. The members of the Brokenhead reserve in Manitoba, for example, held a meeting to consider restrictions placed upon Native people seeking employment by NSS regulations. Their spokesperson, Chief Richard, informed the NSS board of the position taken by band members that no permit be required of them in seeking employment.[45]

Gabriel Sylliboy, Grand Chief of Eskasoni, Chapel Island, on Cape Breton Island, cited discrimination as the reason for his people's refusal to abide by government regulations. 'I am proud and always endeavoured to be a loyal Canadian Indian, under the British flag; but I am certainly not recognized as a Canadian Citizen, or an "Ordinarily Resident" in Canada. I am not an immigrant, and according to the Indian Act, I am not even recognized as a "person." Consequently, in my humble judgement the words "Ordinarily Resident" as used in NSS Regulations, is not applicable to an Indian.'[46]

Native leaders from British Columbia, Quebec, and Nova Scotia objected to Ottawa's move to keep labour in Canada by requiring exit permits from Canadians travelling to the United States. The new regulations clashed with the practice of Native workers of using their right to move across the border freely to obtain more lucrative employment or better working conditions than those available in Canada.[47] Andrew Paull, who had organized Native agricultural labourers in the British Columbia interior before the war, explained to Minister of Labour Humphrey Mitchell that these workers travelled to pick fruits and hops in the United States because wages were higher and conditions were better than in British Columbia. Paull also pointed out that the employment opportunities of Native people were already seriously limited by the discrimination that excluded them from war industries.[48]

Not only their leaders but Native workers themselves recognized that the need for their labour gave them the ability to bargain with their employers and the government. In the Kenora Indian Agency, Natives employed in logging, the pulp industry, fishing, and trapping sought and obtained deferment of military service by emphasizing the importance of their contribution to the war effort on the home front.[49] Native trappers, aware of the indispensability of their labour for maintaining and repairing railway lines in the same district, agreed to perform this work on condition that they be permitted to fit such wage employment into an annual cycle of work involving their return to their more lucrative lines in trapping season. In Saskatchewan, Native women and men agreed to help out with the harvest in 1942 on condition that farmers would not cut wages or in other ways discriminate against them.[50]

Some Native workers also saw labour unions as agencies to obtain equality with non-Native workers. The most prominent advocate of this strategy was Andrew Paull. Even before the war, Native longshoremen (Paull among them) had formed their own longshoring union local in North Vancouver. According to one estimate they constituted about 40 per cent of the longshoring union membership.[51] Under Paull's leadership, Native workers in British Columbia established the Native Brotherhood in 1931 to look after both the interests of Native workers and wider community interests. During the war years, the brotherhood collaborated with the United Fishermen's Federal Union, a communist-led industrial union, to push for improved living conditions for Native cannery workers. Paull saw such a move as urgent because while cannery owners maintained sanitary conditions during production, they housed workers in 'antiquated, cramped quarters infested with rats

'Pictou Shipyard, Pictou, NS. A woman worker in the Pictou shipyard, Mrs.
Martin Malti, Mic Mac Indian, and papoose, 1943.'
Library and Archives Canada, National Film Board of Canada, WRM-2504.

and insects, and minus proper sanitary facilities.' Such quarters were
breeding grounds for tuberculosis and other illnesses. Paull pointed
out the hypocrisy of employers and the officials of the BC Provincial
Board of Health who, amidst such circumstances, blamed the outbreak
of epidemics among cannery workers on their failure to maintain clean-
liness in their living quarters. The union could also be used to protest
against exploitation by company stores.[52] Paull described the move as
'a glowing indication that native Indians of this province and of this
country are ready to take their places beside other citizens.' He wrote:
'They are no longer willing to live as government wards, eking out a
miserable existence on a government "dole." They have learned that in
union there is strength. And we are out to build our union.'[53]

While he obviously had no objections to integrating Native workers
within the broader Canadian labour movement on terms of equality,
Paull saw the DIA's assimilationist policy as hypocritical. 'Indians never
know just when they are British subjects,' he pointed out. 'They are British subjects when income tax is levied, and they are British subjects
when it comes to military callup. But when it comes to old age pensions
and relief allowances, Indians are just "wards of the government."'[54]

Andrew Paull's protest about the baselessness of the rhetorical extension of citizenship rights to racialized minorities when their labour or
service in the armed forces was needed echoed that of other disenfranchised minorities. Although officials did not describe them as 'wards'
of the government, during the war the concept of 'wards' was also
applicable to the condition of Japanese Canadians. That is why their
mobility in the labour market could be formally circumscribed by the
state. As Japanese Canadian activists pointed out, however, given the
denial of citizenship rights to them, they could not be subject to NSS
regulations governing other Canadians. Although state complicity in
discrimination against them was less visible, Chinese and Sikh Canadians also used both the state's wartime role in the labour market and
the discrepancy between the professed democratic war aims and the
discriminatory practices by the state and members of civil society to
fight for their citizenship rights.

PART THREE

Ambivalent Allies: Anglo-Saxon Critics of Discrimination

In August 1942 a *Toronto Daily Star* editorial, reporting on a CBC broadcast by Dr W.C. Perry, pastor of the African Methodist Episcopal Church in Toronto, acknowledged and denounced racist employment discrimination in war production.[1] A few months later, a *Globe and Mail* editorial responded to minority complaints by unequivocally condemning employment discrimination:

> Employers, short as they are of help, are refusing to hire individuals because of their color or because of their religion. While that is bad enough for private employers, it is even worse in Government-owned plants and plants having government orders. The money for the war contracts and for the Government plants is collected from all Canadians, English, French, Protestant, Catholic, Jew, white, black or yellow.[2]

A year later, the 'assimilation' of races was one of the topics discussed at the Lake Couchiching Conference, an annual gathering initiated in 1932 by the Canadian Institute of International Affairs, which brought together Canadian intellectuals and activists concerned about domestic and foreign affairs.[3] That such issues were taken up by leading Canadian dailies and influential groups like the Canadian Institute of International Affairs suggests that minority group members were not alone in challenging racism in wartime Canada.

The critics of racism included academics such as Henry Angus, head of the Department of Economics and Political Science of the University of British Columbia; George Grube, professor of classics at Trinity College and editor of *Canadian Forum*; W. Jarvis McCurdy, associate professor of philosophy at the University of Toronto; F.R. Scott, professor of law at McGill University; George Tatham, professor of geography at the University of Toronto; Malcolm Wallace, principal of University College; Watson Kirkconnell, professor of literature at the University of Manitoba and later McMaster University; T.F. McIlwraith and C.W.M. Hart, professors of anthropology at the University of Toronto; and adult educators A.E. Corbett, Watson Thomson, Robert England, and Norman Black. In addition to academics, the group included journalists such as B.K. Sandwell, editor of *Saturday Night*, and Eleonor Godfrey of the *Canadian Forum*, intellectuals connected to the press, publicists for the railway companies, and novelists Gwethalyn Graham and Morley Callaghan.

These Anglo-Canadian critics of racism were linked through a variety of professional and voluntary associations. Some of these asso-

ciations were well established and well known, such as the Canadian
Political Science Association, the Canadian Institute of International
Affairs, the League of Nations Society, the Association of Canadian
Clubs, the Canadian Association for Adult Education, and the Fellowship of Reconciliation. Others were local, more narrowly focused, and
shorter-lived, established specifically to fight racism, such as the Canadian National Committee on Refugees and Victims of Political Persecution, the Civil Liberties Association of Toronto, and the Cooperative
Committee on Japanese Canadians. These associations expressed their
views in scholarly journals such as the *Canadian Journal of Economics
and Political Science*, the *University of Toronto Quarterly*, and *The Dalhousie Review*, and in more popular magazines such as *Saturday Night* and
the *Canadian Forum*. The civic mindedness of the people connected to
these associations was inspired variously, and sometimes simultaneously, by socialism, pacifism, Canadian nationalism, and social gospel
ideals. Although the group was not politically homogeneous, activists
linked to the CCF, such as Andrew Brewin and E.B. Joliffe, and to the
labour movement, such as C.H. Millard and Percy Bengough, figured
prominently in the fight against prejudice and discrimination.

Although many of the Canadian critics of racism were scholars and
educators, most found their way into anti-racist campaigns not through
the academy, but rather through involvement in the CCF and voluntary organizations. Accordingly, it is worth exploring how the question
of race came to the fore in some of these organizations. Developments
within the Canadian Association for Adult Education (CAAE) illustrate
the route of English Canadian activists into the human rights campaigns.
The association became involved in campaigns against employment
discrimination as a result of the denial of licenses to Japanese Canadians
who wanted to open small businesses in Toronto.[4] The war also led the
CAAE's members to pay close attention to such questions of citizenship
as where immigrants fit into Canadian society and how the Canadian
public viewed them. As a national organization which brought agencies
and organizations interested in adult education together, with links to
provincial departments of education, the CBC, and the National Film
Board, the CAAE was particularly well suited for publicizing the cause
of human rights. Not surprisingly, it saw study and education as the
main means of combating racism. Towards the end of the war it became
involved in a number of conferences on how to combat racism. The Canadian Jewish Congress and the Jewish Labour Committee played a
leading role in this dimension of the CAAE's work.[5]

Wartime developments also led the Fellowship of Reconciliation to become engaged in the fight against racism. The fellowship was a pacifist organization, founded during the First World War in England, with branches in Canada and the United States. Because they saw racism as a leading cause of violence, fellowship members became committed to eradicating it during the Second World War. That is when the fellowship's Committee for Non-Violence changed its name to the Race Relations Committee and began to organize discussions and publish a bulletin on the subject. The fellowship included such leading Ontario human rights activists as George Tatham (professor of geography at the University of Toronto), John Finlay (minister of Toronto's Carleton Street United Church), J. Lavell Smith (superintendent of the United Church's Church of All Nations in Toronto), and folklorist Edith Fowke and Margaret Boos (founding members of the Cooperative Committee on Japanese Canadians). It is significant, however, that in Canada and elsewhere members of ethnic minorities were influential members of the fellowship. Leaders of the non-violent protest during the early Civil Rights Movement in the United States, such as A. Philip Randolph and Bayard Rustin, received their training in the fellowship. In Canada, the fellowship, at the urging of Jewish human rights activist Rabbi Abraham Feinberg, adopted the campaign for anti-discrimination legislation as a priority in 1947.[6] Once the fellowship embarked on this campaign, it deliberately included representatives of the Jewish, Japanese Canadian, African Canadian, and Chinese Canadian communities in its Race Relations Committee and sought to include Native people and French Canadians as well.[7]

The importance of this group is great, not only because of its unswerving commitment to fighting racism, but also because its members brought their convictions to mainstream Anglo-Canadian organizations. They belonged to some of the leading Protestant churches, the CCF, the League for Social Reconstruction, the Student Christian Movement, the YMCA, and the YWCA. As a result of close ties to their American counterparts, moreover, the Canadian members of the fellowship introduced to Canada the tactics of non-violent protest against discrimination and segregation that were at this time being developed in the northern United States.[8] But despite the strong convictions of its members, the fellowship's ability to influence developments on its own was limited. It was small, had limited financial resources, and because pacifism was its driving force its appeal diminished during and after the Second World War.[9]

The development of the Civil Liberties Association of Toronto, established in March 1940, illustrates the transition from defending civil liberties to protecting human rights. The association initially sought to protect what it saw as the fundamental democratic rights of freedom from arbitrary arrest, the right to habeas corpus and a fair trial, freedom of speech and the press, and the freedom of workers to organize and to speak through representatives of their own choice. Its members included writers, journalists, academics, clerics, lawyers, members of the CCF, and labour unionists, and its goals were endorsed by leading businesspeople such as Sir Ellsworth Flavelle. At its inception the association feared that civil liberties were endangered by the federal government's extensive powers under the Defence of Canada Regulations. Specifically, it opposed the government's proscription of the Communist Party of Canada and its newspapers, the arrest of some of its members, and the confiscation of the halls of the Ukrainian Labour-Farmer Temple Association. B.K. Sandwell, conservative editor of *Saturday Night*, for example, who wanted to prevent communists from monopolizing the civil liberties campaign, argued that the confiscation of the Ukrainian Labour temples was a violation of property rights, 'sacred' for everyone in Canada, even 'enemy aliens.' Even before the association was founded, some individuals who became its leading members had expressed concern over racism. But it was in reaction to the treatment of Japanese Canadians that the association as a whole undertook to fight 'race prejudice and discrimination' in 1943. In 1944 it established a committee to study and promote intercultural relations to help prevent racial and religious discrimination. Recognizing that the task required great human and material resources, the association called together a wide variety of educational, religious, professional, and social organizations, clubs, and societies, and planned a number of conferences to promote intercultural relations. Much of the material for these conferences was provided by a Jewish member of the association, Ben Lappin, who also belonged to the Joint Public Relations Committee, one of the two key Jewish organizations in the anti-discrimination campaigns.[10]

Other organizations, such as the Canadian National Committee on Refugees and Victims of Political Persecution and the Cooperative Committee on Japanese Canadians, were created in response to the rise of Nazism in Europe and the Second World War. The National Committee on Refugees grew out of the efforts of the League of Nations Society, headed by Senator Cairine Wilson, and the CJC to gain admission to Canada for Jewish refugees from Nazism.[11] The League of Nations Society was in fact revitalized by the campaign on behalf of refugees. Some of its members, disturbed by the inhumanity of Canada's policy towards Jewish refugees, decided to pressure the government to change its immigration policy. They received intellectual, moral, and financial support from the CJC. Having tried in vain to convince federal politicians to open Canada's gates to their suffering co-religionists, the CJC decided that its campaign to admit Jewish refugees would be strengthened if led by a non-Jewish organization comprised of influential Canadians. Senator Wilson assumed the organization's leadership. Other notable members were United Church minister Claris Silcox and Anglican canon W.W. Judd. In addition to lobbying the government, the National Committee on Refugees also aimed to publicize the fate of European Jews among Canadians and thereby to mobilize them on behalf of refugees. While their efforts were largely unsuccessful, they did contribute to public discussion and hence awareness of anti-Semitism and racism.

The Cooperative Committee on Japanese Canadians was established in June 1943 to counter prejudice and discrimination against Japanese Canadians. Members of the national YWCA, the Toronto YWCA, and the women's missionary societies of the four large Protestant denominations founded the Cooperative Committee to assist Japanese Canadian girls who were coming to Toronto from the relocation centres in BC. Committee members pointed out that Japanese Canadians were singled out in a way that other enemy aliens, such as Germans and Italians, were not. A writer for the *Canadian Forum* wrote: 'The acid test of Canadian democracy is: Are we going to treat our Japanese Canadians as citizens or are we going to continue to discriminate against them solely on account of their racial origin?'[12] The Cooperative Committee's ranks expanded when the Student Christian Movement, the Fellowship of Reconciliation, the Roman Catholic Archdiocese of Toronto, the Metropolitan United Church, and the Church of All Nations sent representatives to extend assistance to Japanese Canadian men and boys. Believing that other Canadians would be more receptive to Japanese Canadians if they were familiar with their predicament, the Cooperative Committee commissioned Norman Black, an educator and CCF member from Vancouver, to publicize the situation of Japanese Canadians. Ten thousand copies of Black's pamphlet, *A Challenge to Patriotism and Statesmanship*, were distributed throughout Canada. Members of the Cooperative Committee also met with various city councils in southern Ontario to underscore the discrimination that Japanese Canadians faced. These efforts helped to diminish resistance to the settlement of Japanese Canadians in Ontario.[13] The Cooperative Committee nevertheless remained convinced that only by preventing the concentration of Japanese Canadians in specific regions or urban neighbourhoods could the group gain acceptance.[14]

Although the members of such organizations all promoted tolerance and unity among Canadians, regardless of race, religion, or national origin, they agreed neither on the nature and extent of racist discrimination in Canada, nor on the best means to combat it. Given that those who fought racism during the war included members of Canada's corporate and political elite, as well the leaders of left-wing parties and labour unions, their divergent views are not surprising. As the following chapters will show, political ideologies played a significant role in shaping campaigns against racism. The very concept of race, as understood by Anglo-Canadian activists, was often riddled with inconsistencies and contradictions. Racial classification was so deeply rooted, for example, that even many commentators who declared it to be meaningless, and sought to substitute other concepts such as ethnicity and culture for it, continued to be influenced by racist assumptions.

5

Mainstream Critics and the Burden of Inherited Ideas

The names of Claris Silcox, Murray Gibbon, Watson Kirkconnell, and Robert England seldom appear in contemporary studies of mid-twentieth-century campaigns against discrimination and racism. The reason for their omission is that their efforts on behalf of minorities, frequently limited to those of European origin, are unknown or deemed irrelevant, even racist, by students of racism. In the Canada of the 1930s and 1940s, however, these men were widely considered the leading experts on the question of race. Their emphasis on environment rather than biology as determinants of difference, and their focus on cultural rather than racial diversity among Canada's people, marked an important shift in the understanding of race.[1] In promoting cultural diversity rather than Anglo-conformity, they saw themselves and were perceived by others as the champions of minority groups of eastern and southern European origin. Not only were these critics of racism Eurocentric in their focus, they were also socially conservative. Indeed, some of them were motivated to fight racism at least in part by the desire 'to prevent the subject of racial discrimination becoming a special property of the CP [Communist Party].'[2] Their social conservatism and opposition to communism may have helped to broaden the appeal of their conceptions of race among English Canadians. At the same time, however, their ideological leanings meant that they paid relatively little attention to employment discrimination.

Claris Silcox

Consider United Church minister Claris Silcox. Deemed the 'United Church's most vigorous and effective foe of anti-Semitism,'[3] Silcox trained as a sociologist as well as a minister, and served churches in the United States following his ordination in 1914. In the 1920s he was a staff member of The Inquiry, a New York group of social scientists and religious leaders dedicated to fighting prejudice. Silcox wrote and lectured about the relationship between·Catholics, Protestants, and Jews in the United States. After he returned to Canada in 1934 to serve as the general secretary of the Social Service Council of Canada, he continued to write and lecture extensively about the problem of anti-Semitism. With Rabbi M.N. Eisendrath, he also co-chaired the Committee on Jewish-Gentile Relationships in Toronto, which modelled itself on the American National Conference of Christians and Jews. The committee brought the practice of 'brotherhood days,' which celebrated religious tolerance through interdenominational meetings, from the United States to Canada and distributed literature promoting religious harmony and decrying anti-Semitism. It also organized seminars for Christian and Jewish leaders to improve relations between the two religious groups.[4] In 1940 Silcox became the director of the Canadian Conference of Christians and Jews, whose main goal was to foster harmonious relations among Canada's different religious denominations. Such members as E.A. Corbett, Watson Kirkconnell, W.W. Judd, University College Principal Malcolm Wallace, Senator Cairine Wilson, and B.K. Sandwell linked the conference to the intellectual community that provided leadership to the anti-racist campaign. Many of its members were also active on the Canadian National Committee on Refugees. The conference's funding came primarily from the Canadian Jewish Congress, Central Region.[5]

Silcox's concern did not stop with anti-Semitism. He believed the fair treatment of all minorities, racial or religious, to be a true measure of democracy. By contrast, persecution of minorities was the spearhead of totalitarianism – both of the communist and of the fascist variety.[6] He noted the arbitrariness of classifying human beings by skin colour, pointing out that in the United States 'anyone with "negro blood" is adjudged negro although he may look white and easily pass as white, while in Brazil, anyone with white blood, even if he be seven-eighth black, is classified as white.'[7] Advocating the admission of refugees from Europe, Silcox tackled the biology–culture controversy; he wrote: 'Above all, what do we need most on this continent – the Anglo-Saxon blood or the Anglo-Saxon spirit?' He apparently believed that European, primarily Jewish, refugees could acquire the Anglo-Saxon spirit, noting that refugees from Austria and Czechoslovakia in particular would become a bulwark of Canada's democratic institutions.[8] Moving beyond the rights of people of European origin, Silcox also spoke out against the mistreatment of Native people. He complained that they had been isolated on reserves, and white people did not mix with them socially or treat them as equals. In order to have a political voice, Silcox maintained, 'Indians' should have the chance to elect a representative of their own to the House of Commons in Ottawa.[9] He also advocated extension of the franchise to the East Indian people in Canada.[10]

Yet Silcox continued to adhere to the practice of racial classification. His writings suggested that racial attributes were both physical and mental, shaped by environmental factors, especially climate and soil. Silcox also held that some races were superior to others. 'It is not racial arrogance but sheer common sense,' he maintained, 'when we assert that no people have made any greater contribution to civilization than the white man.' Silcox believed the 'Negroes' had failed to attain an advanced level of culture because the abundance of nature in warm climates meant that they did not have to become physically and mentally energetic. In tropical climates they required minimal clothing and could 'satisfy their hunger easily from the neighbouring banana-tree.' The 'oriental' developed his capacity to survive on a low general standard of living 'such as the white man would be unwilling to endure' by long experience in heavily populated areas. Yet even among white people a hierarchy existed. Silcox subscribed to the idea of Nordic superiority. Northern European climate and soil had given birth to an energetic, persevering, far-sighted people; though not Anglo-Saxons by blood, northern Europeans had the 'Anglo-Saxon idea.' Southern Europeans, by contrast, should be kept out of Canada. Their inferiority was manifested by their politics. A tendency to authoritarianism was notable among them. By virtue of climate, religion, and language they were, in any event, more suited for Latin America, where Northern Europeans would find it difficult to survive.[11]

Silcox's objections to the introduction of family allowances in Canada revealed that his racist ideas were intertwined with social conservatism. Writing in the Canadian Association for Adult Education publication *Food For Thought* in 1942, he argued that the 'subsidizing of children might create undesirable rivalry between ethnic groups in Canada aiming at the increase of political power for minority groups through expansion of population at public expense.' Money to support the children of 'prolific' minorities would be taken from those who 'deliberately restrict their children to a number which they feel capable of supporting adequately.' This argument seems to be a recapitulation of 'race suicide,' a widely held idea among English Canadians earlier in the century. Silcox's opposition to family allowances was based on class prejudice, as well as preconceptions of 'race.' He believed that the middle class, who acquired a stake in property through their thrift, including restricting their number of children, were a stabilizing element in any culture. Clearly their worth as citizens was far greater than that of licentious minorities.[12] In a CBC broadcast entitled 'Are Canadians Racially Intolerant?' Silcox indicated that he also opposed the presence of minority groups such as Poles, Italians, Ukrainians, and Czechs if they 'tried to upset' existing political institutions by supporting fascism or communism.[13]

Watson Kirkconnell

Watson Kirkconnell, a professor of literature and university administrator, was another widely recognized expert on minority relations in interwar and wartime Canada. Kirkconnell was perhaps best known for his remarkable command of dozens of European languages which permitted him to translate the poetry of immigrants from Europe into English. In recognition of the usefulness of linguistic prowess for interpreting developments in ethnic communities to mainstream Canada, the Canadian Institute of International Affairs gave him a grant to subscribe to forty newspapers in fourteen languages.[14] Kirkconnell was closely linked to other Anglo-Canadian champions of minorities through membership in the Canadian Institute of International Affairs, Canadian National Committee on Refugees, Association of Canadian Clubs, YMCA, Canadian Authors' Association, League of Nations Society, and Writers' War Committee.[15] These and other associations frequently invited him to speak on the subject of new Canadians.[16] He also spoke to ethnic organizations about the place of minority groups in Canada. Kirkconnell believed that through such undertakings he was contributing to nation-building and Canadian unity. His concern for new Canadians formed part of a broad sense of civic responsibility. He was active with prisoners' aid, for example, and he was the chairman of the Social Service Subcommittee of the Board of Social Service and Evangelism of the Baptist Convention of Ontario and Quebec.[17] As a devout and socially active Baptist, Kirkconnell also served on the board of the Committee on Jewish-Gentile Relationships (chaired by Claris Silcox and Rabbi Eisendrath), which was renamed the Canadian Council of Christians and Jews in 1940.[18]

Kirkconnell spoke out against racism during the war. In late 1940, for example, he ascribed fifth column hysteria among Canadians to 'the belief ... that a nation or a language group is in some mysterious way united by the blood kinship of race.' Although Kirkconnell describes the 'myth of race' as 'one of the most dangerous myths of our times,' rather than repudiating the idea of race altogether, he maintained that racial difference was based entirely on physical characteristics, just as cows were classified as 'Aberdeens or Guernseys.' He believed that among members of the white race, such differences had become meaningless because of the extent of intermixing over time. Because Anglo-Saxons, the French, and Germans no longer existed in pure form, there were 'no innate defects of mind or heart,' no congenital depravity that would have prevented collaboration among them.[19]

Distressed over the Canadian government's refusal to admit Jewish refugees from Nazi Europe, Kirkconnell wrote 'The Agony of Israel' in June 1943, and sent the poem to English-language Jewish newspapers in Canada. 'Bow your heads all ye nations / And humble yourselves, all ye people,' he wrote about the slaughter of European Jews by the Nazis, 'In the presence of sorrow unspeakable / At the sight of anguish beyond measure.' The poem listed the 'gifts' that Jews had given to all nations: in the fields of literature, medicine, music, and physics. Drawing Canadians into the circle of guilt, Kirkconnell pointed out that not only the slayers of the Jews, but also those who failed to stay the slayer's hand contributed to the agony of Israel.[20]

By and large, however, Kirkconnell's analysis seemed to apply to European 'races' only. In a pamphlet written to promote national unity in which groups of non-European origin received scant attention, Kirkconnell wrote: 'A very important conclusion for us here in Canada is that none of our national groups from Europe is really alien to the rest of us. All, by nature, are just as kind, just as honest, just as capable of serving and suffering, as any others. It is one of the darkest crimes of our modern world that some evil-hearted men have sought to preach that one nationality (they would falsely say 'race') is superior to others and is entitled, because of that superiority, to insult and enslave and exterminate others.'[21]

Kirkconnell was not unaware that immigrants to Canada from eastern Europe, their children, and even grandchildren encountered harsh economic and social realities, exacerbated by discrimination. He also noted that such discrimination could not be blamed on feelings of insecurity in wartime. 'Gifted and dependable students, Canadian-born youngsters with foreign names, have, even in peace-time, been turned down by employers as soon as it was discovered that they were not Anglo-Saxon.' Kirkconnell blamed ignorance for employment discrimination on the 'exasperating assumption of racial and cultural superiority on the part of the older Canadians.' He believed that if Canadians learned of the contributions that European nations have made to Canadian 'common stock of civilization,' they would be more accepting of immigrants and their descendants. Indeed, he believed that the perception of immigrants as 'European coolies, imported to do heavy work for which [Anglo-Saxon] hands had already grown too delicate' was already beginning to fade.[22] He appears to have believed eastern European immigrants completely capable of assimilation. Offering a humorous example of this process, Kirkconnell recalled the composition of a Canadian 'Scottish' regiment:

> In the spring of 1940, the Queen's Own Cameron Highlanders were in training at Winnipeg and used to march one thousand strong down Portage Avenue past my college, with their bagpipes skirling and their kilts a-swing, and I used to smile proudly to think that more than half of the 'Highlanders' were Ukrainians, Poles and Magyars.[23]

Yet, like Silcox, Kirkconnell also believed that some groups of European origin were superior to others. In *Canada, Europe and Hitler*, a work published in 1939, Kirkconnell wrote of the 'Anglo-Saxons' political genius' that led to the establishment of responsible government and federalism in Canada. Despite denouncing Nazi racism earlier in the same book, and explaining that the term 'race' was meaningless 'unless it is scrupulously reserved to designate people belonging to a common type in such matters as stature, skull-shape, colour of eyes, skin and hair, and texture of hair,' Kirkconnell argued that Anglo-Saxons could 'scarcely view with equanimity the replacement of their own stock by that of alien groups.' Their political genius was seemingly inheritable because its survival was imperilled by the failure of Anglo-Saxons to take parenthood as a serious duty. By having fewer children, the 'potential mothers of the race' were not perpetuating their blood and institutions. Meanwhile French Canadians and Canadians from eastern and southern Europe who did not possess this 'political genius' were having many children. Kirkconnell wrote: 'Unless we are prepared to take parenthood as a serious duty, *la revanche du berceau* will speedily submerge us in both East and West – and deservedly, when the potential mothers of our race mistake comfort for civilization.'[24]

Kirkconnell also shared Silcox's social conservatism. Canada was a classless society, he insisted, using as evidence his own school-day recollections about the Lindsay Collegiate Institute, attended by 'pupils from a variety of backgrounds' who played together 'without the slightest consciousness of any social castes.'[25] The venom of class hatred was injected into this harmonious society by communists. Indeed, fear and loathing of communism led Kirkconnell to speak of Jews and eastern Europeans in terms that could be easily confused with racist utterances. Amidst the tensions of war, Kirkconnell did not hesitate to accuse Jews of being 'the dynamic nucleus' of the Communist Party, the 'back room boys' of a party fronted by English Canadians. He set about exposing the 'foreign' leadership of the party by lifting the veil of anglicized names to reveal their original, 'foreign' names, thus disclosing the Jewish and Ukrainian identities of leading communists such as Norman Freed (Freedenthal), Sam Carr (Cohen) and John Weir (Wevursky).[26]

Kirkconnell's comments about Jews, other eastern Europeans, and communism angered minority and Anglo-Canadian activists alike. By far the most insightful criticism came from Reverend Mutchmor, secretary of the Board of Evangelism and Social Service of the United Church, himself rather patronizing towards minority workers, and by no means a political radical. He told Kirkconnell that his understanding was distorted by a limited class perspective on the lives of Ukrainian Canadians; he wrote: 'You met intelligent and religious leaders and came to know them well. You shared their point of view, appreciated their culture and enjoyed their music.' Mutchmor underlined his own exposure to the 'unschooled, low class Ukrainian working people and their families.' Having seen the 'seamy side of Ukrainian city life,' Mutchmor explained, he sensed 'something of the conditions out of which the Communistic movement among Ukrainians developed.'[27]

Such criticism failed to sway Kirkconnell. His vehement anti-communism led him to denounce industrial unions, the very agencies that working-class members of racialized minorities saw as most effective in ending employment discrimination. Kirkconnell described the CIO as a communist-dominated 'vast class political machine' intent on helping the Communist Party take power in Canada and make the country subservient to the Soviet Union. Consequently, he denied the legitimacy of workers' demands that inspired wartime strikes, denouncing them as acts of sabotage. Speaking to the Canadian Club of Toronto on

1 February 1943, for example, Kirkconnell described workers' actions in the steel industry as 'blackmail' strikes intended as 'a fight for power in Canada.' He believed that they could take place because by 1943 the Soviet Union's control of Europe seemed assured.[28]

Robert England

Robert England first developed an interest in European immigrants as a result of his work as a teacher in a Ukrainian school district in rural Saskatchewan and later as continental superintendent of the CNR's colonization department in London and western manager of the CNR's Department of Colonization and Agriculture in Winnipeg. Widespread Canadian opposition to immigration from central and eastern Europe was a key factor prompting the publication of his first book, *The Central European Immigrant*, in 1929.[29] Many years later, in his memoirs, England reflected that his first book 'argued against exploitation and patronization and concepts of racial superiority and political hegemony, and pleaded for reciprocity in cultural exchange, the sharing of the Dominion, better understanding of the dual French and British heritages, rural community development, and better rural schools.'[30] The controversy about the assimilation of European immigrants also motivated the publication of his second book, *The Colonization of Western Canada*, in 1936.[31] In the eyes of English Canadian contemporaries, his work with immigrants and his publications made England an expert on minorities of European descent. In 1938, for example, Leonard Brockington, chairman of the CBC and England's friend, asked him to prepare a programme for the CBC about these groups. The focus of the series ('Ventures in Citizenship') was on 'citizenship, race and ethnic differences, and the problem of integration and assimilation.' It publicized the cultural contributions of minority groups to Canada by describing their rich cultural traditions, their role as pioneers in the West and as soldiers in the Canadian Expeditionary Force during the First World War.[32] Ideas of cultural pluralism that began to emerge in the United States in the 1920s clearly influenced the programme's approach. Unlike the concepts of the melting pot or Anglo-conformity, this new approach permitted minorities to preserve, even celebrate, aspects of their culture.[33] In the hopes of fostering national unity, the series was revived during the war under the title 'Canadians All.'[34] It was to accompany wartime broadcasts that Kirkconnell wrote his pamphlet *Canadians All: A Primer of Canadian National Unity*.

England's contact and friendships with many of the other men and women who spoke up on behalf of minority groups just before and during the Second World War underscore the nature of the community of civic intellectuals in Canada at this time. In Winnipeg his friends included John Dafoe, editor of the *Winnipeg Free Press*; CCF MP Stanley Knowles; Watson Kirkconnell; and Mrs R.F. McWilliams, social worker, Winnipeg city councillor, and wife of Manitoba's lieutenant governor. Like many other members of this community, England participated in the Canadian Institute of International Affairs. He was also president of the Canadian Club of Winnipeg and vice-president of the Canadian Association for Adult Education.[35] In Vancouver, where he worked in the University of British Columbia's extension department, his friends included Henry Angus, professor of political science and fellow Institute of International Affairs member, who was one of the most vocal advocates of equality for Canadians of Asian descent. England also had connections to the Workers' Educational Association.[36]

England's writings about immigrants disclose some of the confusion and contradictions of thinking about race in Canada during the 1930s and 1940s. On the one hand, he dismissed permanent hierarchical distinctions among races, maintaining that all human groups shared basic characteristics. On the other hand, he stated: 'If we mean by assimilation a process that moulds racial stocks into something else we are flying in the face of what every stock-breeder knows ... No melting pot can make a Slav, an Italian, or Frenchman, an Anglo-Saxon. Racial qualities, vices and instincts will remain.'[37] England subscribed to the view that races manifested different stages of evolutionary development.[38] These stages ascended a ladder from a primitive state at the bottom rung to civilization at the summit. In his eyes, then, allegedly civilized races were clearly superior to allegedly primitive ones. That is why he argued, for example, that the dispossession of Native Canadian property by European settlers was 'sound.' Due to their primitive stage of development, 'Indians' neglected to cultivate and build on the land and therefore had no claim to it.[39] Not surprisingly given his views on the colonization of western Canada, England supported British colonial undertakings in other parts of the world as well. He believed that colonial administrators who brought progress and civilization to the colonies were both sensitive to the needs of natives and recognized that their social life 'must be touched with care.'[40]

But while he believed that all Europeans had clearly reached a relatively advanced level of civilization, England detected great variations

among them as well. He described the central European peasants either
as 'primitive' or as living in the Middle Ages. They were 'lovable' in
their native environment since they were 'immature' and had 'limited
power of continued mental growth.'[41] That is why he accepted the classification of central Europeans as 'non-preferred' immigrants, admitted
to Canada to work on farms for wages that British immigrants would
not accept.[42] He saw the relegation of peasant immigrants to menial,
poorly paid jobs as simply reflecting their capabilities. At the same
time, he believed that racial characteristics, including physical attributes, could be modified by environment.[43] The rigours of the northern
climate made Nordic groups such as the Scandinavians 'clear-blooded,
thrifty, ambitious and hardworking.' By contrast, the 'Ruthenian' was,
in his native land, 'personally unpractical, unenterprising, and unambi-
tious with regard to wealth, ease and worldly advantage.' By coming
to Canada, however, eastern European peasants were putting their feet
on the 'first rung of the ladder of progress.' Their children could be assimilated through being taught superior Canadian 'habits': speaking
English, maintaining good hygiene, and having 'greater mental freedom and a stronger moral fibre.'[44]

England believed that Canada, given its large agricultural sector,
was in a good position to assimilate peasant immigrants from eastern
and central Europe. One indication of their successful assimilation was
that these groups obeyed Canadian laws; they were under-represent-
ed among jail inmates in Canada. England also maintained, however,
that both English Canadians and the immigrants themselves needed
to help this process along. English Canadians would have to abandon
their prejudices, which led them to view these immigrants as 'cattle,'
and they would have to refrain from materially exploiting minorities of
European descent.[45] But while he noted both the exploitation of immigrants and the fears that their use as 'cheap labour' awakened among
Canadians, he paid little attention to industrial and urban immigrant
workers. Perhaps that is why he could believe that cultural change
was much more effective for eradicating discrimination than economic
change. Activists could hasten assimilation by educating immigrants
and their children, not just through schools, but also through community activism. Immigrants, especially their children, would have to take
educational efforts seriously. England's belief that the goal of education
was to teach everyone that no service was demeaning and to teach him
to claim his place in the world with self-respect, courage, and a sense of
purpose reflected his social conservatism.[46]

England believed that folk arts (such as handicrafts, folk dancing, music, and dramatic arts) were exceptionally well-suited to aid the integration of European immigrants. The beauty of folklore would teach English and French Canadians to appreciate the creativity of peasants from Europe, while immigrants would derive satisfaction and self-esteem from the survival of their traditions and the recognition that they enjoyed from the wider society.[47] An added, unspoken advantage of this approach was that the promotion of the pleasing, colourful face of ethnicity would obscure the harsher realities of working-class immigrant life.

John Murray Gibbon

Another widely recognized authority on European immigrants, John Murray Gibbon, a publicist for the CPR, also saw race as a significant marker of difference. In fact, his 1920 novel, *Conquering Hero*, invoked negative stereotypes of Jews. It described a 'pushy' Jewish passenger on a train forcing his way into the dining car out of turn. The novel also suggested that Jews were not white. Asked whether the novel's female romantic lead, a Polish princess, is Jewish, the English Canadian hero replied 'No, white.'[48] Gibbon's best-known book, *Canadian Mosaic*, published in 1938 to dispel fears about different ethnic groups in Canada, indicates a shift in his attitude towards race. Tellingly, Gibbon wrote only of groups of European origin, making no mention at all of groups of Asian and African backgrounds. Since fear about the unassimilability of immigrants was the book's chief target, Gibbon's omission suggests that he may well have shared widely held views about the unassimilability of non-white groups. His *Canadian Mosaic*, moreover, reinforced the notion that each minority group had distinguishing 'racial' characteristics. He accepted the classification of Europeans into Nordic, Mediterranean, and Alpine races, distinguishable by physical characteristics.[49] While he praised the characteristics of other European groups he examined, Gibbon voiced reservations about Jews. No longer resorting to overt anti-Semitism, he nevertheless still cast doubt on the assimilability of Jews: 'unlike most of the racial groups from Europe, the Jews had acquired a mentality and mode of living which could not readily be adapted to those of other races.'[50]

Gibbon shared Reverend Mutchmor's belief that employment discrimination against Ukrainian Canadians was one factor that made them receptive to communism.[51] But his proposals for solving the problem of discrimination did not address economic and political inequality. Like Robert England, Gibbon believed that culture in general, and the folk music and crafts of European immigrants in particular, could hasten the acceptance and integration of European immigrants into Canadian society. When he organized a series of folk-song, folk-dance, and handicraft festivals throughout the country, Gibbon, drawing on his experiences as general publicity agent of the CPR, argued that communication between Anglo-Canadians and immigrants whose knowledge of English was limited would be facilitated by musical performances and handicraft exhibits.[52] Thus, when Leonard Brockington asked Gibbon, roughly at the same time he approached Robert England, to suggest new programmes for the CBC to promote the integration of minorities, Gibbon suggested and prepared a series on the folk songs, dance tunes, and 'composed instrumental music and art songs' of continental European groups. His introductory comments about these groups formed the basis for the book *Canadian Mosaic*.[53]

Gwethalyn Graham

Although the feminist novelist Gwethalyn Graham could hardly be described as socially conservative, her protest against racism was also circumscribed by its focus on the middle class. Introduced to *Saturday Night* readers as 'a hater of every kind of race prejudice' who wrote fiction because she knew it to be 'the most effective means of getting ideas into the public mind,'[54] Graham targeted anti-Semitism in her 1944 novel, *Earth and High Heaven*. The novel explores the anti-Semitism of Montreal's anglophone upper middle class, to which Erica Drake, the novel's heroine, belongs. She learns about the depth of anti-Semitism in her social circles when she falls in love with a Jewish lawyer whom her family, especially her father, refuses to accept. Trying to convince her that the relationship is doomed, her father expresses widespread stereotypes about the Jews. 'The most persistent violators of the price ceiling were the Jews,' he tells his daughter. Jewish lawyers, 'shysters' who sought social contact with gentiles only to advance their careers, were so pushy that 'once they get their foot in your door, if you treat them the way you would anyone else, either they deliberately take advantage of it, or simply misunderstand it, and before you know it, they're all the way in and there's no way of getting rid of them.'[55] Erica angrily condemns such views: 'we Canadians don't disagree fundamentally with the Nazis about the Jews, we just think they go a bit too far.'[56]

Graham's focus on prejudice and discrimination against Jews is not surprising. Given the date of publication and the fact that Jews made up the largest non-English, non-French ethnic group in Montreal, English Canadian intellectuals critical of racism naturally identified them among the main victims of prejudice and discrimination. As Graham's most recent biographer points out, moreover, Graham and her family were intimately involved in trying to open Canada's doors to Jewish refugees and helping the few who managed to win entry.[57] Yet Graham's description of Montreal society as divided 'roughly into three categories labeled "French," "English" and "Jewish"' had the unintended consequence of rendering invisible other minority groups in the city, who together were more numerous than Montreal Jews.[58] Whether Graham was unfamiliar with these groups, or whether her novel simply reflected the implausibility of their interaction with Montreal's English Canadian elite, the absence of eastern and southern Europeans and Blacks from the pages of *Earth and High Heaven* reflects their marginalization. The number of educated, middle-class men and women in these groups was smaller than among the Jews. Consequently, when members of the elites of these groups encountered the same kind of discrimination as the novel's hero – exclusion from better housing, quotas and social isolation on university campuses, exclusion from elite law firms – their tribulations drew even less attention than those of the Jews. As a novelist, Graham was of course not required to expand her exploration of anti-Semitism to a consideration of racism in general. That her determination to use her creative ability to fight against racism led to the invisibility of so many victims of racism in Montreal is nevertheless indicative of a certain sensibility among English Canadian intellectual critics of prejudice and discrimination, especially the gulf that separated them from working-class immigrants from the 'peripheries' of Europe.

Henry Angus

Most of these defenders of human rights remained curiously silent about the treatment of Japanese Canadians, arguably the Canadian minority group most in need of protection during the 1930s and 1940s. Persistence of racist ideas was one reason that some of the anti-racists did little to protect non-European minorities, especially Japanese Canadians, from the intense discrimination that they faced. The small numbers and uneven dispersal of the group in Canada also contributed to its marginal status. Not surprisingly, activist intellectuals in British Columbia, where the majority of Japanese immigrants and their descendants lived, were most acutely aware of the intense discrimination that groups of Asian origin faced.

Professor Henry Angus, head of the Department of Economics and Political Science of UBC, was one of the few critics of discrimination against people of Asian origin who was not directly linked to the Left. He became involved in efforts to improve the position of immigrants of 'Oriental race and their descendants' in British Columbia in the late 1920s through his involvement in the Institute of Pacific Relations.[59] With the intention of dispelling 'violent prejudices' of British Columbians against these minorities, he helped to organize a group that studied immigration from Asia to BC and the cultural assimilation of immigrants in the province.[60] Seeking to find a wider audience and field of action than an informed study group provided, Angus began to write articles on these subjects for scholarly and professional publications and to lecture on the subject to scholarly and community groups. He told a group of Christian clergy, for example, that he thought it 'detestable that they should have separate churches for Japanese or Chinese instead of mixing them with Christians of other races in one community of worship of God.'[61] He also acted as advisor to the Japanese Students Club of UBC, whose members tried to document the hardships experienced by Japanese Canadians in the 1930s in support for their campaign to obtain the franchise.[62]

To Angus it was abundantly clear that economic competition and the colour bar were at the root of the problems Japanese Canadians confronted in BC. Canadians welcomed immigrants if there was 'a probability of their being confined, at any rate for a time, to occupations which Canadians ... tended to avoid, such as domestic service or labour in the beet fields. If they were likely to be competitors, however, immigrants were unwelcome.'[63] Racist ideas – which he explained had been discredited by scientific thought and ran counter to Christian ideology and democratic tradition – were used to rationalize the exclusion of Japanese Canadians from certain occupations.[64] Angus noted that the use of racism to maintain cheap labour persisted during the war, even in eastern Canada. 'Far from being invited to join the local University Women's club, Japanese women graduates might find themselves expected to be available as domestic servants, and men to be available as farm labour.'[65]

Angus put great store by the extension of the franchise to Canadians of Asian origin. He believed that British Columbia would not be able to hold out indefinitely against granting people of Asian origin the vote. With full citizenship the legal economic barriers against them would fall.[66] But Angus, convinced that de facto employment discrimination would not automatically follow the elimination of such legal barriers, insisted that ending employment discrimination was crucial to integrating Asian minorities in Canada. As long as Japanese Canadians had to accept inferior jobs and incomes, the Japanese Canadian elite would be discontented and would influence the entire community.

Contradictory Perceptions of Native People

Some Anglo-Canadian critics of racism paid special attention to Native Canadians. The ensuing public discussions reflected some of the contradictions and inconsistencies that characterized discussions of minorities of European descent. Given the centrality of this question for anthropologists during the period, social scientists not surprisingly played a key role in such discussions. A number of scholars from the University of Toronto, T.F. McIlwraith and Philleo Nash of the Department of Anthropology and C.W.M. Hart, supervisor of studies in sociology in the Department of Political Economy and special lecturer in the Department of Anthropology, saw the racism of white people as responsible for many of the problems that beset 'Indians' and denied them equality. At a 1939 conference on 'The North American Indian Today' at the Royal Ontario Museum, they maintained that assimilation into the mainstream of Canadian society was the only way to attain such equality. When they argued that to attain equality Native people would have to gain equal access to jobs and income, they implicitly acknowledged employment discrimination against Native people.[67] The assimilationist policies they envisioned were gradual and respectful of the importance of indigenous cultures. They nevertheless believed that industrialization and population growth in southern Canada rendered aspects of Native culture such as tribal organization obsolete.[68]

Several representatives of Natives from Canada and the United States attended the conference at the invitation of its organizers. Judging from the published record of the conference, however, most of the discussion was by white academics and government administrators. Native participants expressed their displeasure with this arrangement by passing a resolution that thanked conference organizers for inviting them, but added:

It is the democratic ideal in Canada and in the United States to develop a wide measure of self-expression and self-determination among all the various local, social, political, cultural, and other organizations and groups composing the nations, be it, therefore RESOLVED, that we hereby go on record as hoping that the need for an All-Indian Conference on Indian Welfare will be felt by Indian tribes, the delegates to such a conference to be limited to the *bona fide* Indian leaders actually living among the Indian people of the reservations and reserves, and further, that such a conference remain free of political, anthropological, missionary, administrative, or other domination.[69]

But some people outside the academic world and the federal bureaucracy, especially those residing next to reserves, were also concerned about the place of Natives in post-war Canada. The Okanagan Society for Revival of Indian Arts and Crafts of Oliver, BC, for example, submitted a proposal for the rehabilitation of Native Canadians to the Committee on Reconstruction and Re-establishment in Ottawa.[70] The submission is interesting because it focuses on economics and foreign affairs. The training of Native people for only the lowest-paid labour, the Okanagan society argued, was a major cause of their economic hardship. They dismissed any attempts to perpetuate the racialization of Native Canadians by preventing them from acquiring modern skills. They wrote:

We desire to see a Canada made up of many racial origins, and we want no theories of holding aboriginal inhabitants down to the quaintness of the past, isolating them in picturesqueness for the tourist trade, or limiting them to the 'Laboring Classes.'[71]

An end to discrimination was important not only for the benefit of Native people but also for the sake of Canada's standing in the world. If Canada did not accept the racial equality of Natives, it would find itself alienated from Latin America with its large indigenous populations. Canada needed trade relations with these nations. The high praise that this submission received in *Saturday Night* suggests that these views were shared by other members of the English Canadian intellectual elite. It is worth noting, however, that even such progressive critics spoke for the 'Indians' rather than reporting Native plans for post-war reconstruction.

The Intellectual Context of English Canadian Criticisms of Racism

The thinking of Canadian critics of racism becomes easier to understand if we consider that the ideas of leading anthropologists, biologists, and geneticists who studied race in Britain and the United States in the 1930s and 1940s were at times also inconsistent and ambiguous. Elazar Barkan, author of *The Retreat of Scientific Racism*, attributes this inconsistency to the fact that during the interwar years, scholars in Britain and the United States, motivated by both scientific and political concerns, were in the process of rethinking the meaning of race. The inability of scientists to find consistent demarcations of racial typology cast doubts on the previous understanding of race. Scholars in the new field of human genetics, for example, provided no support for the physical distinctions used for racial classification. Psychologists found no connection between visible differences such as skin colour and innate mental capacities. Anthropologists argued that culture, rather than biology, determined human behaviour. Yet some notions of race persisted even among the most vocal critics of racial thinking. One reason for the persistence of such notions was that the conventions of racial science were deeply rooted. Developments in one discipline did not immediately affect thinking in another, and even within disciplines conceptions of race that had prevailed for more than a century were not immediately undermined by the incremental awareness of the anomalies surrounding the question of racial types.[72]

Concern over the status of African Americans, opposition to the imposition of quotas on immigration to the United States, the desire to counter the rise of Nazism and anti-Semitism in Europe and the United States, and the desire to gain sympathy for the plight of refugees from Nazism were some of the political reasons that drove scholars to repudiate racism. Thus they publicized the decline in the scientific respectability of the prevailing views on race before a new understanding could develop. This helps to explain the contradictions even in the works of the most outspoken critics of racism, such as British biologists Julian Huxley and J.B.S. Haldane and American biologist Herbert Spencer Jennings. When Jennings spoke out against the exclusion of some groups of European immigrants from the United States, for example, he did not challenge notions of a racial hierarchy, but held instead that since Irish immigrants had been admitted, despite the fact that there were more 'defectives' among them than among other groups of Europeans,

they should not be excluded.[73] Huxley offered environmental explanations for the backwardness of Africans: they were isolated from the
rest of mankind and the 'excessive luxuriance of nature, the heat of the
climate, the prevalence of insidious and chronic disease, combine[d]
with the ease of gaining some reasonable livelihood with very little effort' stood in the way of progress. Yet he also argued that races differed
'in the average of their inborn capacities as they do in their physical
traits.'[74] Population geneticist J.B.S. Haldane continued to believe even
in the late 1940s that there were biological differences among races –
different races were more adaptable to different environments and possessed special talents.[75]

Such contradictory thinking entered even into publications penned
by these scholars to eliminate racist thinking among members of the
general public. In *We Europeans*, one of the most influential anti-racist
pamphlets published in the 1930s which was read in Canada as well,
Huxley and anthropologist Alfred C. Haddon wrote that the 'scientific
concept of "race," as applied to humans, "has lost any sharpness of
meaning."'[76] But while they proposed the substitution of the concept
of ethnicity for race, they continued to hold that some ethnic groups
possessed a low average of innate intelligence.[77] Ruth Benedict's *Races of Mankind*, perhaps the most influential of the wartime anti-racist
publications in North America, asserted that European groups such as
Jews and Italians were not races. Benedict nevertheless accepted the
division of humankind into 'Caucasians,' 'Mongoloids,' and 'Negroid,'
thereby implying that 'race' somehow remained a meaningful category
for distinguishing among people.[78] Though she herself opposed ranking races, her continued reliance on the classification lent support to an
analytic criterion that might invite such ranking.

The absence of such inconsistencies from the public statements of
the two Canadian academics whose scholarly interests were directly
linked to the question of race is therefore noteworthy. T.F. McIlwraith,
of the University of Toronto and the Royal Ontario Museum, was one
of them. His discussion of 'race and race concepts' in his presidential
address to the Royal Canadian Institute on 2 November 1942, received
attention in the daily press. He stated categorically that 'no group is
mentally superior and that there is no correlation between physical and
mental types of man.' Australian-born C.W.M. Hart, McIlwraith's col-
league in the University of Toronto's Department of Anthropology, also
attempted to counter the 'Race Myth' during the Second World War. He
publicized the latest findings of American and British social scientists

such as Franz Boas, Raymond Firth, Julian Huxley, A.C. Haddon, and Margaret Mead. But he also pointed out that the myth of race persisted despite scholarly refutations because blaming social problems on innate racial causes excused the public from acting to solve them. 'If the Negro is naturally lazy and stupid ... we are absolved from worrying about it,' he wrote, 'reform, education, raising his standard of living, are useless.'[79] He believed that the introduction of 'more modern' social science in primary and high schools would be required to dispel such 'racial nonsense' as the 'natural genius of the Anglo-Saxons for democracy,' or 'the inherent manliness of the Nordic races.'[80]

In the case of such Canadian critics of racism as Claris Silcox, Watson Kirkconnell, and Robert England, confused, even contradictory ideas of race combined with social conservatism, or a liberal belief in the inevitable rewards of hard labour, to reinforce racist stereotypes and to obscure the full extent and consequences of racial discrimination in Canada. The social and intellectual distance that separated most of these critics from working-class members of minority groups impeded greater understanding.

6

Labour and the Left

Not all English Canadian activists or members of Canadian voluntary associations who tackled racism and discrimination shared the social conservatism of Silcox, Kirkconnell, and Gibbon. A number of them believed that class divisions were a significant and sometimes decisive feature of Canadian society and that racial inequality was closely linked to class inequality in Canada. These activists insisted during the war that overcoming racism was a prerequisite of building a more egalitarian and democratic society.

Critics from the Left

One such activist was Scottish-born Watson Thomson, director of adult education for the University of Manitoba, a member of the Workers' Educational Association and the Canadian Association for Adult Education, and a well-known commentator on the CBC. Thomson pointed to the economic advantages that Canada derived from exploiting 'non-preferred' immigrants. Canada sought immigrants primarily as cheap labour, but while immigrants fulfilled this goal by building railroads and highways, Canadians did not incorporate immigrant workers into their communities. Thomson ascribed this failure to Canada's 'racial principles.' Such principles justified classifying some groups of immigrants as non-preferred, while allowing others to enter Canada only with a special permit. These principles rested on the 'gross error of associating ... moral, cultural, psychological values with a certain physical breed.' Thomson believed that science, above all the new science of genetics, found no evidence that supposed qualities of race other than physical features (such as the colour of eyes, shape of the nose, and texture of hair) were 'permanent qualities' passed along inevitably 'in the blood.' Hostility towards minorities in Canada and resistance to future immigration, he believed, were at odds with Canada's war aim to respect diversity and promote cooperation among minorities.[1]

Unlike socially conservative critics of racism, who saw the middle class as the basis of social stability, Thomson looked to organized labour groups as the representatives of 'the plain people of this world' to identify with the 'humiliated and oppressed of every race and creed.' Acknowledging that the labour movement traditionally opposed immigration because of fears of economic competition, he noted that some unions, such as the UAW, had nevertheless spoken up for Jewish refugees and human rights. Thomson believed that in the future the working class and labour unions would continue to be key players in the fight against racism in Canada.

During the Second World War, Thomson focused mostly on the Jews. *I Accuse*, probably his best-known work against racism, condemned the Canadian government's failure to help Jewish victims of Nazism and urged individual Canadians to fight racism and to pressure their officials to admit Jewish refugees. His pamphlet dealt with anti-Semitism not because it was 'so much more hateful than anti-Negroism, or any other brand of ignorant race passion,' but because he believed that no other group was as endangered by racism during the war as the Jews. *I Accuse* was published by left-wing Jewish publisher Harry Gutkin in Winnipeg.[2]

A critical review of *I Accuse* in *Food for Thought*, the publication of the Canadian Association for Adult Education which was generally critical of racism, suggests that the inclusiveness of Thomson's criteria was still not widespread in Canada. The review, which appeared in a section dealing with race, refugees, and immigration, argued that his proposals could be criticized on sociological grounds. The review stated: 'A culture, like an individual, has an inherent right to safeguard its own perpetuity and to adopt immigration policies which will provide these safeguards.'[3]

The experience of working with immigrant workers allowed Reverend Harvey Forster, superintendent of the All People's Missions in the Niagara peninsula, to speak in less abstract terms than some of the immigrant workers' academic defenders about problems in immigrant communities. Forster believed that crime and disease among immigrants were attributable to unemployment and poverty rather than racial characteristics. Citing a study of immigrant workers in Buffalo, he

explained that prejudice and discrimination perpetuated the marginalization of immigrants and their children by relegating them to the least
skilled, lowest paying, lowest status jobs.[4] He publicized the unhealthy
working conditions that destroyed the bodies of industrial workers,
using examples such as the immigrants who stoked the furnaces in steel
plants, the polluted air that immigrant families breathed because of the
proximity of 'foreign' quarters to factories, and the failure of municipalities to provide proper sewage and roads for such neighbourhoods.

Like Thomson, Forster was a strong supporter of industrial unions.
He believed that while craft unions historically reinforced discrimination and exclusion of immigrant workers, industrial unions organized
by the CIO would reverse this process by organizing all workers, including the unskilled.[5] In practice, he and other United Church workers in the Niagara peninsula openly supported labour unions. Forster,
himself active in the CCF, encouraged the participation of immigrants
in local politics and urged their children to continue their education
through high school and university as additional ways to counteract
their marginalization. He also urged officials at all levels of government to consult more fully with members of minority groups when developing or implementing policies that affected them.[6] Forster's views
were influential, despite his left-wing sympathies. Perhaps because of
his familiarity with working-class immigrants, some civil servants and
members of Anglo-Canadian voluntary organizations saw Forster as an
expert on non-Anglo-Saxon people and turned to him for advice and
assistance in their dealings with such groups.[7]

Norman Black, educator and author of the first Canadian book devoted to 'the educational aspects of the immigrant problems,' was
another social democrat who repudiated racism generally and employment discrimination in particular. He wrote numerous articles for
magazines and newspapers and lectured widely on 'racial problems.'[8]
Black paid special attention to anti-Semitism and to discrimination
against Japanese Canadians. President of the Vancouver Consultative
Council, an organization that aimed to safeguard the rights of citizens
in wartime, Black was intent on convincing Canadians that responsible
scientists no longer supported the 'myth' of race. 'Character, ideas,
ideals, habits, attitudes and the like' were not transmitted by physical
inheritance, but 'acquired after birth and shaped by human contacts.'
Thus, Canadian-born and educated people of Japanese descent were 'as
thoroughly and as obviously Canadian in their thinking as anyone in
this Dominion.' They should, therefore, be offered jobs in keeping with

their training and expertise, including white-collar jobs. Black went so far as to dismiss fears about miscegenation. Geneticists knew 'that where the blending of racial strains involves no social disapproval – as in Hawaii – the children of such marriages are as clever and beautiful and as lovable and as good raw material for citizenship as the children of the strictest racial purists.'[9]

The Co-operative Commonwealth Federation

Understandably, Anglo-Canadian supporters of left-wing parties and the labour movement were most deeply concerned about the economic manifestations of racism, specifically employment discrimination. The CCF expressed its commitment to the defence of civil liberties and human rights from its inception. The party's founding programme, the 1933 Regina Manifesto, called for 'equal treatment before the law of all residents of Canada irrespective of race, nationality or religious or political belief.' Implicit in the manifesto's preamble was the view that intolerance – racist, religious, and political – was the product of competitive capitalism. The new cooperative social order envisioned by the CCF, by contrast, would be a tolerant and pluralistic one in which racial and religious minorities would be free to enjoy their cultural rights. The collective organization of economic resources – the socialist foundation on which the new social order would be built – would make possible the building of such a society.[10]

Responding both to Canadian and international developments, CCF members grew increasingly concerned about safeguarding civil liberties and human rights during the 1930s and 1940s. Domestically, they were reacting to the intensification of anti-Semitism in the late 1930s and early 1940s: Duplessis' 1937 anti-communist Padlock Law, the detention of communists and the seizure of Ukrainian Labour-Farmer Temple Association halls at the outbreak of the Second World War, the expulsion of Japanese Canadians from the west coast in 1942 and the deportation of many of them to Japan at war's end. Internationally, they were reacting to the rise of fascism and Nazism in Europe. As they considered the forces that endangered civil liberties and human rights, the centrality of economics to their analysis became more clearly articulated. Delegates at CCF conventions during the Second World War, for example, argued that the treatment of Japanese Canadians was not simply the consequence of wartime tensions, but the product of long-standing racism that had for decades offered economic advantages to capitalists. Since they saw economic insecurity in a competitive society as the main cause of racial antagonism, social democrats believed that such antagonism would disappear with the introduction of full employment and a social security net to provide, for example, insurance for those whose earning capacity was interrupted through illness.[11]

The belief that state-guaranteed social and economic rights provided the basis for protecting human rights distinguished CCF human rights advocacy from the plans of the Conservative and Liberal parties. A key factor behind the Liberal government's failure to endorse a national bill of rights in the late 1940s, for example, were fears that such a bill might imply state responsibility for guaranteeing the right to medical care and employment.[12] Since the CCF advocated such rights in any event, it could promote a Canadian bill of rights without reservations. Indeed, social democratic plans for an interventionist state account for the CCF's unequivocal support for a national bill of rights as a means to ending racism and discrimination in Canada. Yet, as left-wing critics have pointed out, the CCF's proposals for such legislation stopped short of including social and economic rights. The omission of such rights at this stage, however, did not signify a retreat from socialist principles. Rather, Canadian social democrats believed that incorporating such rights in a bill of rights would be unenforceable. Separate social security and health insurance legislation would be far more effective in guaranteeing social and economic welfare.[13]

CCF members also introduced a class perspective to wartime discussions of racist discrimination. M.J. Coldwell spoke in the House of Commons of the danger of blaming fifth column activities on the poor and discontented. Social democrats were afraid that wartime hysteria would be used to deny labour the right to organize and make its voice heard. The *Canadian Forum* pointed to C.D. Howe's depiction of the strike at the Arvida, Quebec, plant of the Aluminum Company of Canada in 1941 as a case of 'enemy sabotage.'[14] During the same year CCF MP Angus MacInnis challenged employers' right to ask about the religion of prospective employees.[15]

Because they believed that racial tensions served the purposes of Canada's 'ruling cliques' by sowing divisions that prevented Canadians from concentrating on social improvement, social democrats did not underestimate the difficulty of eliminating racial discrimination. The difficulties were especially great in wartime, when racial antagonisms against Canadians of 'foreign' origin were fanned.[16] To social democrats the case of the United States illustrated that legislation alone would be ineffectual 'when public opinion or the opinion of the judges happens to be opposed to the liberties of unpopular minorities.'[17] A massive effort composed of 'all known means' of propaganda and education – home education, schools, radio, citizens' forums, legislation, and research – would also be required.[18] Recognizing the need to build broader public support for their cause, some social democrats joined organizations established specifically to defend civil and human rights, such as the Cooperative Committee on Japanese Canadians and the Civil Liberties Association of Toronto. Activists also promoted cooperation with groups of ordinary Canadians in churches, trade unions, and cooperatives, through which propaganda and educational materials could be distributed.

Social gospel ideas inspired some social democrats to stand up for racialized minorities at a time when racism still informed state policy in Canada. M.J. Coldwell, the CCF's leader from 1942 to 1960, for example, argued that 'racialism' was incompatible with Christianity: 'All men, being the children of God,' he maintained, 'are brothers.' Protestant ministers and their congregations composed a notable segment among social democrats who fought to counter racial discrimination. Commending provincial Premier Tommy Douglas for his stand against the deportation of Japanese Canadians, one of them, Reverend H. Christensen, a United Church minister from Webb, Saskatchewan, expressed their views in colourful and original language. 'The way we have treated these unfortunate people is simply a crime,' Christensen wrote, adding, 'our boasted Christian civilization must stink in the nostrils of the angels of God.' Saskatchewan CCF MPP Warden Burgess maintained that in contrast to established churches, the cooperative movement in Canada 'had never recognized any difference on racial or religious grounds and by so doing it evidenced a true appreciation of Christian principles.'[19]

Secular humanist ideas, as well as evolving notions of Canadian citizenship, also motivated CCF human rights advocates. British Columbia MP Angus MacInnis believed that 'accepting an individual because he is a human being and has rights and privileges with every other human being, regardless of race,' was 'of the essence of socialism.'[20] Norman Black argued that 'distinctions made on the basis of racial stock are contrary to the spirit of Canadian institutions.'[21] Speaking out in parliament against the deportation of Japanese Canadians, Alistair Stewart, CCF MP from Winnipeg, employed the language of rights. 'Any citizen of this country, whether he be Jew or Gentile, Catholic or Protestant, black, white or yellow, believer or unbeliever,' he argued, 'has exactly the same rights as any other citizen.'[22]

Alone among political parties represented in the British Columbia legislature, the CCF took the part of minorities of Asian origin, demanding that they be given the franchise. In 1938, when the British Columbia executive of the CCF temporized, suggesting that the question of the franchise be referred to a plebiscite, the party's national executive argued that such a plebiscite was not in keeping with the CCF's principles which supported equality of status regardless of race or colour.[23] Divisions within the party concerning the 'Oriental' question persisted during the war years. Some caucus members were determined to oppose discrimination against British Columbians of Asian descent, while others, afraid of losing electoral support, tried to sidestep the issue, and a few openly took an anti-Oriental stand.[24]

Even Angus MacInnis and his wife Grace MacInnis, who were among the most steadfast supporters of the CCF's anti-discrimination policy, believed they had to make allowances for anti-Oriental racism in wartime Canada. In a pamphlet sympathetic to the Japanese Canadians (entitled *Oriental Canadians – Outcasts or Citizens*) they supported the exclusion of Japanese Canadians from coastal British Columbia, on the grounds that their concentration on the west coast would single them out for discrimination. When the national executive of the CCF reviewed the pamphlet in manuscript form, only George Grube, president of the Ontario CCF Civil Liberties Committee, objected to this position.[25]

The election of a CCF government in Saskatchewan in 1944 provided social democratic advocates of human rights with the opportunity to put their convictions into practice. Given that the province, with its exceptionally high proportion of people of continental European descent, had witnessed intense anti-foreign movements during the 1920s and again at the outbreak of the Second World War,[26] the Douglas government's actions in this regard were both innovative and courageous. Shortly after the election, the Ministry of Education distributed a pamphlet it received from the Canadian Jewish Congress, *The Races of Mankind*, to five thousand Saskatchewan teachers.[27] Written by Columbia University anthropologists Ruth Benedict and Gene Weltfish, the pamphlet debunked widespread misconceptions about race. Despite federal jurisdiction over Native affairs, the new provincial government, concerned with the plight of Native peoples in Saskatchewan, encouraged the formation of the Union of Saskatchewan Indian Chiefs to speak on their behalf.[28] Even before the end of war with Japan, Premier Douglas invited Japanese Canadians to settle in Saskatchewan. The wording of his invitation rankles today, and it evoked criticism from some rank-and-file CCF members in 1944. 'We did not think that British Columbia should be saddled with the entire Japanese population of this country,' Douglas explained, 'but that these people should be allocated to each of the provinces so that all will be accepting their fair share of responsibility, rather than asking British Columbia to assume the entire burden.'[29] But at a time when communities throughout Canada attempted to prevent Japanese Canadians from settling in their midst, or admitted them only on condition that they would leave at the end of the war, Douglas's offer was remarkable. His government followed up the invitation by retaining lawyer Andrew Brewin – a leading member of the CCF – to fight against Ottawa's attempt to deport Japanese Canadians.[30]

The Communist Party of Canada

The Communist Party of Canada (CPC) also protested against racist discrimination generally and employment discrimination specifically. Key to the CPC's interest in this question was its belief that immigrants were becoming increasingly important among Canadian workers. It aimed to recruit immigrant and minority workers to the Communist Party and to communist-led trade unions. Not only the CPC, but such divisions of the Comintern as the Anglo-American Secretariat and the Red Unions International, noted that in the 1920s Canada replaced the United States as the chief destination of migrants from Europe. They remarked that immigrants composed a large number of workers in the automobile industry, and anticipated that they would come to dominate other key Canadian industries such as lumbering, mining, and textiles. Communists also noted that in British Columbia workers of Asian descent made up a substantial proportion of the working class.[31] During the interwar years, CPC activists called on minority workers to transcend racial and ethnic boundaries in a united working-class campaign against organized capitalism.[32] They believed such a campaign to be particularly urgent, since the promotion of chauvinism by 'fascists' within a number of minority groups was blinding workers to their shared class interests. Once the Soviet Union entered the war on the allied side, a call for national unity against fascism replaced the emphasis on class struggle. Nevertheless, the CPC's foreign-language press continued to promote the unionization of workers.

International developments also motivated communist interest in minority workers. During the 1930s CPC functionaries believed, for example, that 'Oriental' workers in British Columbia could be used to protest Canada's sale of war materials to Japan. They feared that the purpose of such trade was to strengthen 'imperialist' build up against the Soviet Union.[33] During the same period, they sought to recruit Italian Canadian workers to strengthen a campaign against fascist Italy, especially to protest Mussolini's imperialist campaigns in Africa.[34]

From the CPC's inception, its membership was composed overwhelmingly of workers of European origin, Ukrainians and Finns foremost among them. The party was successful in recruiting additional immigrant and minority workers because it paid more attention to such workers than the mainstream labour movement and other political parties did. Through the Comintern, the CPC solicited materials in foreign languages from the Italian, Hungarian, and Chinese communist parties. During organizing drives in Canadian industries, it relied on its language groups to publish materials in the languages of the largest groups of immigrant workers, and for unorganized ethnic groups it requested the aid of organizers from Europe (in the case of Italians) and the United States (in the case of Hungarians). Foreign-language papers carried articles about such topics as 'What does a union mean?' in which a Hungarian miner from Rothwell, New Brunswick, explained that workers enjoyed higher wages, heated bathrooms, and a workshop to sharpen miners' tools thanks to unionization.[35] These papers contrasted genuine labour unions and company or 'fink' unions, against which they warned their readers.[36] Such warnings were especially important because through the wartime Industrial Disputes Inquiry Commission, a tripartite body empowered to investigate and try to settle industrial disputes, Ottawa endorsed substituting employee committees – viewed by the labour movement as company unions – for independent unions.[37] Employers used this endorsement to counter organizing drives by encouraging formation of employee committees and, at times, even signing agreements with the committees while stalling negotiations with supporters of independent unions.[38] Very significantly, the CPC's promotion of unionization persisted even after the German invasion of the Soviet Union in June 1941, when the party adopted a 'no strike' policy. The papers also paid close attention to women workers, and urged the inclusion of workers from all backgrounds in strike committees and unions. John Wier, himself of Ukrainian background, observed in the Canadian Tribune in

1943 that the cooperation among workers of various backgrounds in Windsor should serve as a model for the rest of Canada. 'At the work benches and on the benches at union meetings you find Anglo-Saxon and Ukrainian, French and Yugoslav and all the national groups which make up and build Canada, side by side,' Wier wrote, although he also noted that discrimination against 'Negroes' persisted to mar this inspiring unity.[39]

The CPC's advocacy of cooperation with workers of Asian descent offers a clear example that class analysis informed its anti-racism. It referred repeatedly, for example, to the 1932 Fraser Mills strike, in which shingle workers of English, French, and Asian origin, organized by the CPC, succeeded in obtaining recognition for the Union of Shingle Workers.[40] Similarly, the union's publication, *The Shingle Worker*, commented on the success of a work stoppage at the Sterling Shingle Company in the reinstatement of two Chinese workers who had been fired without cause: 'This is a wonderful lesson to all shingle mill workers, that we must not stand for discrimination regardless of "creed, color or nationality." That the Chinese workers' interests are identically the same as ours.'[41] Five years later, when workers at Blubber Bay, BC, gained recognition for the Lumber and Sawmill Workers' Union, the communist-affiliated *BC Lumber Worker* commented:

> If ever a concrete example has shown that racial problems are no barrier to the unity of workers fighting for benefits to their class brothers, Blubber Bay is it. The division of the plant is almost 50-50 Oriental and white, and throughout the strike, Orientals and whites conferred, planned, canvassed and worked together without a hitch.[42]

The CPC concerned itself with the most marginalized groups of workers during the interwar period. It conducted campaigns among sugar beet and tobacco workers, migrant labourers, female domestic servants, and the unemployed.[43] The communist press reported on discrimination against African Canadians, recording both individual instances of discrimination and resistance against it. For example, it covered A. Philip Randolph's organizing tour in Canada.[44]

Convinced that nearly half of Canada's youths were of foreign extraction, the CPC promoted the formation of 'broad democratic anti-fascist organizations' among them.[45] Organizers used cultural activities, such as dances, songs, and games, to attract young people. Until they were banned in 1942, young communists took an active part in Canadian youth congresses, where they called for an end to economic and political discrimination against racial minorities.[46]

The *Canadian Tribune* denounced the racist treatment of Native people in Canada. The communist publication pointed to the 'absurdity' of the legal definition of who was an 'Indian' in Canada: 'a white woman who marries an Indian man has Indian children, who share in the "treaty money" and have the right to have a house on the reservation. An Indian woman who marries a white man has white children, who become citizens and cannot claim rights on the reservation.' It is worth noting and significant that the article questioned only the racist, not the gender, assumptions behind this policy.[47]

Communist policies toward minority workers, however, were not without contradictions, most obviously in the case of Japanese Canadians. When the *Canadian Tribune* called for the extension of democratic rights to 'Oriental minorities,' it specified only the rights of 'Chinese and East Indian Citizens.' Its failure to mention the Japanese Canadians is particularly noteworthy, given their treatment during the war.[48] In April 1944, *The People*, a communist paper published in British Columbia, denounced the provincial Liberal Party for fomenting race hatred by petitioning the federal government never again to allow settlement of Japanese in British Columbia, to forbid employers to employ persons of Japanese ancestry, and to remove all such persons from Canada.[49] A month later, however, the paper accused the CCF of trying to divide Canadian workers for partisan ends and to distract them from the major tasks of the war by advocating the enfranchisement of Japanese Canadians. While not all Japanese Canadians in British Columbia were fascist, the paper claimed, 'all of them were to some extent under the influence of their fascist leaders.' Accordingly, their removal from the west coast had been necessary, and the plans to disperse them throughout the country rather than allowing their return to British Columbia were also justified.[50]

In the case of Native workers, communist MP Dorise Nielsen was among the few Canadians who addressed the issue of employment discrimination. She objected to restricting the training and education of young Native people to making traditional handicrafts or to performing menial labour, such as domestic service. The 'Indian people,' she told a fellow MP, 'have the same right to employment as anybody else.'[51] The solutions she advocated, however, did not take the plans of Native people into consideration. Full assimilation rather than the preservation of Native rights was the CPC's goal. Nielsen compared the situation of Native people to that of European immigrants. She urged that every member of the young generation of indigenous people should be given adequate education to get jobs and 'become really a part of our nation.' She stated: 'We do as much for people who come from European countries ... they come here, they are educated, and they are no longer Hungarians or Austrians or from European countries; they have become Canadians. Just the same way I think it is equally important that Indians should be educated to become Canadians themselves.'[52]

This assimilationist goal echoed earlier communist plans for workers of European descent. As part of the Comintern's 'bolshevization' programme in the 1920s, CPC functionaries denounced the alleged petty-bourgeois nationalism of the CPC's language federations, and forced immigrant workers with limited knowledge of English to join factory nuclei of the party.[53] Displaying little understanding of the traditions, practices, and needs of minority workers, party functionaries claimed that Ukrainian workers ignored the all-important goal of labour organizing, preferring instead to invest their energies in social activities within the Ukrainian Labour-Farmer Temple Association (ULFTA). Despite Comintern directives, however, experienced Ukrainian Canadian activists such as John Boychuck and Matthew Popovich insisted that the social and cultural 'mass' organizations were crucial for transmitting communist ideology to immigrant workers and thus for winning the workers' support. They pointed out that organizers holding competing ideologies, ranging from nationalism to fascism, were at work in immigrant communities and that the cultural work of communist mass organizations was essential to counter competing campaigns.[54]

Having attended meetings in various factories, where workers who shared sympathy with the party could not communicate with one another, some English Canadian CPC members also concluded that attempts to reorganize the party were impracticable. In 1926, even Tim Buck, generally depicted by historians as the chief proponent of bolshevization, apparently acknowledged that the programme had been ill-conceived. Evidence suggests that the bolshevization policy had the effect of demoralizing minority party members and driving some of them out of the party.[55] By 1933, a communist organizer pointed out that organizing among Slavic workers in their own languages helped union campaigns among miners in the west and in the Sudbury area.[56]

The CPC's ideological twists and turns also diminished the ability of minority workers to fight against discrimination. On the one hand, the leadership criticized language associations for not giving enough attention to the labour movement. On the other hand, it denounced minority labour organizations whose ideological orientation differed from its own. In 1931, for example, it denounced the Japanese Camp and Mill Workers' Union as reactionary because of its connections to the CCF.[57] While fighting against the economic exploitation of workers in the early 1930s, the party-organized Workers' Unity League unions also served to divide workers in such industries as clothing and mining.

By the war years, however, the CPC's torturous route towards building worker internationalism among some minority groups did assume the form of a programme for intergroup collaboration. During the Great Depression, the CPC had established a multi-ethnic fraternal organization modelled after the communist-affiliated International Workers' Order in the United States. These organizations provided health and life insurance to their members and supported foreign-language newspapers as well as social and educational activities. The CPC's plan was motivated by practical considerations as well as the desire to promote inter-ethnic cooperation. It aimed to unite small, impoverished, ethnically based benefit federations with larger, somewhat more prosperous ones such as the Ukrainian Labour-Farmer Temple Association and the United Jewish People's Order. When these plans failed, Hungarian, Slovak, German, Polish, and Italian groups, as well as an English Canadian and a French Canadian group, united to form the Independent Mutual Benefit Federation.[58] During the war, the federation underwent structural reorganization, establishing national sections in response to what it described as an 'upsurge in national identity,' in the hope that 'this would help rally people of each nationality.' Along with catering to the economic and social needs of its members, the federation's conventions and publications provided a forum for campaigning against racist discrimination. Its bulletin, *The Guide*, reported and denounced the loss of jobs by naturalized workers of European descent following the declaration of war, even if they traced their origins to countries allied with Canada.[59] At the federation's 1944 convention in Hamilton, fraternal delegate Paul Kirzner of the Jewish Labor League pointed out that the war had produced a measure of unity in Canada, but added that 'there cannot be national unity when national minorities face economic and social discrimination.' He described the Ontario government's 1944 Racial Discrimination Act as merely a step towards outlawing such discrimination.[60] The federation's grand council commended the Hungarian and Slovak sections for fighting against 'the racial hatred that throws one group of people against another.'[61]

The Labour Movement

Influential unions in both of Canada's large labour federations publicly condemned racial discrimination even before the outbreak of the Second World War. They included unions with large minority membership, such as the International Ladies' Garment Workers' Union (with many Jewish members) and the Brotherhood of Sleeping Car Porters (with African Canadian members), but also unions with ethnically diverse membership, such as the United Automobile Workers; the United Gas, Coke and Chemical Workers; the United Electrical, Radio and Machine Workers; and the Steel Workers Organizing Committee. Union constitutions and by-laws, like that of the United Gas, Coke and Chemical Workers, declared membership open 'to all working men and women regardless of race, creed, color or nationality,' and added a commitment on the part of each member to do all in his or her power to defend 'fellow workers against discrimination because of color, creed or nationality.'[62] Workers joining Local 529 of the United Electrical, Radio and Machine Workers Union in St Catharines, Ontario, were required to take an initiation oath, declaring their 'solidarity with Brother or Sister workers regardless of Race, Creed, Sex, Color, Nationality, Political belief or Affiliation.'[63] Throughout the war years, both social-democratic and communist unionists raised their voices against racist discrimination. At its 55th annual convention in October 1939, for example, the Trades and Labour Congress (TLC) declared itself in favour of unrestricted racial and religious liberty and condemned propaganda promoting discrimination on the grounds of race or creed.[64] The following year, Aaron Mosher, of the Canadian Brotherhood of Railway Employees, declared that he believed the labour movement to be the most potent instrument for overcoming the economic, racial, and political differences that divided the people of Canada.[65] In the summer of 1941 the Packinghouse Workers' Organizing Committee campaigned among 'foreign' workers in Toronto by telling them that joining its ranks was their chance to assert themselves. In May 1942 the conference of international unions (affiliated with the American Federation of Labor) adopted a resolution denouncing anti-Semitism and race hatred.[66] In October 1942, when unions with a large number of Jewish workers, such as the International Ladies' Garment Workers' Union, travelled to Ottawa to protest against discriminatory hiring practices in war industries, they were accompanied by Percy Bengough, acting president of the TLC.[67] In August 1943, the Vancouver Trade and Labor Council wrote Prime Minister King to condemn Wetaskiwin Social Credit MP Norman Jacques's fomenting anti-Semitism.[68] Appearing before the Ontario Select Committee to Inquire into Collective Bargaining between Employers and Employees in the same year, a representative of the Packinghouse Workers' Organizing Committee characterized his union as an agency for integrating immigrant workers and their children in Canadian society; he reported:

> In the packinghouse field there is another special situation, in that a large number of the workers are either foreign-born or the children of foreign-born parents. The union can render service to these new Canadians that perhaps no other organization can give – if it is not kept preoccupied by the struggle for existence. In the first place, it brings together good, bad and broken English speakers for common activities and the discussion of common problems. This not only trains our members in self-expression but creates a feeling of unity and fellowship. In the second place, the union meeting gives the new Canadians, as well as others, information about national and international events of general interest to all citizens. For the local union does not confine its discussions to the affairs of its own plant. It can debate and pass resolutions on anything from the foreign policy of our Government to the desirability of tablecloths in the lunch-room. It can thus be an integrating medium for different racial groups in the community and a training-school in the techniques of democracy.[69]

In 1944 the TLC convention resolved to appoint a permanent committee 'to promote the unity of Canadians of all racial origins, and to combat and counteract any evidence of racial discrimination in industry in particular and in life in general.'[70]

Unions also played an active role in protesting against such practices as the refusal of tourist homes and hotels to serve members of minorities.[71] The United Electrical, Radio and Machine Workers union representing workers in the Niagara region sent a strongly worded protest to the Port Elgin town council when it contemplated endorsing the exclusion of Jews from local tourist homes.[72] When George Drew's government limited its Racial Discrimination Act to prohibiting the publication of racist materials, George Burt of the UAW called on Drew to expand the law's coverage to include the prohibition of job and housing discrimination.[73]

International unions drew on American experience and even publicity materials to convey anti-racist ideas to their members. One example

of such materials was a comic book, published by the publicity department of the CIO, *They Got the Blame: The Story of Scapegoats in History*.[74]
The introduction emphasized the centrality of the CIO's goal of overcoming racist divisions among workers:

> The basic purpose of the CIO, as expressed in its constitution, is to bring
> about the effective organization of the working men and women of Ameri-
> ca regardless of race, creed, color or nationality, and to unite them for com-
> mon action into labor unions for their mutual aid and protection.
>
> To win this war against fascism and tyranny, and to win the peace as
> well, all who believe in democracy must stand united WHATEVER THEIR
> RACE, CREED OR COLOR if they would preserve the blessing of freedom
> and human dignity.[75]

Labour unions did more than simply talk about ending discrimination. In contrast to racist employers, they provided opportunities for
advancement to talented members of minority groups. Armenian Canadian Hygus Torosian was a founding member of UAW Local 199 in
St Catharines, and was one of the most active members of the local's
educational committee. In recognition for his contribution, the UAW
awarded Torosian a scholarship to study at the Workers' Educational
Association's training school in England so that he could prepare himself 'for even more effective work in his organization and community.'[76]
The same UAW local fought for the reinstatement of Joseph di Mercurio. An Italian Canadian employee of McKinnon Industries, di Mercurio came to Canada in 1913, had been working as a foundry man
at McKinnon Industries since 1916, and had been naturalized in 1923.
After Italy's entry into the war, the RCMP removed di Mercurio from
the plant. He was interned at Camp Petawawa until June 1941. Following his unconditional release from internment, di Mercurio applied
for re-employment at McKinnon Industries. He was refused on the
grounds that he was 'not entirely free from suspicion.' The president
of McKinnon Industries told di Mercurio that he would employ him if
he obtained authorization from the government to return to work. Di
Mercurio applied to the Ministry of Justice for authorization, but while
waiting for a response he took a job elsewhere. The company then argued that it had no further obligation to di Mercurio. The UAW con-
tended that di Mercurio, having worked for McKinnon Industries for
fifteen years, and having been released from internment unconditio-
nally, was entitled to re-employment by the company. Only economic ne-

cessity had compelled di Mercurio to take another job while waiting for the government's response. The union saw workers as extremely vulnerable under wartime security regulations, and believed that insisting on di Mercurio's re-employment would serve the interest of all workers. 'Anybody might be picked up under the new regulations for some unknown reason,' the union's representative argued, 'and the manager would not re-employ us because we were once under suspicion.'[77]

During the war years, moreover, both CIO and AFL unions actively recruited minority workers. Given the high concentration of immigrant workers in certain industries, such a policy made practical sense. As an English Canadian steel worker at Fittings Ltd. in Oshawa pointed out to the Steel Workers Organizing Committee, 80 per cent of the workers in two of the company's plants were 'foreign speaking.' Since almost half of these workers were already expressing their sympathy toward unionization by attending meetings, an organizer who could speak to them in their own languages would improve the situation of the workers' meetings '100%.'[78]

A commitment to egalitarian principles became part of union culture during the war years. By then the ranks of union organizers included immigrants or the children of immigrants. Where needed, interpreters were present during union meetings. In Welland, for example, the United Electrical Workers organized 'special meetings' in the languages of the French, Hungarian, and Croatian workers. They also organized a meeting for women workers.[79] In Oshawa, Steel Workers Local 1817 published its newsletter, *Melting Pot*, in a number of European languages.[80] Local 199 of the United Auto Workers of America brought in a French Canadian organizer from Quebec to work among French Canadian workers.[81] In Port Colborne a discussion on the history of labour unions was interpreted into minority languages and, for those unable to attend, a summary was provided in foreign-language newspapers.[82]

At a time when Ontario communities mounted public protests against the introduction of Japanese Canadian workers, labour organizations ranging across the AFL-affiliated trade councils of Port Arthur and Fort William, the Candian Congress of Labour–affiliated London Labour Council, Hamilton Trades and Labour Council, and Steel Workers Organizing Committee distinguished themselves by publicly welcoming Japanese Canadians and insisting that they be treated and paid like other workers.[83] In Brantford, Ontario, UAW representative Robert Stacey declared that Japanese Canadians should be treated the same as all other Canadians by the National Selective Service, employers, fellow employees, and the general public, adding: 'to do otherwise would be to endorse the Nazi principle of race distinction, one of the fallacies we are fighting a war to erase.'[84] In 1944, Charlie Millard, an organizer for the Steel Workers Organizing Committee and a CCF member, protested against the government's effort to perpetuate the disenfranchisement of Japanese Canadians by substituting racial origin for place of birth as a qualification in Section 5 of Bill 135. His letter to Prime Minister King described uniting working men and women 'regardless of race, creed, color or nationality' as the Steel Workers Organizing Committee's first goal, and warned that just because the bill affected only Japanese Canadians did not mean that it would not be used in the future to discriminate against other racial groups.[85]

In Vancouver, Local 28 of the Hotel, Restaurant and Culinary Bartenders Union brought together Chinese Canadian workers with English Canadians and workers of southern and eastern European descent. In 1943 the local's president was a Chinese Canadian woman: Pearl Chan. Towards the end of the war the local appointed a Chinese Canadian organizer in recognition of the large percentage of workers of the same background among the kitchen staff in hotels and restaurants.[86] Unions also protested when NSS officials discriminated against Chinese Canadian workers by sending them to work in laundries and restaurants rather than to better paying jobs in the automobile plants. The UAW's Local 195 in Windsor pointed out that Chinese workers at the local Ford plant were doing an excellent job and that one of them had been elected sub-steward.[87]

The record of unions was of course not unambiguous in this respect. Labour's human rights campaign was initiated by minority workers and the union leadership. We do not know how widely the remaining membership shared these goals. We do have evidence of racist attitudes and behaviour among organized workers. Early in the war Vancouver longshoremen protested against employment of 'enemy-born persons and their sympathizers.'[88] R. Eggleton, secretary of the Port Arthur Trades and Labour Council, wired Prime Minister King and Munitions Minister C.D. Howe in 1942 to argue that bringing Japanese nationals to northern and northwestern Ontario was 'unnecessary, unwarranted and unwanted.'[89] Edmonton's Trades and Labour Council was sufficiently aware of labour's official anti-racist position to claim that racial discrimination was not their motive when they objected to the admission of Japanese Canadians to Alberta. But its spokesman nevertheless blamed minority victims of exploitation for their predicament, falling back on labour's traditional justification for racist exclusivism. Claiming that 'the Japanese are not fair competitors to organized labour,' he asserted that the Trades and Labour Council's protest against their importation to the province was simply an attempt to protect the rights of organized labour.[90] The Alberta Federation of Labour also objected to the allegedly low standards of Japanese Canadian workers.[91] Similar reasons were probably behind protests from the Coaters' Union and the Pulp, Sulphite and Paper Mill Workers Union when two Georgetown companies proposed to import Japanese Canadian machinists for their factories. Neither union resorted to racist comments, but they made it clear that 'Canadian' skilled workers were entitled to these jobs.[92] The UAW's Local 199 in St Catharines opposed the hiring of Japanese Canadians by McKinnon Industries in 1944.[93]

Despite such instances of discrimination by labour unions, many minority workers, as we saw in Chapter 3, still saw membership in the labour movement as the most effective way to put an end to employment discrimination. Their numbers were large enough that English and French Canadians recognized the necessity of incorporating them in organizing drives. Minority workers served on organizing committees. Those who spoke both English and one (or more) of the languages of immigrant workers were especially useful. Indeed, unions employed interpreters and multilingual publications to draw in even those workers who did not speak one of Canada's two official languages. Anti-racist resolutions introduced by minority activists at labour conventions were generally adopted. Left-wing intellectuals and political activists, who concerned themselves with the interests of minority workers and sought their electoral support, saw labour unions as their most effective allies.

PART FOUR

Anglo-Saxon Guardianship

7

Anglo-Saxon Guardianship

Even as state officials and agencies colluded in various forms of employment discrimination, the federal government initiated new agencies and programmes to integrate minority groups within the body of the nation. Two main objectives shaped the federal government's minority policies in wartime. The first major impetus behind these initiatives was the belief that special efforts would be required to unify a population of diverse origins and to rally the large number of Canada's inhabitants whose origins were neither British nor French behind the war effort. From the outset a key consideration behind government plans was the potential of employment discrimination against minority workers to undermine Canada's wartime productive capacities.[1] Immigrant and minority group workers, after all, were concentrated within such important sectors of the economy as mining, agriculture, and heavy industry. Their labour would be indispensable for Canada's war effort. At the beginning of the war officials feared that the inability of such workers to find or retain employment would inflict great hardship upon the unemployed workers and their families. Once employment became more plentiful, officials worried that Canadians eligible for conscription and their families would resent enemy aliens and minority group members who, prohibited from enlisting, would hold on to their civilian jobs. The second major factor shaping Ottawa's wartime minority policies were security considerations.[2] Not only did federal officials suspect the loyalties of immigrants and Canadians with origins in enemy countries, they also worried that the activities of such minorities might sour relations with Canada's allies. In fact, in the eyes of Canadian officials, security considerations and concerns about employment discrimination intersected. The victims of employment discrimination, 'who were good citizens when usefully employed,' might well become receptive to the overtures of enemy agents and propagandists and thus constitute a danger to Canadian security.[3] As workers in mines, forests, and factories they would have ample opportunity for sabotage.

As we have seen, a large number of government departments and committees, including the departments of labour, external affairs, justice, defence, and above all, national war services, participated in Ottawa's dealings with ethnic and racialized minority groups. Late in 1941, however, the Department of National War Services established the Nationalities Branch (NB), and in January 1942, it appointed an advisory committee – The Committee on Cooperation in Canadian Citizenship (CCCC) – to lend support to the Nationalities Branch and all government departments dealing with minorities. The part of the mandate of these bodies and of the wartime Bureau of Public Information (BPI, later the Wartime Information Board [WIB], the agency in charge of propaganda and censorship) that dealt with minorities had two purposes: to mobilize minority groups behind Canada's war effort and to lessen social tensions by increasing the understanding of the nature of these groups and their contributions to Canadian society among English and French Canadians. Mobilization involved both Canadianizing the immigrants and discovering the sources of dissatisfaction among them which might impede assimilation. From the very first meeting of the CCCC employment discrimination was mentioned as a major source of dissatisfaction among immigrants.[4]

The paradoxical feature of these new state agencies was that their programmes did not intersect with the campaigns by minority groups engaged in fighting prejudice and discrimination. Indeed, participants in the CCCC and the NB appeared oblivious to some minority group campaigns and hostile to others. These parallel developments within the state and civil society reflect the marginalization of ethnic and racialized minority groups even while public policy for their closer integration into Canadian society was being articulated. The reasons for this paradox form the focus of this chapter.

The scholarly literature on state initiatives inadvertently reproduces the paradoxical wartime situation. Because the efforts of the NB, the CCCC, as well as the BPI/WIB marked the first formal attempt by the federal government to integrate ethnic minorities into the nation, they have attracted a great deal of scholarly attention. The many studies about them should not obscure the fact that these agencies, not a high priority for wartime planners, were so underfunded and understaffed that they virtually ceased operations for two crucial years during the war. Nevertheless most studies of state–minority relations in wartime have focused entirely on the state's approach to minorities, paying little attention to the simultaneous development of programmes to combat prejudice and discrimination by a number of minority groups during the war. The neglect of a minority perspective in these historical works reflects the virtual silence of government records about minority anti-discrimination campaigns. Because it offers a clear illustration of the limitations of state policy towards minorities during the Second World War, this disregard of minority campaigns calls for an explanation.

Even the assessments of the work of the NB, CCCC, and BPI/WIB are contradictory. According to Leslie Pal, these agencies and that policy constituted the basis of 'modern citizenship development' in Canada.[5] N.F. Dreisziger believes that these programmes marked the first step in Canada's progress towards a tolerant and inclusive national policy of multiculturalism.[6] Others, by contrast, see these same programmes as indicative of the limitations of Canada's treatment of ethnic and racial-ized minorities during the war. William R. Young and John Thompson point out that the programmes did not address the most serious minor-ity problem in wartime Canada – that of Japanese Canadians. Indeed, Thompson believes that some state propaganda, such as the NFB film *Mask of Nippon*, perpetuated racist stereotypes of Japanese Canadians.[7] Not surprisingly, therefore, state initiatives failed to mitigate Can-adian chauvinism. As Young's work indicates, the surveys of the WIB revealed that prejudice against 'foreigners' in general, and especially against Jews, had actually grown during the war. Moreover, even with-in minority communities of European origin the red-baiting on the part of some of the programme's advisors and officials fomented discord. In *Plateaus of Freedom: Nationality, Culture, and State Security in Canada, 1940–1960*, Mark Kristmanson analyses the security dimension of the wartime activities of these agencies. He sees these agencies as examples of the inseparable link between cultural policy and security concerns in multicultural states and the resultant encroachment by the state on cultural, artistic, and intellectual freedom.[8] Ivana Caccia's *Managing the Canadian Mosaic in Wartime*, the latest interpretation of the work of these government agencies, suggests that disappointment in the results led the government to reorient its approach to integrating Canada's im-migrant population.[9]

Establishing the Nationalities Branch and the CCCC

As early as December 1940, the National Labour Supply Council warned that persons of foreign birth who were loyal to Canada 'should not be discriminated against.'[10] The findings of the Labour Supply Investigation Committee, appointed in July 1941 to uncover sources of labour for growing demand in the armed forces and war production on the home front, provided a new incentive for dealing with employment discrimination. As labour pools in central Canada were being exhausted by enlistments and new openings in war production, the committee reported that some of the most promising reserves of labour were among non-Anglo-Saxon workers in the prairie provinces. Yet prejudice against non-Anglo-Saxons, as we have seen, prevented the maximum use of this labour power. Investigators emphasized that even when workers from such backgrounds took advantage of the War Emergency Training Programme, prejudice prevented their employment in Ontario.[11]

Meanwhile, in response not only to employment discrimination, but also to the intensification of hostility towards 'foreigners' that accompanied German advances in Europe and Italy's entry into the war, the BPI made plans in the fall of 1941 to establish a special section to make Canadians of foreign birth and foreign extraction 'feel that they are truly Canadian.' The BPI hoped to accomplish this goal by changing the attitudes both of Canada's inhabitants of foreign descent and of the members of Canada's charter groups. An early proposal to call the section 'Committee on Cultural-Group Cooperation' suggested an inclusive, non-racist approach. In fact, however, the emphasis on culture was a continuation of pre-war assimilationist goals, intended to minimize distinctive group identities. As a memorandum outlining the purpose of the proposed division explained, the term 'cultural' is used in a strictly scientific sense in order to exclude the idea of racial or political particularism.'[12] It was probably no coincidence that the emphasis on culture allowed for the exclusion of groups perceived as unassimilable because of racial distinctiveness. From the outset, the DNWS conceived of this agency as 'dealing with the element of our population who have come to our shores from the European continent.'[13] The plans for a 'cultural committee' eventually led to the establishment of the NB and the CCCC.

The CCCC's work would indeed be cultural. It planned to use the CBC, the NFB, public lectures, and the press to supply 'cultural' groups with material deemed to be of special interest to them. Such material would focus on Canadian public policies – not only war-related ones, but also policies governing naturalization, health, and educational services. Cultural groups would also be encouraged to pursue their specialized gifts, especially in the area of handicrafts and folk culture, to strengthen their sense of dignity and self worth. The CCCC would supply the foreign-language press with news items of special interest and significance to their readers and to the government. The CBC, NFB, and the English- and French-language press would in turn be used to familiarize English and French Canadians with the achievements of these 'cultural' groups as a way of fostering cooperation and mutual respect. The CCCC would also 'provide a clearing-house for evidence of unfair discrimination against foreign-born Canadians and non-Canadians which appear[ed] on various fronts – industrial, military, educational and the like.'[14] But no plans other than persuasion and education through cultural activities were made to deal with such discrimination.

The mandates of these two bodies are not easy to disentangle. Both were meant to act as intermediaries between minority groups and the government, monitoring developments within these groups as well as the relationship between minorities and dominant groups in Canadian society, and interpreting developments within these groups to government officials.[15] They were also expected to transmit the government's goals to members of minority groups. The NB's staff consisted of George Simpson, professor and chair of the Department of History at the University of Saskatchewan, hired as senior adviser; Tracy Philipps, an upper-class Englishman who was, according to his curriculum vitae, a distinguished ethnologist, journalist, and employee of the British Colonial Office in eastern Europe, the Middle East, and South America, hired on a contract basis to act as the branch's European adviser; a clerk; and a stenographer. Simpson and Philipps were to work closely with Vladimir Kaye, the BPI's liaison officer with the foreign-language press. Kaye was a historian and journalist who had immigrated to Canada in 1925, but had been head of the Ukrainian Press Bureau in London from 1930 until he returned to Canada to work for the BPI.

Simpson also chaired the advisory CCCC when he was appointed in January 1942. Its name was adopted, as Simpson explained at the first meeting, 'to avoid a name which might suggest the perpetuation of particularism within the Canadian nation, although, at the present period of evolution, one had still to deal with non-English and non-French self-conscious ethnic groups in Canada as an existent fact.'[16] The

CCCC's other members were selected on the basis of their expertise on various minority groups or their interest in citizenship development. Their ranks included at various points: Henry Angus; Robert England; J. Murray Gibbon; Watson Kirkconnell; C.H. Blakeny, New Brunswick's minister of education and founding member of the Committee on Education in Canadian Citizenship; Major J.S.A. Bois, a professor of philosophy at the University of Montreal; Professor Jean Bruchesi, author and educator; D. Cameron, director of extension work at the University of Alberta; Mrs R.F. McWilliams, social worker, former Winnipeg city councillor, and wife of the lieutenant governor of Manitoba; and Mrs O.D. Skelton, author, educator, and widow of the former undersecretary of state for foreign affairs.[17]

Not only did all committee members belong to the educated elites of Canada's two dominant ethnocultural groups, but some of the most active among them, such as Watson Kirkconnell, Robert England, and J. Murray Gibbon, represented the socially conservative critics of discrimination and prejudice in Canada, whose ideas we examined in Chapter 5. In their dealings with minority groups, the CCCC's members interacted primarily with the small number of educated elites whose social standing and level of education were closest to their own. The committee's members were not very familiar with the conditions of working-class people, who composed the overwhelming majority of minority groups, and some of them were unsympathetic if not hostile to the politically left-leaning segments of minority groups.

The ideological orientation of George Simpson was not unlike that of Gibbon and of Kirkconnell. He had developed an interest in Slavic studies as a result of his interaction with Ukrainian Canadian nationalists belonging to the group's small educated elite: students of Slavic origin at the University of Saskatchewan and members of the educated elite in the Ukrainian nationalist camp.[18] He dismissed the official 'racial origin' classification of Canada's inhabitants as unscientific and inaccurate and hoped that minorities of European origin would assimilate rather than perpetuate group consciousness.[19] His opposition to communism was somewhat milder than Kirkconnell's.[20]

Despite the fact that DNWS officials such as T.C. Davis were concerned only with minorities of European background, within the NB and CCCC there was some initial confusion about the minority groups whose integration fell within their mandate. At its establishment, the CCCC defined its goals broadly. It was supposed to 'interest itself in situations which appear[ed] to be producing misunderstanding, dissatisfaction or discord among groups of Canadians of European origin, non-French and non-British, or between these groups and other Canadian citizens' and to report 'such situations to the appropriate bodies or authorities.' Henry Angus, appointed because of his expertise on Asia and Asian Canadians, wondered at the first CCCC meeting whether the body was going to concern itself with these minority groups. More than a year following the Nationalities Branch's and the CCCC's establishment Angus also asked if the NB had been in touch with Jewish groups.[21] Department of Labour officials also believed, like Angus, that the CCCC should tackle discrimination against Japanese Canadians as well as groups of European origin. They suggested that the 1941 circular advising employers and labour unions not to discriminate against workers of European origin be revised to 'refer specifically to Japanese and that there should continue to be public education along this line.' These officials also advised that a special subcommittee of the CCCC be established to deal with the problems of French Canadians, many of whom also faced discrimination in employment.[22] None of these suggestions was adopted. The decision not to address the condition of Chinese and Japanese Canadians was based on directions from the minister of national war services.[23] Nor did these government agencies deal with the predicament of African Canadians, Native Canadians, or Jews. Their focus remained throughout the war on Christian minorities of European descent.[24]

The failure to take action against anti-Asian prejudice and discrimination – arguably the most intense expressions of racism in Canada – reflected the opportunism of some state officials. They were much less concerned with eliminating racism or improving the situation of those disadvantaged by it than with ensuring the smooth functioning of the war effort. The comments of a member of the Special Committee on Orientals in British Columbia offer a blatant example of this type of opportunism. The official maintained that it was not necessary to deal with discrimination against the Chinese because 'they accept discriminatory treatment with a minimum of expressed resentment,' and thus 'do not constitute a serious problem.'[25]

The Eurocentric focus of many of the government's experts on minorities goes a long way towards explaining the state's lack of commitment to combating discrimination against non-White minorities. Even Henry Angus followed his question about the CCCC's involvement with 'Japanese and Chinese in Canada' with the observation that were the CCCC to fight discrimination against Japanese and Chinese Canadians, 'its general viewpoint might be found at variance with the attitude of the ... government of British Columbia.'[26] In his unpublished autobiography he revealed that he nearly resigned over the Canadian government's decision to relocate Japanese Canadians, but eventually decided against it. He wrote: 'I felt that a civil servant, albeit temporary, should not resign in wartime except under the most extreme circumstances.'[27]

The absence of minority representation in these government agencies also helps to explain the impractical nature of their programmes. Several minority groups sought representation on the CCCC. The officers of the Ukrainian Canadian Committee, which had been created with state support, maintained that 'ethnic groups desire participation not dictation.'[28] Lazarus Phillips, a prominent Montreal lawyer, approached the minister of national war services offering collaboration with the Canadian Jewish Congress, as did Sigmund Samuel, an influential member of Toronto's Jewish community.[29] Winnipeg's Canadian Unity Council, representing twenty-two ethnic groups in western Canada, explained that its members believed 'that mutual understanding and cooperation between the various ethnic groups which make up Canada's population can best be achieved when the efforts of the ethnic groups themselves ... are encouraged and recognized.'[30] Yet no minority group representatives were taken on, largely because of the patronizing attitude of most CCCC's members towards them. On the few occasions when the possibility of including them came up, the idea was quickly dismissed on grounds that minority groups were too divergent in size, the educated among them were too fractious or partisan,[31] and that the manual workers and peasants who constituted the majority of immigrants sharing 'the ancestral habit of looking for a lead' would fall into a void in the absence of proper guidance.[32]

The lack of working-class representation in these agencies, despite the fact that most minority group members belonged to that class, reflected the views of its organizers about the appropriate guardians of Canadian identity. This became clear when health concerns forced George Simpson to withdraw from directing the NB. He proposed that Tracy Philipps, the upper-class Englishman, be consulted 'on matters of broad principles,' and that an additional 'woman secretary' be recruited. Simpson added that if possible the new staff member should be 'from some well-known Canadian family,' explaining that 'this latter qualification would strengthen the Canadian character of the organization.' Clearly, he saw social standing as an important component of the best features of Canadian character.[33]

In the eyes of a number of members serving on the CCCC and the NB, peasants and workers of eastern and southern European origin were not prepared to determine the best course of their own integration into Canadian society. Murray Gibbon's admiration for the industry and creativity of peasant immigrants, for example, really expressed socially conservative views that prevented him from appreciating the problems of immigrant workers, including employment discrimination. At a time when immigrant workers in ever-increasing numbers were asserting their claim to decent jobs and good wages in the urban industrial work force, especially because they feared loss of employment following the war, Gibbon envisioned for at least some of them a return to pre-industrial peasant self-sufficiency. Such immigrants, he suggested, could provide a sound economic base for themselves in rural areas by supplementing farm production with home industry and thus minimizing their dependence on manufactured goods.[34] Tracy Philipps and George Simspon joined the government's Arts and Crafts Interdepartmental Committee on Canada's Homecrafts to hear Allen Eaton of the Department of Arts and Social Work of the American Sage Foundation. Eaton, like Gibbon, believed that home crafts would help an important part of Canada's population to improve their economic position. Eaton suggested that the inability of such Canadians to budget their limited cash incomes, rather than the low wages they received, made them economically vulnerable. If they could be taught to make money by craft production, they would not require relief. At a time when Canadian workers were struggling to ensure their standing in the post-war economy through unions, Eaton, like Gibbon, promoted 'self-sufficiency' programmes as a way of dealing with prospective unemployment after the war.[35] Given the acceptance of economic marginalization of peasant immigrants evident in these plans, it is especially significant that discussions of 'home crafts' were the only occasions at which officials concerned with Native Candians were invited to take part in planning for other minority groups.

An intense fear of radicalism and of labour militancy accompanied the conservatism of some members of the CCCC and the NB, as well as others in state agencies they advised. As we saw in Chapter 5, men like Watson Kirkconnell were deeply suspicious not only of communists but also of organized labour. In his book *Seven Pillars of Freedom*, Kirkconnell described the CIO as an outlaw industrial union bent on becoming some kind of Soviet super-union.[36] Although Kirkconnell maintained that radicalism was limited to extremists within European minority groups, his frequent writings and talks on this subject both exhibited and encouraged the association many Canadians made between 'foreigners' and radicalism.[37] Moreover, he was all too quick to see anyone who sympathized with the anti-racist efforts of organized labour as a communist.[38] Apparently he found it difficult to distinguish between legitimate grievances of exploited workers and disloyalty to Canada.

While they aimed to integrate people of European origin, the racism of some members of the CCCC and the NB combined with class and ideological biases to prevent them from understanding the needs and goals of their purported clientele and offering effective programs to improve their situation in wartime Canada. At the first meeting of the CCCC, Gibbon, for example, proposed that the committee publish a forty volume series of the treasures of world literature. The CCCC itself did not adopt Gibbon's plan, since its more practical members pointed out that this was not the time to undertake such an expensive, purely educational project. It did recommend the project to the Royal Society of Canada. Ann Grant, an editorial assistant in the Nationalities Branch from Calgary, who was hired because of her experience in newspaper and radio work,[39] turned to the Department of Mines and Resources in Ottawa asking for information about non-English-speaking prospectors or mining engineers. She hoped that such material for stories would make non-English-speaking people 'feel that they are part and parcel of this country' by making 'them feel they know quite a bit about it.' Grant was either unaware that a large proportion of Canada's mineworkers belonged to minority groups, or she could not imagine that such workers could take pride in their own work or derive satisfaction from public recognition of the importance of their contribution to the Canadian economy.[40]

The notably few cultural materials that the CCCC eventually disseminated, moreover, reflected similarly patronizing and unrealistic approaches.[41] 'What it Means to Be Canadian,' an article distributed to foreign-language newspapers, assured its readers that there were many ways of feeling Canadian, even if they worked 'on a farm, in factories or in mines.' The article provided examples illustrating what it meant to be Canadian. In one of these, a young Canadian woman arrives to a party a bit late, explaining that she set out to post a letter from the main post office. Fortunately, she tells her hostess, she fell into conversation with the woman seated next to her on the streetcar, and upon learning of her concern that she might be late for a party, the woman offered to mail the letter for her. Clearly astonished by the story, another party guest, a Czech refugee, asks whether she understood correctly that the Canadian guest entrusted her letter to a total stranger. When the Canadian replies in the affirmative, the Czech 'girl' exclaims: 'It is marvellous that here in Canada you count on friendliness and good will, that you trust one another.' The article concludes by stating: 'This is what we understand by being Canadian, to offer and receive kindness as a matter of course, to be good natured and act with unconditional trust towards one another.'[42]

A year later an article entitled 'It's Women's War Too,' noted the contribution of ethnic workers in war industries. Its dismissive tone concerning the discrimination that such workers had encountered was unlikely to give them the sense that more established members of the host society empathized with their plight:

> The names on the payroll look as if this were an amateur League of Nations – and perhaps it is just that. The names may be diverse but the girls don't care about that. They feel that they are all Canadians fighting Hitler. The government feels that too. As long as they are British subjects, there is no silly fuss about how many decades or how few, have been spent by the family in Canada.[43]

Such superficial treatment of a serious and pervasive problem was also sharply at odds with the analysis of racist discrimination in minority group campaigns.

The NB and the CCCC's most consistent contribution was to supply foreign-language press with news releases starting in June 1942. From 1 May 1943 they also provided foreign-language newspapers with brief biographies of famous Canadians. To the English- and French-language newspapers they sent stories about outstanding European figures from the countries of origin of minority groups, such as Ukrainian poet Taras Shevchenko.[44] After the reorganization of these agencies in 1944, they also circulated stories about men of southern and eastern European origin who enlisted or rendered notable service in other ways.[45]

The NB and CCCC collaborated with the WIB's work with minorities, which was also primarily cultural. Ironically, although it did not specialize in relations with minorities, some of the initiatives of the Bureau of Public Information, the WIB's predecessor, were far more practical than those of the NB and CCCC. G.H. Lash, director of public information, for example, requested the editors of Canada's leading dailies to use their editorials to condemn the refusal to hire men and women because of their foreign surnames. Such intolerance towards 'fellow-Canadians' made 'a hollow mockery of the very principles of democracy which we are fighting to preserve,' he argued in a letter to *Globe and Mail* editor A.A. McIntosh.[46] McIntosh complied, condemning such discrimination using not only the public information director's reasoning but much of the wording of his letter of request.

Much of the WIB's minority work was very similar to that of the NB and CCCC. It sponsored the radio series 'Canadians All,' which followed the lines of Robert England's 1938 programme 'Ventures in Citizenship' by paying tribute to the contributions of 'New Canadians' to Canada.[47] To accompany this radio series, 296,000 copies of Watson Kirkconnell's pamphlet 'Canadians All' were printed.[48] While we cannot tell what effect this material had on ordinary Canadians, its almost exclusive focus on minorities of European origin is significant.

The ideas and language of the 1941 foreign-language posters promoting the purchase of victory bonds among minority groups echoed the social conservatism of the NB and CCCC. They also revealed how little Canadian bureaucrats generally knew about the lives of racialized immigrants and their children. Oblivious to the job discrimination that immigrants of Hungarian descent faced, the Hungarian-language poster encouraged them to buy victory bonds by reminding them that Canada, 'the promised land,' offered them freedoms and their children opportunities that they had never enjoyed in their native land. Even while Canada's doors remained closed to Jewish refugees from Nazi Europe, the Yiddish-language posters reminded Jews that Canada had welcomed them with open arms. While Jews of all ages were excluded from many jobs, and young Jews faced quotas in Canadian universities, these posters spoke of the freedom, equality, and educational opportunities that Canada supposedly offered them. Only the extent of discrimination against Chinese Canadians seems to have sufficed to restrain the propagandistic claims of victory bond promoters. The Chinese-language poster urged Chinese Canadians to purchase bonds to help defeat the Japanese aggressors against China. It made no claims about benefits offered by Canada to its residents of Chinese descent.[49]

In 1940 the National Film Board began the production of the series 'The Peoples of Canada,' a series focused on the cultural traditions and heritage of select groups. The films were meant to appeal to English-speaking audiences and to cultivate a feeling of pride among members

Chinese version of a poster encouraging the purchase of Victory bonds. This item was produced by the National Committee Victory Loan, 1941.
Library and Archives Canada, acc. no. 1983-30-1378.

of the groups that they depicted. The first film, 'Peoples of Canada,' an overview of immigration and settlement, set out to show that in no other country were 'inter-racial' relations better than in Canada. The film adopted the 'immigrant gifts' approach, stressing the contributions of different groups to Canadian society through pioneering, construction, culture, art, and leadership. By starting with the arrival of the French, and including immigration from Britain as well as from continental Europe, the film emphasized that most Canadians were 'transplanted Europeans.' This Eurocentric focus was not accidental, the film's programme notes referred to the work of Watson Kirkconnell, mistakenly identifying him as a noted Canadian ethnologist.[50] The film's initial version may have included a reference to Chinese immigrants as the 'unofficial bankers of the Prairies,' but this reference elicited negative responses as it implied that the Chinese and the 'Japs' were antisocial and sent 'all their profits out of the country.'[51] Subsequent films covered only a few groups individually: Icelanders, Poles, and Ukrainians, all of them European. As Robert England and George Simpson explained – underscoring the cautious and limited character of the cultural programme – this was because the series covered only groups 'that can be dealt with without misunderstanding.' They attributed the exclusion of other European groups to the fact that their homelands were at war with Canada, but did not think it necessary to explain why non-European groups were not covered.[52] In this cautious, conservative environment, tentative steps taken at the recommendation of David Petegorsky, a Jewish employee of the WIB, to prepare a film about employment discrimination (based on the material uncovered by the Canadian Jewish Congress) led nowhere.[53]

The NFB did attempt to tackle job discrimination against minority workers, including people of colour, through striking photographs it distributed to the press. Some of the captions accompanying these photographs simply identified workers in canning, lumbering, manufacturing, mining, and shipbuilding by their national or ethnic descent and described their work. Others, however, were so blatantly at odds with the treatment accorded such workers that their potential for enhancing understanding among diverse groups of workers is doubtful. In 1943, when African Canadians found it difficult to obtain jobs in war industries, for example, the caption accompanying the picture of African Canadian Cecilia Butler of Lucan, Ontario, working at the John Inglis Company in Toronto, stated that 'Negro girl workers are highly regarded in majority of munition plants, [and] display exceptional aptitude for work of precision nature.'[54]

'War Workers with interesting pre-War Jobs (December 1943). Cecilia Butler of Lucan, Ont. Working on reamer at Small Arms. Negro girl workers are highly regarded in majority of munitions plants, [and] display exceptional aptitude for work of precision nature. Cecilia is a former night club singer and dancer.'
Library and Archives Canada, National Film Board of Canada, WRM-4036.

Tracy Philipps

The November 1941 appointment of Tracy Philipps to act as the main contact between the Nationalities Branch and CCCC on one side and eastern and southern European immigrant workers in Canadian industrial centres on the other offers a clear illustration of the great distance that separated Anglo-Canadian academics and civil servants from minority groups in Canada. Philipps, a highly controversial figure, has received a great deal of attention from scholars, at least partly because his voluminous records are available for research at Library and Archives Canada.[55] He is especially important for present purposes, however, because other members in the NB and the CCCC saw him as their main link to working-class immigrants.[56] Since such immigrants composed the bulk of groups with origins in eastern and southern Europe, as Philipps himself never tired of repeating, his ideas and actions constituted a major obstacle to greater understanding and cooperation between state agencies and minority groups.

Neither Philipps's contemporaries nor scholars agree about the circumstances of Philipps's arrival in Canada and his subsequent appointment to the Nationalities Branch. George Simpson believed that Philipps had come to the United States to attend a congress of Ukrainian Americans and then crossed the border on a speaking tour.[57] T.C. Davis, associate deputy minister of the DNWS at the time of Philipps's appointment to the Nationalities Branch, later claimed that the Englishman came to Canada under the aegis of the National Council of Education of Canada, that the undersecretary of external affairs strongly recommended him for his Canadian appointment, and that a confidential report from Great Britain confirmed that Philipps was a 'reliable and responsible person, clearly charged with the duty of making his contribution to the war effort of the United Nations.'[58] Yet, in the records of the DEA, someone wrote 'No' beside Davis's claim concerning its undersecretary recommendation.[59]

According to some scholars he arrived in Canada at the behest of the British government to collect intelligence about the attitudes of European immigrants in the United States and Canada,[60] to strengthen North American support for British war objectives,[61] or to conduct propaganda work among immigrants. They see the Canadian invitation as a cover for the Englishman's work on behalf of the British government. These scholars appear to have accepted at face value the very impressive curriculum vitae that Philipps circulated in Canada. In it Philipps attests that 'England's third oldest university' had conferred an honorary doctorate upon him 'for his public work with special reference to minorities.'[62] On his own account, Philipps was on the verge of taking up a diplomatic position in eastern Europe when the outbreak of war forced allied diplomatic missions to leave the area. At this point, in response to a request from Canada, the British government selected him as one of three specialists who would travel through Canada to explain 'the background of the actual and potential war zones' to Canadians.[63] Philipps claimed that no less a figure than a 'Cabinet Minister (Lord Lloyd)' informed him that it was his duty to accept the invitation to Canada for at least six months, and without pay – the work was to be done for 'a dollar a year.'[64] This account seems unlikely, given that the causes of Philipps's departure from England reportedly precluded him from future employment by the British government, either in Britain or anywhere else (as Ottawa officials would discover only in 1944).[65] Indeed, unemployability in England or by the colonial office may help to explain the desperate lengths to which Philipps went to obtain a permanent position in Canada, even after his appointment to the NB in November 1941 on a limited contract. In fact, Philipps's correspondence with his friend Vladimir Kaye suggests that he established a connection to Ukrainians in Canada through Kaye and that Philipps himself approached the DNWS and DEA.[66]

In January 1941, Philipps and Kaye were involved in the establishment of the Ukrainian Canadian Committee (UCC) which brought together all Ukrainian Canadian organizations except those linked to the Communist Party. Government officials, who believed that they would be able to rally Ukrainian Canadians behind the war effort more easily through the UCC, greeted its formation with enthusiasm.[67] When lack of funds, ostensibly because war conditions prevented him from gaining access to his private funds in England, led him to importune his Canadian contacts for employment, Philipps pointed to his role in the formation of the UCC as evidence of his qualifications for working with minority groups in Canada.[68]

In March 1941 Philipps undertook, on his own initiative but with the sponsorship of the Association of Canadian Clubs, a speaking tour in western Canada about European nationality problems.[69] To boost his credentials as an expert on minority groups, he attempted at roughly the same time to establish contacts with American and Argentinean officials in charge of fostering national unity and tolerance among multiethnic populations, claiming to have been appointed by the Canadian government to carry out similar work. Philipps also arranged a speaking tour in the United States, primarily in 'Negro' colleges, in April and May 1941. He claimed to have met with officials of the State Department and the FBI to lay the groundwork for collaboration between the United States and Canada in rallying immigrants from east-central Europe behind the war effort.[70] Philipps next bombarded Canadian officials with proposals, ostensibly based on his exchange of views with British and American officials, for setting up programmes for the 'foreign-born' in Canada, coordinating such programmes with the United States, and even establishing hemisphere defence by foreign-born populations of the Americas.[71] Philipps, who lived in the same Ottawa apartment building as several cabinet ministers, apparently ambushed them in the corridors to share his expertise on European nationalities.[72]

Once he obtained a three-month contract from the RCMP in May 1941, Philipps launched a campaign to get a permanent civil-service position based on his alleged expertise in dealing with 'foreign-born' workers. To convince officials that his services were essential, Philipps did not hesitate to exaggerate the propensity of 'foreign-born' workers for unrest. He informed the Department of Labour that 'Croats, Slovaks and several larger ethnic groups do not now necessarily regard capitalist democracy as a boon and a blessing to men, for instance, in oriental Europe.'[73] He referred to the susceptibility of 'foreign-born' workers to 'unexpected influences' as 'a factor in slow-downs in production and strikes.'[74] He then travelled to several industrial centres in Ontario, Quebec, and Nova Scotia to uncover the role of the 'foreign born' in labour strife through his purportedly good contacts among immigrant workers. Philipps went so far as falsely attributing labour unrest to 'foreign' workers. In informing his superiors about his plans to visit Sydney, Nova Scotia, because of growing tensions between workers and Dominion Steel and Coal Corporation, for example, Philipps conveniently neglected to mention that the company's president had assured him in a letter that workers of 'foreign racial origin are not giving us any trouble at the present time.'[75] A year later Philipps would claim that he was instrumental in bringing about a settlement of the slow-downs in Cape Breton and thus laying the foundation for the NB work with 'foreign-born' workers in war services.[76] On another occasion, he reported that Hamilton was, for minority groups, 'one of the most difficult, fanatical and neglected war-industry centres.'[77] As officials for the DEA later discovered, one 'dangerous' pan-Slavic meeting in Hamilton on which he reported was actually 'an innocuous gathering of Yugoslavs' concerned with 'the forthcoming visit of King Peter!'[78] But Philipps maintained that efforts to create pan-Slavic solidarity among North American workers constituted preparations for class war. He wrote: 'This solidarity is conceived as utilizable both in constitutional elections and in paralyzing strikes. It has been jocularly described by some of its organizers as "our Hunky block as a set-off against the ruling classes," meaning the Anglo-saxon element in industry and government. But there will be nothing funny about it if high wages cease or the Soviet Empire has to change direction.'[79]

Another strategy that Philipps employed was to emphasize the difficulty of working with the 'foreign-borns.' He described the challenge as a 'delicate process of transmuting over 2 ½ million souls to a Canadian current,' and as 'technical and complicated as the work of any electrical engineer.'[80] Philipps maintained that these communities were 'almost closed' and that 'an individual of French or Anglosaxon stock' was unlikely to be invited to establish contacts with these community members unless he happened to have 'recent and personal knowledge of their motherlands and their temperament.'[81] Philipps's own expertise on the mental capacities of peasants and workers of European descent was what supposedly rendered him an authority on 'labour and industry.' But even for someone with his qualifications, argued Philipps, it would not be possible to carry out 'far-seeing planning' and devise the 'necessary machinery' to consolidate minority groups into a new nation under a contract of short duration.[82]

That Philipps's shadowy past was not revealed until some years following his appointment suggests the enduring status and credibility of someone with British upper-middle-class background in Canada. The officials who sponsored and eventually hired him apparently dispensed with any background checks on Philipps.[83] Even if they did not know about Philipps's past, the decision of federal officials to appoint an Englishman with supposed expertise in Russian and mid-eastern affairs to work among Canadian ethnic minorities scarcely a year following his arrival in Canada gives one pause. Only one of them, Donald Cameron, of the Department of Extension of the University of Alberta, objected to putting a non-Canadian in charge of this exercise of nation-building.[84] In light of state officials' unwillingness to appoint Canadians of 'foreign' background to act as intermediaries between the state and minority groups, Philipps's appointment underscores the officials' deep distrust of minority group members. Even educated, middle-class emissaries from Europe seemed more acceptable than local leaders for rallying minority groups behind the war effort. Around the time that Philipps began his work in Canada, associate deputy minister Davis, in conjunction with the Institute of International Affairs and the Association of Canadian Clubs, invited Joseph P. Jonusza, a Polish academic connected to the Polish government in exile, to give a speaking tour in western Canada in an effort to rally Polish Canadians behind the war effort.[85]

Had officials been better informed about and more sympathetic to the plight and goals of minority workers in Canada, and had many of them not shared some of Philipps's views, the content of the Englishman's missives and plans alone would have dissuaded them from employing him in any capacity. Philipps's view of immigrants from eastern and southern Europe was patronizing and often racist. He classified not only immigrants, but even their Canadian-born and educated children as 'foreign-born;' implying that they were primitive or backward. He compared the problem of guiding the assimilation of these children to the 'Europeanizing and Anglicizing of Africans.'[86] The immigrants' children, who 'between the Volga and the Saskatchewan' had been 'whirled overnight through so many centuries that their heads' were 'dizzy,' were assimilating too quickly and superficially, Philipps maintained, and hence needed supervision. Both the immigrants and their children had the 'ancestral habit of looking for a leader;' it was the absence of 'proper' guidance that led them to crime and to become communists.[87]

Although comments about discrimination against 'foreign-born' workers appeared like a mantra in Philipps's voluminous correspondence and memoranda, his understanding of discrimination was very much at odds with the views of minority anti-discrimination activists. At times he suggested that discrimination against citizens whose names did not 'happen to be Anglo-Saxon' was 'against the name as such.'[88] Hence, the remedy he proposed was either a change of name, or familiarizing Canadians with the meaning of foreign names. Presumably if English and French Canadians knew that the Hungarian name 'Kovács' and the German name 'Schmidt' meant 'smith' they would stop discriminating against the 'foreigners' bearing these names. At other times Philipps cast doubt on the legitimacy of claims of discrimination, suggesting that 'among foreign-born labour,' with whom he mixed, there existed, 'however mistakenly, a feeling of neglect.'[89] Consequently, these groups needed 'nursing.'[90] One way to alleviate this sense of neglect, according to Philipps, was to explain to 'foreign-born' workers 'the "romance" of destination and exotic usages and "adventures"' of the products they made.[91]

For a supposed expert on eastern and southern Europeans, Philipps sometimes resorted to some fairly crude ethnic or racial stereotypes to explain their behaviour. He claimed, for example, that Italian Canadians, guided by their tradition of vendetta, saw their treatment in Canada as the result of the desire of the governments of the British Commonwealth to 'get their own back' against 'people of Italian blood for the public humiliation inflicted on the British groups of peoples by the failure of their sanctions and their inability to prevent even the unsupported Italian government from taking Abyssinia.' Philipps also claimed that one could not expect 'Latin (French, Italian, Rumanian, Belgian) Canadians' to approach problems 'by the same thought processes and by the same paths as Anglo-Canadians.'[92]

Philipps's claim to expertise about Jews is equally jarring. He allegedly gained this expertise while he was charged with reporting on 'the quality and character of the human raw material wishing to emigrate from Russia, Rumania and Poland to the Jewish National Home,'[93] yet a number of his references to Jews smacked of anti-Semitic stereotypes. Offering a seemingly objective explanation of why many Jews were communists, Philipps noted that acting as a communist agent was 'a well-paid job.' He also claimed that 'past experience holds a very grave warning that, in times of national emergency, Jews should not be employed anywhere in censorship or government information, especially radio.'[94]

Philipps's warnings of the urgent need for government intervention – with himself as an intermediary – among 'foreign workers' because the CIO was making headway among them undoubtedly increased his appeal to CCCC members such as Watson Kirkconnell. According to Philipps:

The CIO are explaining and are interpreting all the time. Their way of it is not always reassuring. One of the results is that the state of spirit induced in the manual man, not the artisan or shift-boss (who most often informs us), is leading him to think: 'If I don't get a good settlement now, when I know "they" need me, "they" will excite public opinion and a (middle) CLASS-WAR against us, and whip up a war spirit and war legislation, to keep us down. And then, after all, we shall only be kicked around again just as we were before.'[95]

Philipps's intervention in this area was doubly pernicious. On the one hand he exaggerated the radicalism of the 'foreign-born,' and on the other, he attempted to discredit their genuine support for CIO unions. Philipps purported to know of a systematic campaign, funded by the Russian GPU and the Germans Gestapo to influence foreign-born workers through the CIO, which was relying on American-born organizers of foreign origin. The plan ostensibly consisted of four phases: 1) sabotage; 2) strikes; 3) slowdown of production; and 4) a whisper campaign against the administration and against persons whom the enemy finds 'inconvenient.'[96] Although he referred to 'Communazis' in his correspondence, Philipps said next to nothing about right-wing agitators. Yet by 1942, after Canada and the Soviet Union became allies, he claimed to have been responsible for establishing close contacts with the CIO through 'Sibley Barratt' [sic] and to have enlightened the United Mine Workers organizer concerning industrial workers of European origin.[97]

The RCMP apparently found Philipps's rather astonishing views about the CIO perfectly credible. In the summer of 1941, when Philipps was working for the force, he was corresponding with the RCMP about 'B,' an active organizer of the Packinghouse Workers' Organizing Committee (probably Adam Borsk), whom the RCMP believed to be a Nazi sympathizer using the CIO's organizing efforts to slow down production at Canada Packers.[98] It is not irrelevant that the personnel director of Canada Packers had the same view of union activities and of Borsk as Philipps did.[99]

The confidence with which Philipps advised the government about minority workers in Canada is especially astounding because, not surprisingly given his background and recent arrival in Canada, he had little contact with such workers. The three men engaged at the behest of Simpson and Philipps to act as intermediaries between their communities and the government – Béla Eisner among Hungarian Canadians, Alfred Fossati among Italian Canadians, and Peter Taraska among Polish Canadians – were all middle class and none had well-established relations with organized immigrant workers. Philipps appointed Eisner and Fossati to provide information about people of Hungarian and Italian origin in Canada and to encourage the establishment of organizations to unite all non-communist members of these groups. Fossati was secretary of the Mazzini Society of Canada, an anti-fascist organization concerned primarily with developments in Italy. He was a self-employed accountant, who seemed to have few connections with Italians outside Montreal or with working-class Italians anywhere. When Philipps asked him to visit Italian Canadian communities to investigate conditions and publicize the war effort, Fossati asked Philipps to supply him with the names and addresses of contact persons in such communities. An example of his plan to disseminate 'democratic ideals among Italo-Canadians' and unite them to support Canada and its allies was to give a lecture commemorating Dante, in which he stressed that 'according to Dante's classification of evildoers, Mussolini, Hitler and Hirohito are assured a place in the nethermost circle of the Infernal Pit.'[100] Philipps's

Italian contact in Toronto, Carlo Lamberti, president of the local branch of the Mazzini Society, suggested that the best way to rally Italian Canadians behind the war effort would be to find a patroness, such as Lady Eaton, to hold a garden party for the friends of Italy.[101] Béla Eisner, an employee of Sun Life Insurance Company who was given leave with pay for three months to travel to Hungarian communities throughout Canada and to report about conditions within them, provided Philipps with richer information.[102] Eisner shared Philipps's hostility towards the CIO. Accordingly, he noted with alarm that employment discrimination against Hungarian and other minority workers led them to embrace the CIO. He reported: 'The CIO is becoming stronger every day. They are most certainly striving for supreme political power and, if they are not checked in time, the end of this War may bring them dangerously close to their dreams.'[103] The cultural organizations in which Eisner and Fossati were active engaged primarily in ceremonial occasions. Philipps claimed that through his involvement in the establishment of a Hungarian organization, he played a key role in shaping that community's affirmative vote in the national plebiscite that freed Prime Minister King from his promise not to send Canadian troops overseas.[104]

George Simpson's choice of Peter Taraska, a Liberal school trustee in Winnipeg, as an intermediary with Polish groups reveals his ideological affinity with Philipps. Like Philipps and Eisner, Taraska's vision of uniting Polish Canadians excluded group members with connections to the communists. Taraska's exaggerated fear of communism is perhaps best conveyed by his belief that Norman Robertson, undersecretary of State for External Affairs, and Arthur MacNamara, NSS director, were both Marxists.[105] Surprisingly, given such fears, he was somewhat less antagonistic than Philipps and Eisner towards labour protests, simply observing (following visits to Fort William–Port Arthur, Sault Ste Marie, and Toronto) that Polish immigrants who had come to Canada between the two world wars appeared sympathetic to the left, and that in Sault Ste Marie they seemed to take pride in being out on strike with the Steel Workers Organizing Committee.[106] In any event, Taraska's intervention was scarcely necessary to organize Polish Canadians. Given the devastating German attack on Poland, efforts to organize Polish relief from within the community were well underway by the time of Taraska's appointment. The fate of Poland, rather than Canadian concerns, provided the focus for organizing.

To appease immigrant workers, Philipps proposed the formation of labour advisory committees comprised of the Ukrainian Canadian

Committee, the Cultural Committee of Canadians of Hungarian origin, and the Mazzini Society. None of these organizations represented labour. The two eastern European ones, moreover, deliberately excluded communist organizations.[107] But in Philipps's scheme, even these politically reliable bodies would have little say in shaping government policy. Instead they would provide valuable information to the government, and their existence would give minority group members the impression that the government concerned itself with their welfare; Philipps reported:

> This commits us to nothing. But it would gain for us a valuable added source of specialized advice and reliable information of which we can never have too much. At the same time, it would give these Canadians, men of good will who are contending against great difficulties and sectional intrigues, a feeling of being worthy of consideration by the government. In these communities which feel 'neglected', we cannot expect them to show themselves responsible men unless we ourselves help to give them a sense of responsibility.[108]

Resistance to Anglo-Saxon Guardianship

Given the anti-communist orientation of Philipps, Simpson, and others in the NB and the CCCC, it is understandable that some of the most trenchant criticism of their efforts came from communists. At the time, and since, accusations in the communist press about Philipps's alleged links to Italian and British fascists, and about Philipps's and Kirkconnell's ties to Ukrainian right-wing nationalists, attracted considerable attention. These controversies over international relations have obscured the communists' insightful criticisms of the policies of the NB and Tracy Philipps within Canada. That these criticisms were issued from the communist camp sufficed to discredit them in the eyes of the officials of the Department of National War Services and some members of the CCCC. Yet some of the objections anticipated the views of scholars critical of the state policy of multiculturalism decades following the war. For example, John Wier, a Ukrainian Canadian communist, writing in *The Canadian Tribune*, pointed to the anti-labour orientation of the cultural programmes of the NB and the CCCC:

> Kirkconnell and his ilk 'love' the 'New Canadians'. They have discovered that they too have traditions, culture and histories from the lands from

which they came (surprise!) ... They deign to permit them to keep alive the
memory of these things (even condescending to translate the odd poem
into English) so long, of course, as they keep their proper place at the bottom of the ladder and don't start acting as the citizens of a democratic
country which they are. But once let them act as free Canadians, let them
join trade unions and organize labor societies, let them participate in trying to fashion Canada's destiny in a progressive direction and presto! The
'New Canadians' become 'damned foreigners' again.[109]

In the House of Commons and in the pages of foreign-language newspapers communists insisted that Canadianization must be undertaken
with the full cooperation of ethnic group leaders. 'We have an advisory
committee,' argued Fred Rose in the House of Commons on 27 April
1944, 'composed entirely of English and French-speaking Canadians.
Why should not there be Canadians of European extraction on the
advisory committee, people who have been in this country for a long
time? They know something about their people, they know something
of their problems.'[110]

But communists were by no means the only critics of the NB's and
the CCCC's programmes generally, and of Tracy Philipps specifically.
Even the leaders of the Ukrainian Canadian Committee, whose establishment Tracy Philipps and the DNWS encouraged and aided, believed that the CCCC would be strengthened if the representatives of
ethnic groups were invited to participate in it. 'The ethnic groups desire
participation and not dictation,' they explained.[111] Winnipeg Judge W.J.
Lindal wrote to J.T. Thorson, minister of national war services and a
fellow Icelandic Canadian, in the spring of 1942, arguing that material
to promote understanding between minority groups and Canada's two
dominant groups would carry more weight if it was prepared by Canadians of origins other than French or Anglo-Saxon. He told the minister that, at a meeting he had convened, representatives of Winnipeg's
Foreign Language Press Club unanimously supported this position.[112]
H.W. Winkler, a Manitoba MP, complained that describing 'foreign-
language groups' as 'foreign-born' was 'grossly misleading' since the
vast majority of these people, in Manitoba for example, were born in
Canada. He also protested against the suggestion that too many of the
new Canadians exist in a 'spiritual vacuum.' 'Surely if this statement be
true,' he argued, 'we in Canada live in a virtual Balkan state.'[113]

In 1943, the National Unity Council of Winnipeg, representing local
African, Armenian, Belgian, Czech, Croatian, Danish, French, Hungar-

ian, Icelandic, Italian, Jewish, Polish, Scottish, Swedish, Swiss, Ukrainian, and Welsh Canadian organizations, organized a delegation to complain to John Grierson of the Wartime Information Board about the Nationalities Branch. As we have seen, the mandate of the National Unity Council resembled that of the government agency: 'to create among the Canadian people a greater unity and mutual understanding resulting from a common citizenship, a common belief in democracy and the ideals of liberty, the placing of the common good before the interests of any group, whatever their national or racial origins, as equal partners in Canadian society.' Yet the Unity Council believed that, as a voluntary organization spontaneously created by all ethnic groups, it was in a much better position to promote such cooperation than an agency of the government rendered partisan by its links to the reigning political party.[114] Council members resented the implication they detected in the programmes of the NB that they were not loyal Canadians. They objected specifically to a newcomer such as Philipps telling 'New Canadians,' who may have been in this country as long as sixty years, 'where their Canadianism lies.' The delegation also stated that the 'New Canadians, whether they were Danes, Norwegians, Ukrainians or Poles, resented the undisguised suggestion of an 'Anglo-Saxon' guardianship.'[115] Here again, they placed much of the blame on Philipps, who depicted them as 'helpless and divided and thus in need of such guardianship.' Finally, they objected to Watson Kirkconnell's politics, arguing somewhat disingenuously that his anti-communism sowed discord even within otherwise harmonious communities.[116]

The anti-communist Polish-language newspaper, *Czas*, the official organ of the Federation of Polish Societies in Canada, also objected to the attempts by the state, through the NB, to unify Poles in Canada. The objections were fuelled partly by the view that this action constituted partisan machinations by the Liberal Party and an insult to their ethnic group. *Czas* declared Poles in Canada to be 'mentally developed, politically conscious,' and fully capable of understanding their own political interests.[117] The government agency's failure to involve ethnic groups in its work was unfathomable, and its taking credit for the unification of ethnic groups such as the Poles and for the increasing enlistment from their ranks was not only 'completely unjust and humiliating,' but also indicative of the ignorance of Canadian politicians about 'people who work, fight and die for Canada.' 'Those who went to fight,' the paper stated, 'did not even dream there was a Department "aiding" them to go. They went of their own free will, influenced solely by their sense of duty towards Canada and humanity.'[118]

Individuals from minority groups targeted by the CCCC also expressed their objections. Writing to the *Montreal Gazette* in November 1943, Paul Poremsky, a Ukrainian Canadian who had lived in Canada for forty years, objected to the assumptions behind the establishment of the CCCC. Why, he asked, should Ukrainian Canadians who had 'opened up new lands in the West, built schools, churches and community halls, learned various new trades, educated their children,' and taken 'an active part in the Canadian social and political life,' not to mention the many young Ukrainian Canadians who had enlisted in the Canadian armed forces, be 'regarded by the Canadian government as a foreign element in need of some special committee to instruct them in Canadian citizenship and patriotism?' Like members of the National Unity Council, Poremsky objected to the appointment of 'some entirely unknown newcomers ... at high cost to lead us on the path of righteousness.'[119]

Problems caused by the class character of government agencies were best explained by Reverend Harvey Forster, the superintendent of the All People's Missions, Niagara presbytery:

> The Federal government has proven to be most inept in its dealing with these people. Apparently the government seeks its knowledge of the needs of the foreign-language groups and uses as its media of communication university professors and the like, who may have a more or less adequate knowledge of the various languages and may be conversant with the history of the various nationalities represented, but certainly have no knowledge of the thinking and needs of the great masses of the people of other tongues in Canada today. Indeed many of these so-called government advisers seem to be fascist-minded and this is bitterly resented by the Non-Anglo-Saxon people.

Forster went on to say that the churches should be censured for not having insisted that the government consult with non-Anglo-Saxon workers in the formulations of their policies towards these groups.[120]

Despite such criticisms, and in some cases precisely because of the excessive zeal of communist criticisms, many of those most closely linked to the work of the NB and the CCCC retained confidence in Philipps.[121] George Simpson regretted his departure and believed that it would be very difficult to find anyone with 'similar experience and talent' to replace Philipps.[122] Watson Kirkconnell, clearly very sympathetic to Philipps's anti-communism, also believed that through Philipps's tireless fieldwork the Englishman succeeded in combating discrimination against minority groups from Europe. MP Hlynka believed that Philipps had been the main force behind fighting employment discrimination.[123] Blair Fraser of the *Montreal Gazette* continued to rely on Philipps's analysis of groups that became known as 'New Canadians.'[124]

But by the summer of 1942, almost a year following his appointment, various officials in the DEA were becoming increasingly convinced that Philipps was not providing a useful service for the government. Some scholars believe that these officials were anxious to get rid of Philipps primarily because of protests from the USSR about the activities of Ukrainian Canadian nationalists among whom he had been active.[125] To be sure, government attitudes towards the CPC changed as a result of Canada's alliance with the Soviet Union, and Canada's ambassador to the USSR did urge that Philipps be prevented from meddling in Ukrainian Canadian affairs, and preferably be sent back to Britain, where he could do less harm.[126] To ascribe Philipps's downfall entirely to Soviet protests, however, would be to discredit the reasoning of DEA officials in interdepartmental memoranda in which they had no reason to be untruthful. Norman Robertson, for example, argued that his lack of confidence in Tracy Philipps was not the result of ideological attacks in the communist press. Rather, after a year's observation of Philipps's activities, he had come to believe that Philipps was incompetent. S.F. Rae believed that, instead of reporting on developments within immigrant communities, Philipps was offering his own opinions about foreign policy in Europe. Rae believed that Philipps was 'so perturbed about "Communism"' that he had 'little energy left to devise ways and means of enlisting the cooperation of foreign-born persons of European origin in the common fight.'[127] R.G. Riddell believed that the DEA lost confidence in the NB because of the tensions that developed between Philipps and Kirkconnell on the one hand, and minority groups on the other.[128]

Donald Cameron, who alone among members of the CCCC had earlier objected to the appointment of an Englishman to promote Canadian citizenship, became convinced that both Philipps and Kirkconnell had had an inflammatory influence and hence created disharmony in foreign-language communities.[129] Deputy Minister Payne of the Department of National War Service reported to Major-General LaFlèche:

Pursuant to our conversation of last evening in which I confessed to you my inability to understand what Mr. Tracy Philipps is doing and, what is more discouraging, to get him to express himself in a way which is comprehensible, as illustration, I am attaching two recent memoranda ... they are pretty typical of TP submissions.[130]

Robert England, who agreed to reorganize the Nationalities Branch in February 1944, learned that civil servants who dealt with the NB believed that it should come under the direction of a Canadian, preferably one from western Canada.[131] In a letter to George Simpson, he conveyed the widespread distrust of Philipps. 'No one had any real confidence in his submissions,' wrote England, 'since you left.'[132]

Restructuring

Some civil servants, responding to the criticisms of the Nationalities Branch and its staff, advocated its disbanding. The minister in charge of the DNWS, however, decided to restructure it. Robert England, who had at one time served on the CCCC, was appointed to study the history of the NB and make recommendations for its rehabilitation.[133] No doubt in response to the criticisms of Tracy Philipps, England recommended that the Nationalities Branch be organized as a division of the Department of Citizenship, and be staffed entirely by Canadians with 'an intimate knowledge of Canada.' He recommended that an adequate number of the staff should be able to work among French Canadians. England wrote: 'indeed the most important part of the problem of securing a keener participation in the war effort by minority groups consists in the winning of a greater sympathy from the larger English-speaking and French-speaking communities. To look for achievement in the way of national service from our groups of recent European stock without a greater degree of appreciation of that achievement on the part of the older stocks throughout the Dominion is a form of blind optimism which reckons without human nature.'[134]

But the failure to take meaningful action against discrimination persisted even after Tracy Philipps had been discredited and removed. England recognized that Canadians of German and Ukrainian descent faced difficulties in securing employment in the professions and the civil service. He denied, however, that workers of minority background were otherwise unfavourably treated 'in respect of remuneration and in other ways.'[135]

The way to remedy the marginalization of minority groups, according to England, was to encourage more social contacts between them and Canada's charter groups. As an example of what he had in mind, England pointed to the lieutenant governor of Manitoba, R.F. McWilliams, and his wife, who invited the 'representatives of the larger racial groups' to events at Government House from which they had, until then, been excluded. England also commended visits by the McWilliams to many rural communities inhabited by minority groups and their attendance of church services there. In addition to promoting social interaction, England favoured the continuation of the cultural approach of the CCCC. He commended Murray Gibbon's plans for publishing translations of 'the cream of the literatures of the people represented in the Dominion,' and for including excerpts from these translations in school readers. He also urged that more material about Canada should be provided to the foreign-language press.[136]

Vladimir Kaye, the only member of the controversial group connected to the Nationalities Branch who remained in the government's employ after its restructuring, followed England's cultural orientation. In 1944, for example, he promoted a booklet on basic English as a tool to combat employment discrimination. Kaye maintained that 'what appear[ed] to be cases of discrimination against foreign-born workers in industry [could] very often be traced to the reluctance of English-speaking workmen to serve under a foreman whose English [was] broken.' Thus he was optimistic that the use of basic English should help eliminate the difficulty.[137]

Despite the transformation of relations among the state, workers, and employers as a result of state recognition of workers right to collective bargaining during the Second World War, state policy towards minority workers remained unaltered. Because minority group members were excluded from agencies in charge of state–minority relations, and because when they consulted members of civil society, state officials relied on middle-class, socially conservative experts and racialized minority group members, no effective state policies to counteract employment discrimination emerged during the war. The benefits that racialized workers derived from the state, employer, and worker accord in post-war Canada, especially from the principle of seniority in unionized workplaces, were the products of wartime initiatives in civil society, primarily by minority groups.

Conclusion

Shortly before the end of the Second World War, an editorial in the *Winnipeg Free Press* noted that the persistence of discriminatory employment practices was symptomatic of 'a deep disease' in Canadian society. 'If this nation is to endure,' the editorial warned, such discrimination 'must be quickly rooted out.'[1] The paper was responding to news that employers continued to state a preference for 'Anglo-Saxons' in job advertisements, and that the bearers of foreign-sounding names, even men who had served in the Canadian armed forces, had difficulties finding employment in the city.[2]

That employment discrimination continued to the very end of the Second World War, and beyond, should not come as a surprise. The examination of the fate of racialized minority groups in the labour market between 1939 and 1945 reveals that the crisis of war reinforced pre-existing social and economic inequality based on racist views and practices. War-induced anxieties intensified suspicion of 'foreigners'– a term that encompassed large numbers of Canadian-born and naturalized people of Chinese, Japanese, central, eastern and southern European, as well as Jewish descent – as unpatriotic, disloyal, radical, and incapable of becoming truly Canadian. Wartime developments also reinforced racist assumptions that African Canadians, eastern and southern Europeans, and Native people were fit only for menial jobs; that Jewish, Chinese, and Japanese Canadians were economically aggressive; and that Jews in particular were given to shady practices. Such racist stereotypes appeared to legitimize ongoing employment discrimination.

The state colluded in racist practices. State officials – some of whom held racist ideas – were willing to collaborate with racist employers and workers to ensure the smooth functioning of war production. Not only

Wartime Information Board, Propaganda Poster. Artist: Harry Mayerovitch, 1944–5.
Library and Archives Canada, C-115708.

did officials believe that by acceding to racist preferences they reduced the likelihood of social unrest, they also found that the exclusion of Chinese Canadians, Japanese Canadians, and Native people from well-paid jobs in war production and white-collar jobs offered the important benefit of filling jobs that Canadians with wider options avoided.

Racist assumptions in wartime Canada clearly affected some groups more adversely than others. People of colour, or 'visible minorities,' targets of the most extreme, state-sanctioned racism, continued to suffer most from employment discrimination during the Second World War. Southern and eastern Europeans, however, were also racialized, and hence disadvantaged as workers and citizens. At the same time, state officials were most keenly aware of and most willing to tackle discrimination against these groups. Indeed, the varying extent to which racism shaped the experiences of racialized minority workers during the war serves as an important reminder of the complexity and historical specificity of the meaning of race. On the one hand, limits to the mobility of all these workers amidst wartime labour shortages reflected both the depth of racist views in mid-twentieth-century Canada and the practical advantages of racist assumptions in filling low-wage but essential jobs in the economy. On the other hand, the selective allocation of different groups within the labour market expressed their placement in a racial hierarchy that privileged those from northern and western Europe – especially 'Anglo-Saxons' – while disadvantaging eastern and southern Europeans, people of African and Asian origin, and Native Canadians to differing degrees. Anti-discrimination campaigns by racialized minorities themselves – with the help of their English and French Canadian allies – were required to begin to dismantle this hierarchy after the war and thus to pave the way towards greater, if imperfect, equality for minority groups in Canadian society.

The condemnation of employment discrimination by the *Winnipeg Free Press* was also not new. Influential Canadians sought to end such discrimination throughout the war. A close reading of some of the most outspoken critics of prejudice and discrimination reveals, however, that racism persisted even among them. This was the case not only among socially conservative critics such as Watson Kirkconnell, but also within the labour movement and in left-wing parties. For example, appearing before the Standing Committee on Immigration and Labour of the Canadian Senate in 1946, Percy Bengough, head of the Trades and Labour Congress of Canada, asserted that the labour movement subscribed to the principle that 'there should be no racial discrimination.' At the same time, he also called for immigration policies that would exclude 'all races that cannot be properly assimilated into the national life of Canada,' apparently without realizing the contradiction between these two positions.[3] Such inconsistency in the labour leader's statements, reflecting the deep roots of racist thinking in Canadian society, is especially striking because the labour movement saw itself and was perceived by many minority workers as the key agency in fighting discrimination.

Even some of those critics who believed in equality for all, regardless of skin colour, religion, or national origin, opposed legislation to prohibit racist discrimination. Some of them believed that anti-discrimination legislation violated the freedom of expression and contract, while others dismissed such legislation as ineffectual. When the Ontario legislature passed the 1944 Racial Discrimination Act, a *Globe and Mail* editorial, for example, protested on the grounds that the bill restricted the rights of Ontarians. 'The rights of the few will never be maintained by restricting the rights of the whole.'[4] In 1951, when the Conservative government of Leslie Frost introduced legislation specifically against employment discrimination, the paper argued that the new law would be useless without changes in the attitudes of Ontarians regarding race. It maintained that not laws, but the 'slow, earnest, educative process' was the 'best hope' minorities had.[5]

Minority group members victimized by racist discrimination were understandably less patient. They could not afford to wait until education convinced Canadians belonging to the dominant groups that those of minority origin should possess all the rights of citizenship. Studying employment discrimination during the war years reveals not only the exploitation of minority workers and state complicity in this process, but also the key role racialized minorities played in resisting discrimination. Minority group members did not generally internalize notions of racial inferiority that prevailed among dominant groups in Canadian society. Despite the suspicion and discrimination they faced, they did not doubt their rights as Canadians. In their strategy to end discrimination they adopted three main tactics: the promotion of anti-discrimination legislation, the development of intergroup relations, and support for labour organizations that pledged to make no distinctions based on race or religion.

In civil society, the presence of racialized minorities in ethnically diverse organizations was essential for focusing attention on racist employment discrimination and guiding such organizations to protest against it. In wartime labour conventions, members of racialized minorities, especially Jews, most frequently initiated motions condemning such discrimination and calling for legislation to prohibit it. Delegates from the racialized minority groups were most often behind similar motions at CCF conventions. Minority activists participated in round-table discussions, radio broadcasts sponsored by such organizations as the Canadian Association for Adult Education and the Fellowship of Reconciliation, and they, especially Jewish activists, supplied much of the publicity material that such organizations relied on in campaigns against racism. The activists obtained most of the books, pamphlets, films, workshop guides, and other materials from American human rights organizations. They thus acted as conduits for spreading the more developed American human rights ideas and campaigns in Canada and shaping these ideas to fit Canadian conditions.

During the war, the gulf that separated minority activists, especially working-class and radical ones, from policymakers, however, meant that the ideas and programmes in civil society could have only limited impact on state policy. Some state officials, for example, continued to collude in racist practices even after Ottawa officially condemned racist discrimination. Just as significantly, in sharp contrast to campaigns spearheaded by minorities, the programmes developed by government agencies mandated to promote national unity had very little practical significance in the lives of most minority group members.

Despite widespread criticism of the Nationalities Branch and its reorganization in 1944, the federal government's post-war policy to end racist employment discrimination resembled its wartime policy in many respects. Such discrimination remained a relatively low priority, overshadowed by the goal of 'Canadianizing' immigrants as part of the new project of Canadian citizenship. Insofar as the newly created Citizenship Branch, in charge of the project, tackled this problem at all, it attempted to counter discrimination through cautious, cultural initiatives.[6] Although Ottawa responded to pressure from the advocates of civil liberties and human rights and to the United Nations' human rights policies by establishing special committees in 1947 and 1948 to investigate the possibility of introducing a Canadian bill of rights, it rejected the appropriateness of such a bill for Canada. Officials reasoned that individual rights were adequately protected under British common law, that a bill of rights threatened parliamentary supremacy by giving too much power to the courts, and that Ottawa's passage of such a bill would interfere with provincial jurisdiction. They left unstated another widely held concern, one shared by many of the investigative committees' members, namely that a national bill of rights would com-

mit Ottawa to recognize social and economic rights such as the right to
medical care and employment. Members of the Liberal and Conservative parties did not support state guarantees for such rights.[7]

Even after the Second World War, therefore, well-organized campaigns by minority group members and their supporters were essential for the passage of legislation against employment discrimination.
As the Cold War closed in, however, not all minority groups remained
equally involved in fighting racist employment practices. Because
communist-led associations had conducted the only organized anti-
discrimination protests within such groups as the Hungarians, the
clamp down against communists dampened protest among several
groups of eastern European descent, if it did not silence it altogether.
The link between communists and anti-discrimination campaigns may
also have served to discredit these campaigns in such ideologically
segmented groups as the Ukrainians, Poles, and Hungarians. Roman
Catholic distrust of interdenominational collaboration and secular hu-
manism also weakened support for human rights campaigns in groups
within which the Catholic Church was influential. It fell mainly to Jews,
African Canadians, and Japanese Canadians, whose commitment to
fighting discrimination could transcend ideological divisions, to lead
the post-war fight against racist discrimination.[8]

Because employment fell under provincial jurisdiction, it was at
this level that minority anti-discrimination campaigns had their greatest impact. In the case of Saskatchewan, the CCF government, elected
in 1944, was the key force behind the introduction of the 1947 Bill of
Rights which prohibited employment discrimination and other forms
of discrimination. Jews played an important part in the formulation of
the Saskatchewan bill. A Jewish lawyer, Morris Shumiatcher, drafted
the bill. Shumiatcher's personal commitment to the new Saskatchewan
government rested on his conviction that the CCF would end racist
discrimination by ending capitalist competitiveness and inequality. In
drafting the provincial bill, he drew on social science and legal research
by Canadian and American Jews of various ideological leanings. While
this first recognition that the state had an important role to play in protecting human rights was of tremendous significance, the Saskatchewan Bill of Rights proved disappointing in the long run. Because it was
initiated by the state with little public participation, and because the
new social democratic government, committed to many other projects,
feared arousing antagonism through too much state involvement in society, the bill received little publicity and was scarcely used.[9]

When attempts to introduce bills of rights in other provinces failed, and human rights activists saw that few cases were tried under the Saskatchewan bill, activists chose to follow an incrementalist approach, targeting specific areas of discrimination. In so doing, they adopted the American strategy of fair practices legislation. Canadian activists believed that an important advantage of the American approach was that it relied on civil bodies rather than the courts to monitor and protect human rights. The successful campaign to enact legislation to prohibit employment discrimination in Ontario, the province which introduced the first fair employment practices act in Canada in 1951, launched the new strategy. Some of the same activists who had sought to include employment discrimination in Ontario's 1944 Racial Discrimination Act were key players in this post-war campaign. Other provinces, including Saskatchewan, in turn followed Ontario's example, as did the federal government, and by 1956 legislation prohibited employment discrimination based on race, religion, and nationality through much of the country.[10] The laws themselves, as well as the actors and strategies behind their implementation, illustrate the key role of campaigns by racialized minorities during the war in laying the foundation for Canada's human rights policies. Fair employment practices acts set the tone for other provincial statutes against racist discrimination in the provision of housing and services.

If the success of campaigns against employment discrimination is measured by the passage of anti-discrimination legislation in post-war Canada, the campaigns initiated by minority groups and their allies were clearly successful. By mobilizing men and women in a wide variety of labour and community organizations in support of such legislation, and by mounting far-reaching publicity and educational campaigns on the subjects of racism and discrimination (through delegations to various governments, programmes in public schools, workshops, conferences, articles in newspapers and magazines, pamphlets, and radio programs) minority activists also helped to refashion public discourse about the nature of Canadian society and helped make its institutions more responsive to, and reflective of, the diversity of Canada's people.

Fair practices acts, however, suffered from serious shortcomings. Some of these resulted from activists' decision to make compromises in response to resistance to human rights legislation. The incrementalist approach is a case in point.[11] Even after employment discrimination was legally prohibited, the persistence of discriminatory immigration policies in Canada allowed for a formalized channelling of people of

colour into jobs that had earlier been filled by non-preferred immigrants from Europe. By restricting immigration from the Caribbean to
women willing to serve as domestics, for example, Canadian policy en-
sured that such jobs, generally disdained by women with other options,
were filled. The women forced to take these jobs, some of them well
educated and skilled, were not free to seek other employment. Because
Canada's federal immigration policy legitimated this practice, human
rights activists were forced to mount campaigns against this discriminatory policy on a separate front from their fight against employment
discrimination governed by provincial laws.

The same activists held a rather narrow definition of human rights.
In some respects, the absence of demands to end discrimination on the
basis of disability or sexual orientation at this stage is understandable,
given that campaigns for the rights of groups marginalized on these
grounds did not begin until decades later. The failure to tackle sex discrimination, however, requires explanation. By the war years, the constitutions of some industrial unions prohibited discrimination based on
sex. After the war female activists protested against the omission of sex
discrimination from human rights bills, and the United Nations' Universal Declaration of Human Rights condemned discrimination on the
basis of sex, as well as race, ethnicity, and religion. The highly specific
focus of racialized minority activists on racist discrimination often con-
stricted their awareness of other types of inequality. Although many of
them were able to empathize with racialized groups other than their
own, they seemed to share the prevailing gender norms.[12]

In the absence of studies of the impact of fair employment practices
acts in Canada, the effectiveness of such legislation is more difficult
to evaluate. However, late twentieth- and early twenty-first-century
studies of employment discrimination, not unlike those undertaken by
human rights activists in the 1940s and 1950s, suggest that racist employment practices persist in Canada. Ironically, given the 1941 example of discrimination based on 'foreign-sounding' names with which
this work began, a 2009 study using names as signifiers of racial dif-
ferentiation brought to light that prospective employees bearing such
names continue to encounter racism in the labour market. The study
examined employer responses to six thousand mock resumes sent out
in the Greater Toronto Area for jobs ranging from administrative assistant to accountant. The focus on white-collar occupations reveals the
changing social background of immigrants and their children. Current
immigration policy preference for educated immigrants ensures the ar-

rival of many middle-class immigrants, whereas prior to the Second World War, the majority of 'non-preferred' immigrants were peasants and workers. The study's findings, however, are disconcertingly similar in terms of racist prejudice to those of the 1941 Manpower Labour Supply investigation. It found that those with 'English names such as Greg Johnson and Michael Smith were 40 per cent more likely to receive a call back than people with the same education and job experience with Indian, Chinese or Pakistani names such as Maya Kumar, Dong Liu and Faima Sheikh.'[13] Since the resumes did not reveal whether the applicants were immigrants or natives, the study suggests that not only immigrants, but their offspring as well, continue to face discrimination in employment.

Canada's immigration policy is now officially colour-blind. But, in fact, it sometimes formalizes what was earlier an informal channelling of racialized minorities to jobs at the bottom end of the occupational spectrum. Women entering the country under the Live-In Caregiver Programme, for example, are required to remain domestics for two years. Their long hours of work and limited possibility for learning English prevent many of them from moving into better jobs. The Seasonal Agricultural Worker Programme brings thousands of men and women from the Caribbean and Mexico to work in Canada for many months each year without permitting them to move freely in the labour market or to remain in Canada.[14]

Should we conclude from this state of affairs that in the long run human rights activism in Canada, and its wartime foundations, have made little difference in Canadian society? To do so would be a grave injustice not only to the accomplishments but also to the foresight of Canada's human rights pioneers. They did not naively hold that the mere enactment of protective legislation would end discriminatory practices. From the very beginning, they warned that to be effective, their campaigns would have to be actively and ceaselessly maintained. Seemingly, we have not heeded this warning. While the pursuit of equality in hiring, pay, and promotion has not been abandoned in Canada, an important reason behind the persistence of racist employment discrimination is the change in the agents and methods of resistance to it.

Although human rights activists in Canada never formed a mass movement, in the mid-twentieth century the battle against discrimination relied primarily on volunteers. The limited financial resources of minority and labour organizations could provide only modest salaries for a few full-time organizers.[15] By contrast, the enactment of the Canadian Charter of Rights and Freedoms, and the focus of Canada's policy of multiculturalism on anti-discrimination, led to the professionalization of rights campaigns. Rights groups today rely on expert lobbyists and on litigation to fight employment discrimination. They are also better funded than earlier human rights groups; the federal government, in fact, provides part of their funding. By becoming mainstream, however, human rights advocates have lost some of their effectiveness in educating Canadians to the existence of prejudice and discrimination in their midst and mobilizing them to fight against such sources of inequality.[16]

Developments within the labour movement, whose participants made up one of the earliest and most committed groups in Canada's early human rights campaigns, offer a good illustration of the consequences of changing strategies and their impact. Critics of the tendency of redefining workers' rights as human rights maintain that following the 1982 enactment of the Canadian Charter of Rights and Freedoms – a goal so fervently advocated by human rights activists in the 1940s and 1950s – unions have increasingly relied on lawyers and the courts to settle labour disputes and defend the right to collective bargaining on the basis of the freedom of association. This strategy dispenses with mobilizing and politicizing rank-and-file workers to advance their own rights. Moreover, individual claims to universal rights, or to rights based on such attributes as race or gender, have shifted attention from the labour movement's claims to 'collective advancement of mutual interests,'[17] and labour activism has been replaced with a reliance on experts.[18]

While the trajectory from Canadian labour's anti-discrimination campaigns in the 1940s and 1950s to its adoption of the rights-based approach still awaits examination, it is important to recall that during the Second World War and in its aftermath, labour activists who campaigned for anti-discrimination or human rights legislation did not see a contradiction between such legislation and union democracy and activism. On the contrary, such pioneering activists could see that the seniority system and grievance procedures eliminated many features of racist discrimination in unionized workplaces.[19] This positive feature of the post-war compromise has received little attention from scholars in Canada.

They also anticipated that fair employment practices committees in the workplace would educate grassroots members and prepare them to extend the fight against discrimination and intolerance throughout their communities. Workers' influence in human rights campaigns would extend even further through committees at the municipal and provincial level, and at national labour conventions. Early human rights advocates could not have known how few and short-lived workplace fair employment practices committees would prove to be in Canada. In any event, the focus on human rights did not divert workers from more collectivist labour goals. Rather, the failure of most ordinary workers to participate in human rights campaigns was a manifestation of the more general decline of democratic participation in labour unions and the concomitant bureaucratization of the labour movement. Because neither the majority of its members nor the general public see the labour movement as a key agency for promoting social change, social activists have invested their energies in other social movements.

As in the 1940s and 1950s, many Canadians today deny that racism is a problem here. Unlike in the mid-twentieth century, however, when Canadians could remain oblivious to racist discrimination because the practice garnered scant attention, in the twenty-first century Canada prides itself in being, and is widely seen as, one of the most tolerant countries in the world. This reputation has rendered many Canadians complacent. Pioneering efforts to end employment discrimination clearly had some shortcomings. But to match the accomplishments of the original movement, contemporary human rights advocates would have to inspire ordinary Canadians to confront the sources of inequality in Canada by participating in broad campaigns to end racist discrimination.

Notes

Introduction

1 Library and Archives Canada (hereafter LAC), J.M.L. Ralston fonds (hereafter RF), MG 27 III B11, vol. 113: Manpower Labour Supply Investigation Committee's report to the Labour Coordination Committee, October 1941, F31. My attention was drawn to this important report by Thomas M. Prymak, *Maple Leaf and Trident: The Ukrainian Canadians during the Second World War* (Toronto, 1988).

2 Dominion Bureau of Statistics, *Eighth Census of Canada, 1941*, vol. 1 (Ottawa, 1950), 218–19.

3 Monica Boyd, Gustave Goldman, and Pamela White, 'Race in the Canadian Census,' in *Race and Racism: Canada's Challenge*, edited by Leo Dreiger and Shiva S. Halli (Montreal, 2000).

4 For discussions of racialization in Canada see Vic Satzewich, *Racism and the Incorporation of Foreign Labour* (London, 1991); 'The Political Economy of Race and Ethnicity,' in *Race and Ethnic Relations in Canada*, 2nd ed., edited by Peter S. Li (Oxford, 1999); and 'Whiteness Limited: Racialization and the Social Construction of "Peripheral Europeans,"' *Histoire Sociale/Social History* 33 (November 2000), 271–89. Also see Kay Anderson, *Vancouver's Chinatown* (Kingston and Montreal, 1991).

5 See Satzewich, 'Whiteness Limited;' Constance Backhouse, *Colour-Coded: A Legal History of Racism in Canada, 1900–1950* (Toronto, 1999), 6; and Ian McKay, *Reasoning Otherwise: Leftists and the People's Enlightenment in Canada, 1890–1920* (Toronto, 2008), Chapter 6. In his path-breaking *Patterns of Prejudice*, Howard Palmer used the term nativism to describe prejudice against groups of European origin, arguing that racism was inapplicable to white groups. More recently, *The Colour of Democracy: Racism in Canadian Society*, 2nd ed., by Frances Henry et al. (Toronto, 2000), questioned the

application of 'racism' to groups of European origin on grounds that it diminishes the 'colonization' of coloured people (p. 22), while in 'Immigrants, Ethnicity and Earnings in 1901: Revisiting Canada's Vertical Mosaic,' *Canadian Historical Review* 83 (2002), 196–229, a quantitative analysis of the 1901 census, Eric W. Sager and Christopher Morier suggested that ethnicity had no significant impact on the class position of Canadians.

6 'Peripheral' Europeans is Vic Satzewich's term for eastern and southern Europeans. See Satzewich, 'Whiteness Limited.'

7 James R. Barrett and David R. Roediger, 'Inbetween Peoples: Race, Nationality and the "New Immigrant" Working Class,' *Journal of American Ethnic History* 16 (Spring 1997), 3–44. Another fascinating account of the racialization of European immigrants is Matthew Frye Jacobson, *Whiteness of a Different Color: European Immigrants and the Alchemy of Race* (Cambridge, MA, 1998).

8 Eric Arnesen, 'Whiteness and the Historians' Imagination,' *International Labor and Working-Class History* (Fall 2001), 3–23. See also contributions from David Brody, Barbara Fields, Eric Foner, and Adolph Reed, Jr. in the same issue.

9 LAC, Immigration Branch, RG 76-1-A-1, reel C-7812, vol. 264, pt. 8, file 216882: W.J. Black, Director, Department of Colonization, Agriculture and National Resources, Canadian National Railways, to W.J. Egan, Deputy Minister, Department of Immigration and Colonization, 2 May 1928.

10 See Chapter 3.

11 James Walker, *'Race,' Rights and the Law in the Supreme Court of Canada* (Waterloo, 1997), 190.

12 Canadian Jewish Congress Charities Committee National Archives, (hereafter CJCCCNA), CJC Organizational Records, Chronological File Series (hereafter CJCCF), ZA 1944, box 4, file 87: Hamilton, Memorandum on formations, activities, findings and suggestions and conclusions of the Committee of the Council of Jewish Organizations in Hamilton, in connection with allegations regarding restrictions in Hamilton against Jews owning and occupying lands and occupying apartments and residences.

13 David Roediger, *Working Toward Whiteness: How America's Immigrants Became White* (New York, 2005), Chapter 6, especially 170–1.

14 CJCCCNA, CJCCF, ZA 1944, box 4, file 87: Hamilton, Memorandum.

15 Backhouse, *Colour-Coded*, 9.

16 LAC, Labour Canada (hereafter LC), RG 27, vol. 1484, file 2-141, pt. 2: Rose Prévost to Ministry of National Defense, 18 August 1941.

17 See the discussion of the Nationalities Branch and the Committee on Cooperation in Canadian Citizenship in Chapter 7.

18 LAC, LC, RG 27, vol. 1484, file 2-141, pt. 2: Major General L.R. LaFléche, Associate Deputy Minister of National War Services to A. J. Hills, Chairman, National Labour Supply Council, 1 September 1941.

19 N.F. Dreisziger, 'The Rise of a Bureaucracy for Multiculturalism: The Origins of the Nationalities Branch, 1939–1941,' in *On Guard For Thee: War, Ethnicity, and the Canadian State, 1939–1945,* edited by Norman Hillmer, Bohdan Kordan, and Lubomyr Luciuk (Ottawa,1988), 1–29; Leslie Pal, *Interest of State: The Politics of Language, Multiculturalism and Feminism in Canada* (Montreal, 1993), 64–77; Bohdan Kordan and Lubomyr Luciuk, 'A Prescription for Nationbuilding: Ukrainian Canadians and the Canadian State, 1939–1945,' in *On Guard for Thee*; Bohdan Kordan, *Canada and the Ukrainian Question, 1939–1945* (Montreal and Kingston, 2001).

20 William R. Young, 'Chauvinism and Canadianism,' in *On Guard for Thee*; John Herd Thompson, *Ethnic Minorities during Two World Wars* (Ottawa, 1991). Mark Kristmanson, *Plateaus of Freedom: Nationality, Culture, and State Security in Canada* (Toronto, 2002), sees a link between state cultural policy and security concerns in multicultural states.

21 Ivana Caccia, *Managing the Canadian Mosaic in Wartime: Shaping Citizenship Policy, 1939–1945* (Montreal and Kingston, 2010).

22 Ruth Roach Pierson, *'They're Still Women After All': The Second World War and Canadian Womanhood* (Toronto, 1986); Jennifer Stephen, *Pick One Intelligent Girl: Employability, Domesticity and the Gendering of Canada's Welfare State, 1939–1947* (Toronto, 2006).

23 Ruth A. Frager, *Sweatshop Strife: Class, Ethnicity and Gender in the Jewish Labour Movement of Toronto, 1900–1939* (Toronto, 1992), Chapter 6; Alice Kessler-Harris, *In Pursuit of Equity: Women, Men, and the Quest for Economic Citizenship in 20th-Century America* (Oxford and New York, 2001), especially Chapter 5.

24 I thank Larry Savage for his help with this research.

25 Nelson Lichtenstein, *Labor's War at Home: The CIO in World War II* (Philadelphia, 2003), xix.

1. Employment Discrimination and State Complicity

1 *Montreal Gazette*, 15 September 1939, 22 May 1940; LAC, Department of Labour fonds (hereafter DL), RG 27, vol. 149, file 611-1-15: Margaret Livingstone to L.B. Pearson, 8 August 1940, and Philippe Lukawecki to Ernest Lapointe, 10 February 1941; LAC, Canadian Citizenship Branch sous-fonds (hereafter CCB), RG 26, vol. 36, file: 'German and Italian Unemployable,' Clarence Gillis, CCF MP, Glace Bay South to Ernest Lapointe, Minister of

Justice, 26 September 1940; Acadia University Archives (hereafter AUA), Watson Kirkconnell Papers (hereafter WKP), box 21, file 4: Dorothy Stepler to Watson Kirkconnell, 15 January 1941; *Hamilton Spectator*, 11 June 1940; Windsor Municipal Archives, City Council Minutes, 11 June 1940, and Board of Control Minutes 1940; 'Fifth Column Hysteria is Helping Hitler,' *Saturday Night*, 28 December 1940. On dismissals of Japanese Canadians even before Pearl Harbor see Forrest Emmanuel Laviolette, *The Canadian Japanese and World War II: A Sociological and Psychological Account* (1948; reprinted, Toronto,1978), 45.

2 LAC, Department of National War Services fonds (hereafter DNWS), RG 44, vol. 36, file: 'German and Italian Unemployable,' T.C. Davis, Associate Deputy Minister of DNWS, to Norman McLarty, Minister of Labour, 21 December 1940.

3 W. Burton Hurd, *Racial Origins and Nativity of the Canadian People* (Ottawa, 1937); LAC, DNWS, RG 44, vol. 36, file: 'German and Italian Unemployable,' Harry Hereford, Dominion Commissioner, Dominion Unemployment Relief, Department of Labour, to Justice T.C. Davis, Associate Deputy Minister of National War Services, 18 October 1940.

4 LAC, Department of External Affairs (hereafter DEA), RG 25, vol. 1964, file 855-E, pt. 2: Ernest Lapointe, Minister of Justice, to Prime Minister King, 30 May 1940.

5 LAC, Ian MacKenzie fonds (hereafter IMF), MG 27 III B5, vol. 81(1), file J-25-1: Japanese in Canada problem, January 1942, R.W. Mayhew, Member for Victoria to Prime Minister King, 17 February 1942; LAC, Norman Robertson fonds, MG 30 E163, vol. 12, file 145: E.W. Bavin, Supt. Intelligence Officer, RCMP, memo to interdepartmental committee, 22 June 1940; LAC, W.L. Mackenzie King fonds, MG 26, J1, vol. 325, reel C6806, p. 276562: Olof Hanson MP to King, 1 June 1942; *Winnipeg Free Press*, 19, 20, 21, 23 May 1940; *Montreal Gazette*, 22 May 1940.

6 *Globe and Mail*, 14 October 1939, 4.

7 Ontario Archives (hereafter OA), Department of Labour Papers, RG 29-135-1-15: Enemy Aliens, E.A. Horton, Director Unemployment Relief, Memo to Municipal Clerks, Municipal Relief Administrators, Provincial Relief Administrators, 10 June 1940.

8 *Hansard*, 25 November 1940, 380.

9 LAC, DNWS, RG 44, vol. 36, file: 'German and Italian Unemployable,' Harry Herreford, Commissioner, Dominion Unemployment Relief, to T.C. Davis, Associate Deputy Minister of National War Services, 18 October 1940; OA, Hepburn Papers (hereafter HP) RG 3-9, Gen Cor (Public), box 213, file: Public Welfare Department, Clerk, Town of Kenora, to Hepburn, 11 June 1940.

10 LAC, DNWS, RG 44, vol. 36, file: 'German and Italian Unemployable,' T.C. Davis, Associate Deputy Minister of National War Services, to Norman McLarty, Minister of Labour, 21 December 1940.

11 *Windsor Daily Star*, 22 September 1939, 9.

12 LAC, Citizenship and Immigration, RG 26, vol. 36, file: 'German and Italian Unemployable,' Clarence Gillis, CCF MP, Glace Bay South, to Ernest Lapointe, Minister of Justice, 26 September 1940.

13 Ibid.

14 LAC, RF, MG 27 III B11, vol. 113: Manpower Labour Supply Investigation, Committee's report to the Labour Coordination Committee – with appendix and index, October 1941, F14.

15 Ibid., F31.

16 According to Deputy Minister of Immigration W.J. Egan, the classification guided immigrant selection but was not publicized. *Select Standing Committee of the House of Commons. Standing Committee on Agriculture and Colonization. Minutes of Proceedings and Evidence and Report. In respect to the consideration of the subject of Immigration, the Immigration Act, Regulations and the work of the Department of Immigration and Colonization* (Ottawa, 1928). For an examination of this classification see Donald Avery, *Reluctant Host: Canada's Response to Immigrant Workers, 1896–1994* (Toronto, 1994), and Brian Osborne, '"Non-Preferred" People: Inter-war Ukrainian Immigration to Canada,' in *Canada's Ukrainians: Negotiating an Identity*, edited by Lubomyr Luciuk and Stella Hryniuk (Toronto, 1991), 81–103.

17 John Porter pointed to the connection between immigrants' entrance status and their subsequent placement in Canada's 'vertical mosaic,' in *The Vertical Mosaic: an Analysis of Social Class and Power in Canada* (Toronto, 1965). This type of racialization in early twentieth-century works, such as J.S. Woodsworth, *Strangers within Our Gates* and Edmund Bradwin, *The Bunkhouse Man*, is well known. A dissertation written shortly after the Second World War on the basis of oral interviews in Manitoba illustrates the persistence of such views during the war. See, P.J. Giffen, 'Rural Adult Education in Manitoba,' (master's thesis, University of Toronto, 1947).

18 LAC, RF, MG 27 III B11, vol. 113: Manpower Labour Supply Investigation, Committee's report to the Labour Coordination Committee – with appendix and index, October 1941, F6.

19 Ibid.

20 *Globe and Mail*, 26 December 1941.

21 *Montreal Star*, 30 December 1941.

22 'Foreigners Dig In,' *Vancouver Sun*, 16 October 1941.

23 Laviolette, *The Canadian Japanese and World War II*, 32, note 5.

24 P.J. Giffen, 'Rural Adult Education in Manitoba,' 155. See also LAC, DL,

RG 27, vol. 982, file 15: 'NSS Foreign-born persons in Canada during war,' A.M. Manson, Vancouver, to General LaFlèche, Deputy Minister of DNWS, 11 October 1941; 'Foreigners and Jobs,' *Saturday Night*, 24 May 1941.

25 LAC, DL, RG 27, vol. 632, file 77: Farm Labour Problems, Raymond W. Pincott, Secty, Vancouver Island Farmers' Council to the Honourable Minister of Agriculture, 20 May 1941.

26 LAC, Canadian Authors' Association, MG 28 I 2: Special Projects or Awards, Writers' War Committee, report of Mary Weekes, Cooksville, Ontario, 30 July 1943. The Writers' War Committee, with Watson Kirkconnell as chairman, was appointed in 1942 by the Canadian Authors' Association 'to put the abilities of all Canadian authors at the disposal of the Wartime Information Board.' As part of the committee's efforts, writers from almost every part of Canada submitted fortnightly reports to the WIB, giving their impressions of the trend of public opinion in their districts; Watson Kirkconnell, *A Slice of Canada: Memoirs* (Toronto, 1967), especially Chapter 23.

27 See, for example, *Winnipeg Free Press*, 14 October 1939; LAC, RG 44, vol. 8, file S-3: 'Salvage – Complaints, Problems in Collection,' Chairman, Fort William Voluntary Branch of the National Salvage Committee to William Knightly, Supervisor, National Salvage Campaign, DNWS, 21 January 1941, and A.L. Wickwire, Private Secretary, Minister of Finance to J. A. Hume, DNWS, 7 March 1942; Jeffery Keshen, *Saints, Sinners, and Soldiers: Canada's Second World War* (Vancouver, 2004), 39.

28 LAC, DL, RG 27, vol. 638, file 202: Canada Packers Limited, J.S. Willis, Personnel Director, Canada Packers Ltd., Toronto to Professor Gilbert Jackson, Montreal, 12 July 1941.

29 LAC, Tracy Philipps fonds (hereafter TPF), MG 30 E350, vol. 1: file 22, Correspondence July 1941, M. Black, RCMP, to Tracy Philipps, 25 July 1941.

30 Ross Murray, 'The End of the Canada Packers Myth,' *The Canadian Forum* 21 (February 1942), 334–5.

31 OA, RG 49-116, vol. XI: Submission of St Catharines Citizens' Delegation, 16 March 1943, 1263. According to the UAW's George Burt, the man known as Digger in St Catharines went by the name of Martin in the Windsor area, where he was also involved in anti-union activities. In Nova Scotia, he was known as Dr Michael.

32 *Winnipeg Free Press*, 21 October 1939. The CFL was a small organization formed in the 1930s, when a few members of the All-Canadian Congress of Labour left it in protest over the influx of communists.

33 Donald Avery, *'Dangerous Foreigners': European Immigrant Workers and Labour Radicalism in Canada, 1896–1932* (Toronto, 1979).

34 LAC, RF, MG 27 III B11, vol. 38: Major General (signature illegible) to the Minister, 26 July 1941.

35 OA, Drew Papers, RG 3-17, box 436, file 87-G: Fair Employment Practices Act, 'Brief Presented to the National Selective Service by the Canadian Jewish Congress in 1942,' (hereafter CJC Brief).

36 CJC Brief, Hy Lampert to Mr Hoffman, 31 July 1942; Gertrude Green to Mrs Sherwin, 21 July 1942.

37 CJC Brief, 2.

38 Canadian Jewish Congress Charities Committee National Archives (hereafter CJCCCNA), CJC Organizational Records, Chronological File Series (hereafter CJCCF), ZA 1943, box 3, file 26: undated confidential memorandum by H.M. Caiserman.

39 CJCCCNA, CJCCF, ZA 1943, box 3, file 26, H.M. Caiserman to Mrs S. Levitt, 22 March 1943.

40 Dionne Brand, '"We weren't allowed to go into factory work until Hitler started the war": The 1920s to the 1940s,' in 'We're Rooted Here and They Can't Pull Us Up': Essays in African Canadian Women's History, by Peggy Bristow et al. (Toronto, 1994), 179.

41 Globe and Mail, 31 October 1942; CJCCCNA, CJCCF, ZA 1943, box 3, file 22: note from Bernice Marshall, Verdun, dated 3 February 1943.

42 Pamela Sugiman, 'Privilege and Oppression: The Configuration of Race, Gender, and Class in Southern Ontario Auto Plants, 1939 to 1949,' Labour/ Le Travail 47 (Spring 2001), 89–91.

43 LAC, TPF, MG 30 E350, vol. 2, file 15: Eisner Report.

44 Kanadai Magyar Munkás (Canadian Hungarian Worker), 20 August 1941, 14; Giffen, 'Rural Adult Education in Manitoba,' 157.

45 Jewish Historical Society of Western Canada Collection, CJC collection, vol. 13, file: Publications, Anti-Semitism in Canada, Saul Hayes, 1949, The Facts, Reported monthly by the Civil Rights Division, Anti-Defamation League of B'nai B'rith, vol. IV, no. 5, May 1949, 15ff. 'Discrimination.'

46 CJCCCNA, CJCCF, ZA 1939, box 2, file 15: H.M. Caiserman, General Secretary, to Louis Fitch, KC, MPP, 11 July 1939; Ibid., Louis Fitch to H.M. Caiserman, 13 July 1939.

47 CJC Brief, Norman Cowan to Mrs Sherwin, 17 June 1942.

48 CJC Brief, Adeline Natanson to Mrs Sherwin, Jewish Employment Service, Toronto, 1 October 1942. (Emphasis in the original.)

49 Montreal Daily Star, 8 December 1942, cited in Harold Herbert Potter, 'The Occupational Adjustments of Montreal Negroes, 1941–48,' (master's thesis, McGill University, 1949), 74–5.

50 Potter, 'The Occupational Adjustments of Montreal Negroes,' 119–20. On

discrimination against Jewish and 'coloured' girls in Toronto, see LAC, DL, RG 27, vol. 1522, file XI-2-12, pt. 3: B.G. Sullivan to Mrs Rex Eaton, 5 July 1943.

51 *Globe and Mail*, 30 October 1942. See also Robin Winks, *The Blacks in Canada* (Kingston and Montreal, 1997), 422.

52 LAC, DNWS, RG 44, vol. 35, file: 'Bureau of Public Information – Foreign Section,' Davis to H.R. McMillan, 28 Feb 1942; AUA, WKP, vol. 48, file 20: T.C. Davis, Associate Deputy Minister, Department of National War Services, to Professor Watson Kirkconnell, 3 January 1941.

53 LAC, Department of Munitions and Supply, RG 28, vol. 144, file: Inter-Departmental Committee on Labour Co-ordination, General Correspondence, pt. 3, H.H. Kerr, Regional Director, Ontario, Dominion Provincial War Emergency Training Programme, to J.H. Ross, Regional Director, Alta., 17 November 1941; Joe H. Ross, Regional Director, Alta, Dept. of Ed., to Mr Thompson, Supervisor of Training, Department of Labour, Ottawa, 24 November 1941; R.F. Thompson to A.W. Crawford, Director General of Labour Relations, DMS, 27 November 1941; LAC, Privy Council Office fonds, RG 2, vol. 6, file M5: Re: Armed Services Industry, A.D.P. Heeney analysis of Manpower Supply for Cabinet War Committee.

54 OA, Ministry of Labour, RG 7-16-0-143: Dominion-Provincial War Emergency Training Programme, Conference Proceedings, Ottawa, 16–18 March 1942.

55 LAC, DNWS, RG 44, vol. 36, file: 'German and Italian Unemployable,' Memorandum of the Interdepartmental Committee on the Treatment of Aliens, by Norman Robertson, 13 August 1940.

56 LAC, Robert England fonds, MG 30 C181, vol. 3, file: Report on the Reorganization of Nationalities Branch, Department of National War Services, by Robert England, 12 June 1944.

57 LAC, DNWS, RG 44, vol. 36, file: 'German and Italian Unemployable,' Memorandum to Labour Co-ordination Committee from A.W. Crawford and W.J. Couper, Re: Discrimination in employment against certain nationality groups by war industries, 13 January 1942. The plan is discussed in N.F. Dreisziger, 'The Rise of a Bureaucracy for Multiculturalism: The Origins of the Nationalities Branch, 1939–1941,' in *On Guard for Thee*.

58 LAC, DNWS, RG 44, vol. 36, file: 'German and Italian Unemployable,' T.C. Davis, Associate Deputy Minister, DNWS to Norman McLarty, Minister of Labour, 21 December 1940.

59 LAC, DNWS, RG 44, vol. 36, file: 'German and Italian Unemployable,' to Employers of Labour and Secretaries of Trade Unions from N.A. McLarty, Minister of Labour, Re: Employment of Citizens and Aliens, 14 March 1941.

60 LAC, Ian MacKenzie fonds, MG 27 III B5, vol. 32, file X-52: Committee on the Treatment of Aliens and Alien Property, first interim report; and file 81(1): Japanese in Canada problem, 'Meeting to consider questions concerned with Canadian Japanese and Japanese Nationals in BC, 8 January 1942.'

61 LAC, DEA, RG 25, vol. 3005, file 3464-T-40: Civilian Labour Force, Memorandum for Mr Robertson, Re: the proposed order-in-council postponing the formation of the Canadian Japanese Construction Corps, from HFA [Henry Angus] 1 April 1942; LAC, DL, RG 27, vol. 1500, file 2-K-184: NSS Orientals, 'Report and Recommendation of the Special Committee on Orientals in British Columbia, December 1940; Canada. House of Commons, *Special Committee on Orientals in British Columbia, Reports and Recommendations*, 1940.

62 LAC, DEA, RG 25, box 3008, file 3542-40: H.F. Angus to W.J. Couper, Department of Labour, 28 August 1942.

63 OA, RG 7-16-0-93: R.F. Thompson, Supervisor of Youth Training to J.F. Marsh, Dept. of Labour, 2 May 1940.

64 CJC Brief, CJC, M.W. Wright to Martin Cohn, 22 January 1942; Confidential, the Board of Education, Toronto, 19 March 1942. Sponsored classes in 4 Vocational Toronto Schools.

65 Michael D. Stevenson, *Canada's Greatest Wartime Muddle: National Selective Service and the Mobilization of Human Resources during World War II* (Montreal and Kingston, 2001), 20, 122–3.

66 Walter Reuther Library, United Auto Workers Toronto Sub-Regional Office, box 11, file: Meeting November 1943. Minutes of District Council 26, 7–8 November 1942.

67 LAC, DL, RG 27, vol. 998, file 2-114-6: NSS Employment of Released Italian Internees, L.M. Lymburner, Jr NSS Officer, Montreal to A. MacNamara, Deputy Minister of Labour, and Director NSS, 2 March 1943.

68 Potter, 'The Occupational Adjustments of Montreal Negroes, 1941–48,' 70.

69 Potter, 'The Occupational Adjustments of Montreal Negroes, 1941–48,' 71.

70 CJCCCNA, CJCCF, ZA 1943, box 3, file 26: Conversation with Mr Shecter of the National Selective (*sic*) of Montreal, H.M. Caiserman, 11 March 1943.

71 LAC, DEA, RG 25, vol. 3005, file 3464-V-40: London Japanese Advisory Committee to Prime Minister King, 29 June 1944.

72 CJCCCNA, CJCCF, ZA 1943, box 3, file 26: Confidential memo; CJCCCNA, CJCCF, ZA 1943, box 3, file 26: Conversation with Mr Shecter of the National Selective [*sic*] of Montreal, H.M. Caiserman, 11 March 1943.

73 CJCCCNA, CJCCF, ZA 1942, box 5, file 57: Affidavit by Simon Yasin, 9 September 1942.

74 CJC Brief, J.H. Gringorten to Rabbi Maurice N. Eisendrath, 2 October 1942.
75 Want Congress to Substantiate Charge Made,' *Ottawa Evening Journal*, 13 October 1942.
76 CJCCCNA, CJCCF, ZA 1943, box 3, file 26: Selective Service Circular no. 81, 'Discrimination in Employment,' *Winnipeg Free Press*, 14 October 1942; 'Race Prejudice Stories Result in Ottawa Step,' clipping, Canadian War Museum online exhibition *Democracy at War: Canadian Newspapers and the Second World War.*
77 *Globe and Mail*, 16 November 1942. For a more detailed discussion of the protests, see chapters 2 and 3.
78 JAO, JCRC, MG 8S, file 78: NSS Circular no. 81A, 'Discrimination in Employment.' For a discussion of the new instructions see CJCCCNA, CJCCF, ZA 1943, box 3, file 26: Louis Rosenberg to Saul Hayes, 24 February 1944; LAC, Jewish Historical Society of Western Canada Collection, Records of the CJC, Western Division, MG 28 V114, vol. 3, file: Executive, Louis Rosenberg, 1944.
79 OA, Amherstburg Community Club papers, H.C. Stratton, Manager of the Unemployment Insurance Commission in Windsor, to Alvin McCurdy, president of the ACC, 28 May 1943.
80 LAC, RF, MG 27 III B11, vol. 113: Manpower Labour Supply Investigation, Committee's report to the Labour Coordination Committee, October 1941; LAC, DL, RG 27, vol. 980, file: NSS Minutes Advisory Board, NSS 1943–4.
81 LAC, RF, MG 27 III B11, vol. 113: Manpower Labour Supply Investigation, Committee's report to the Labour Coordination Committee, October 1941, 91–6; LAC, DL, RG 27, vol. 632, file 77: 'Farm Labour Patterns;' LAC, DL, RG 27, vol. 975, file 1: NSS Canning.
82 LAC, DL, RG 27, vol. 998, file: 'NSS Aliens, Chinese,' Minutes of Meeting in Office of Brigadier Sutherland, DAG, 26 March 1943; LAC, DL, RG 27, vol. 999, file 2-114-15: 'NSS Aliens, Chinese,' A. MacNamara to A.M. Manson, 5 May 1944.
83 LAC, DEA, RG 25, box 1964, file 855-E-39, pt. 2: Order in Council, P.C. 1348, 29 February 1942.
84 LAC, DL, RG 27, vol. 650, file 23-2-0-6, pt. 1: 'Road Camps, Mines and Resources,' Kinzie Tanaka to BCSC, 26 May 1942.
85 On the nature of beet work and the difficulty of labour recruitment in this field before the Second World War, see John Herd Thompson and Allen Seager, 'Workers, Growers and Monopolists: The "Labour Problem" in the Alberta Beet Sugar Industry,' *Labour/Le Travail* 3 (1978), 153–74.
86 Laviolette, *The Canadian Japanese and World War II*, 74.

87 LAC, DL, RG 27, vol. 170, file 614-02-11: Re: Placement of Certain Japanese Families in the Province of Alberta, vol. 2, Japanese conditions in Canada generally, Report by Const J.S. Connor, RCMP, Lethbridge, 21 October 1943; Ken Adachi, *The Enemy That Never Was: A History of the Japanese Canadians* (Toronto, 1976), 281.

88 Adachi, *The Enemy That Never Was*, 282.

89 LAC, DL, RG 27, vol. 644, file 23-2-3-7-1, pt. 1: 'Placement and Relocation, Southern Ontario,' Mactavish, Acting Eastern Supervisor, BCSC, to George Collins, Commissioner, BCSC, 15 January 1944.

90 LAC, DL, RG 27, vol. 644, file 23-2-3-7-1, pt. 1: J. Macdonald, Japanese Placement Officer, Unemployment Insurance Commission, to A. MacNamara, Director, National Selective Service, 30 October 1943.

91 LAC, DL, RG 27, vol. 170, file 614-02-11: Transference of Japanese from BC to Province of Manitoba, vol. 2, from 1 December 1942, R.H. Brown, Commissioner's representative for Manitoba, to MacNamara, 22 March 1943.

92 Stevenson, *Canada's Greatest Wartime Muddle*, 35.

93 United Church Archives, Board of Home Missions, General Files, box 27, file 446: 'Report made by Rev. K. Shimizu on resettlement of Japanese Canadians, 21 June 1944.'

94 LAC, DL, RG 27, vol. 1485, file 2-153, pt. 2: DNWS, Native Indians, Memorandum, W.S. Arneil, Inspector of Indian Agencies, to Dr McGill on Indian Reserves and Indian administration in Nova Scotia, 23 August 1941.

95 LAC, Department of Indian Affairs fonds (hereafter DIA), RG 10, vol. 3236, file 600-337: M. Christianson to T.R.L. MacInnes, Secretary of Indian Affairs Branch, 7 November 1941.

96 LAC, DIA, RG 10, vol. 2326, file 600-337: J.P.B. Ostrander, Indian Agent, Battleford, Sask., to M. Christianson, General Superintendent of Indian Agencies, Regina, 6 November 1941.

97 LAC, DIA, RG 10, vol. 7236, file 600-337: J.P.B. Ostrander, Indian Agent, Battleford, Sask., to M. Christianson, General Superintendent of Indian Agencies, Regina, 6 November 1941.

98 Ibid., passim.

99 Ibid., passim.

100 LAC, DL, RG 27, vol. 170, 614-01-11: Transference of Japanese from BC to Man., vol. 1, RCMP Report concerning Sugar Beet workers strike against Manitoba Sugar Co. In Fort Garry, Man., 2–3 October 1942.

101 For reliance on Native labour after the war, see Ron Laliberte and Vic Satzewich, 'Native Migrant Labour in the Southern Alberta Sugar-beet In-

dustry: Coercion and Paternalism in the Recruitment of Labour,' *Canadian Review of Sociology and Anthropology* 26 (February 1999), 65–85.

102 LAC, Canadian Authors' Association, MG 28 I 2, Special Projects or Awards, Writers' War Committee, file: Edmonton district reports from Edna Jaques, n.d.; *Winnipeg Tribune*, 12 March 1943.

103 Steven High, 'Native Wage Labour and Independent Production during the "Era of Irrelevance,"' *Labour/Le Travail* 37 (Spring 1996), 243–64.

104 My attention was drawn to these discussions by Vic Satzewich, 'Indian Agents and the "Indian Problem" in Canada in 1946: Reconsidering the Theory of Coercive Tutelage,' *The Canadian Journal of Native Studies* 17 (1997), 227–57; LAC, DIA, RG 10, vol. 6771, file 452-32, pt. 2, reel C-8515: Correspondence Regarding Post War Rehabilitation for Returned Indian Soldiers, R.S. Davis, Indian Agent, Touchwood Indian Agency, report for the month of December 1943. For a detailed study of changing attitudes toward Native people during the war, see R. Scott Sheffield, *The Red Man's on the Warpath: The Image of the 'Indian' and the Second World War* (Vancouver, 2004).

105 *Special Standing Committee on Reconstruction and Reestablishment, Minutes of Proceedings and Evidence no. 8* (Ottawa, 1944), testimony of D.J. Allan, superintendent of Reserves and Trust Service, Indian Affairs Branch, 242–3.

106 Ibid.

107 Satzewich, 'Indian Agents;' LAC, DIA, RG 10, vol. 6811, file 470-2-8, pt. 1, reel C-8534: W.M. Christie, Indian Agent, Williams Lake, BC, to Glen, 5 Feb 1946.

108 *Special Standing Committee on Reconstruction*, testimony of D.J. Allan, IAB, 243.

Introduction to Part Two

1 Potter, 'The Occupational Adjustments of Montreal Negroes, 1941–48,' 92.

2 *Montreal Gazette*, 14 September 1943.

3 Constance Backhouse, *Colour-Coded: A Legal History of Racism in Canada, 1900–1950* (Toronto, 1999), 11.

4 Stuart Svonkin, *Jews Against Prejudice: American Jews and the Fight for Civil Liberties*, Chapter 1. For a Canadian discussion of this, see Herbert Sohn, 'Human Rights Policy in Ontario: A Case Study,' (PhD diss., University of Toronto, 1975); Irving Abella, 'Jews, Human Rights, and the Making of a New Canada,' *Journal of the Canadian Historical Association* 11 (2000), 3–15; Carmela Patrias and Ruth Frager, 'This Is Our Country, These Are Our Rights,' *Canadian Historical Review* 82, no. 1 (March 2001), 1–35; James

Walker, 'The "Jewish Phase" in the Movement for Racial Equality in Canada,' *Canadian Ethnic Studies* 4, no. 1 (2002); Ross Lambertson, *Repression and Resistance: Canadian Human Rights Activists, 1930–1960* (Montreal and Kingston, 2005); Stephanie Bangarth, *Voices Raised in Protest: Defending North American Citizens of Japanese Ancestry, 1942–49* (Vancouver, 2008), Chapter 4.

2. Jews

1 OA, Drew Papers, RG 3-17, box 436, file 87-G: 'Fair Employment Practices Act,' M. Wolfson to Mrs Jack Sherwin, Jewish Employment Service, 5 October 1942.
2 'The Cartier By-Election,' *Canadian Forum*, September 1943.
3 'Outlaw Anti-Semitism, Unite for Victory: Rose,' *Canadian Tribune*, 10 July 1943, 4.
4 CJCCCNA, CJCCF, ZA 1940, box 1, file 6: Public Relations Round Table, 22 September 1940; ZA 1943, box 5, file 63: H. Guralnick to S. Bronfman, 7 December 1943.
5 On this question, see Ruth Frager, *Sweatshop Strife: Class, Ethnicity and Gender in the Jewish Labour Movement of Toronto, 1900–1939* (Toronto, 1992).
6 CJCCCNA, CJCCF, ZA 1939, box 2, file 15: Minutes of Executive Committee on Economic Problems, 11 May 1939.
7 CJCCCNA, CJCCF, ZA 1939, box 5, file 48: J. Finkelman, Chairman, report of Social and Economic Research Committee.
8 CJCCCNA, CJCCF, ZA 1939, box 2, file 15: Minutes of Executive Committee, 1 June 1939, and Ibid., 27 June 1939. For using labour unions to combat anti-Semitism, see also CJCCCNA, CJCCF, ZA 1939, box 5, file 48: J. Finkelman, Social and Economic Research Committee.
9 Jewish Historical Society of Western Canada (hereafter JHSWC), CJC Collection, vol. 9, file: CJC Conference, Winnipeg, 1940, Address by S. Bronfman.
10 CJCCCNA, CJCCF, ZA 1939, box 5, file 48: Gurston S. Allen, Chairman, Committee on Economic Problems, Canadian Jewish Congress, Central Division, 'Jewish Occupational Difficulties,' n.d.
11 For a discussion of Bora Laskin's role in human rights campaigns, see Philip Girard, *Bora Laskin: Bringing Law to Life* (Toronto, 2005), especially Chapter 11.
12 CJCCCNA, DA 1, box 8, file 17: H.M. Caiserman, Public Relations Work 1941–1944, Michael Rubinstein, Chairman, JLC, to Joseph Fine, Chairman JPRC, Montreal, 20 October 1944.

13 CJCCCNA, CJCCF, ZA 1939, box 2, file 15: Minutes of the Meeting of the Economic Committee of the CJC, 4 April 1939; CJCCCNA, CJCCF, ZA 1940, box 1, file 4: Record of Proceedings, Eastern Division Conference of the CJC, St John, NB, July 1940; CJCCCNA, CJCCF, ZA 1943, box 2, file 13: Report of the Committee on Economic Problems of the Jewish Community Council, Detroit.

14 JHSWC, Records of the CJC, Western Division, vol. 9, file: Western Regional Conference, Saskatoon, Addresses, Proceedings, Resolutions, 1938, Address by Rosenberg on Social and Economic Position of Jews and anti-Semitism in Western Canada, 17 July 1938.

15 CJCCCNA, CJCCF, ZA 1939, box 5, file 48: Gurston S. Allen, Chairman, Committee on Economic Problems, Canadian Jewish Congress, Central Division, 'Jewish Occupational Difficulties,' n.d., 11.

16 CJCCCNA, CJCCF, ZA 1939, box 5, file 48: Gurston S. Allen, Chairman, Committee on Economic Problems, Canadian Jewish Congress, Central Division, 'Jewish Occupational Difficulties,' n.d., 12. Marked 'Speakers' Notes – Confidential – not to circulate – The Economic Problems and Social Research Committee of the CJC.'

17 CJCCCNA, CJCCF, ZA 1939 box 5, file 48: Speakers' notes, 19. Marked 'Confidential.'

18 CJCCCNA, CJCCF, ZA 1939, box 2, file 15: Minutes of the Executive Committee on Economic Problems, 9 March 1939; Ibid., 23 March 1939.

19 CJCCCNA, CJCCF, ZA 1939, box 2, file 15: 'Report of discussion at a meeting of the Committee on Economic Problems, 21 February 1939.

20 CJCCCNA, CJCCF, ZA 1939, box 2, file 15: Minutes of the Committee on Economic Problems, 21 February 1939.

21 CJCCCNA, CJCCF, ZA 1939, box 5, file 48: Speakers' notes. Marked 'Confidential.'

22 CJCCCNA, CJCCF, ZA 1939, box 2, file 15: Minutes of Executive Committee on Economic Problems, 23 March 1939.

23 Ibid., 6 April 1939.

24 Ibid., 21 February 1939.

25 CJCCCNA, CJCCF, ZA 1940, box 1, file 2: Minutes of the Executive Meeting of the Youth Division, Canadian Jewish Congress, 28 March 1940.

26 LAC, Department of National War Services (hereafter DNWS), RG 44, vol. 36, file: 'German and Italian Unemployable,' N.A. McLarty to Employers of Labour and Secretaries of Trade Unions, Re: Employment of Citizens and Aliens, 14 March 1941.

27 CJCCCNA, CJCCF, ZA 1943, box 3, file 26: H.M. Caiserman, 'Employment Discrimination in Canadian War Industries.'

28 CJCCCNA, CJCCF, ZA 1944, box 4, file 73: H.M. Caiserman to Ben F. Levin, Director of Commission on Economic Problems, American Jewish Congress, 23 February 1944.

29 CJCCCNA, CJCCF, ZA 1943, box 3, file 26: H.M. Caiserman, 'Employment Discrimination in Canadian War Industries,' 'CJC representations to the Govt resulted in the circular addressed to the employers of labour and secretaries of trade unions of March 14th, 1941'; CJCCCNA, CJCCF, 1942, box 5, file 60: Minutes of the PRC, Montreal, 24 February 1942.

30 CJCCCNA, CJCCF, ZA 1942, box 5, file 57: press clipping, probably from the Winnipeg Free Press, 13 October 1942; CJCCCNA, CJCCF, ZA 1944, box 4, file 73: Social and Economic Misc., H.M. Caiserman to Ben F. Levin, Director, Commission on Economic Problems, American Jewish Congress, 23 February 1944.

31 CJCCCNA, CJCCF, ZA 1942, box 5, file 60: Public Relations Committee, unsigned resolution.

32 Louis Rosenberg, 'By the Way,' Israelite Press, 23 October 1942.

33 CJCCCNA, CJCCF, ZA 1942, box 5, file 60: Report of JPRC, 9 October 1942.

34 CJCCCNA, CJCCF, ZA 1942, box 5, file 60: Minutes of the National Exec. JPRC, 30 May 1942.

35 CJCCCNA, CJCCF, ZA 1942, box 5, file 57: Unidentified newspaper clipping.

36 Ibid., clipping dated 17 Nov 1942.

37 CJCCCNA, CJCCF, ZA 1944, box 5, file 980.

38 CJCCCNA, CJCCF, ZA 1943, box 2, file 13: Minutes of the Meeting of the Economic Committee of the Canadian Jewish Congress, Montreal, 5 November 1941.

39 CJCCCNA, CJCCF, ZA 1943: Minutes of a Meeting of Committee on Social and Economic Research and Post-War Planning, 26 September 1943.

40 JHSWC, Records of the CJC, Western Division, vol. 1, file: Bureau of Jewish Social and Economic Research, Louis Rosenberg Reports, 1934–1944, L. Rosenberg, 'Post-War Problems,' 23 May 1943.

41 CJCCCNA, CJCCF, ZA 1943, box 3, file 26: L. Rosenberg to H.M. Caiserman, 25 February 1943.

42 JHSWC, Records of the CJC, Western Division, vol. 3, file: Executive, Louis Rosenberg, 1944, Rosenberg to Hayes, 24 April 1944. See Chapter 1, p. 00.

43 CJCCCNA, CJCCF, ZA 1943, box 2, file 13: Louis Rosenberg, 'Do We Need Social and Economic Research Now?'

44 CJCCCNA, CJCCF, ZA 1943, box 4, file 47: Professor Jacob Finkelman, Chairman, Committee on Social and Economic Research, to Louis Rosenberg, 29 January 1943.

45 CJCCCNA, CJCCF, ZA 1943, box 2, file 13: Memo, Re: Committee on Social and Economic Research and Post-War Planning, n.d.

46 CJCCCNA, CJCCF, ZA 1943, box 3, file 26: Caiserman, 'Employment Discrimination in Canadian War Industries.'

47 CJCCCNA, CJCCF, ZA 1942, box 5, file 55: 'Some notes on activities of the Western Division of the Canadian Jewish Congress, 1933–1945.'

48 CJCCCNA, CJCCF, ZA 1945 box 2, file 31: 'A Canadian Approach to Anti-Semitism,' by Joseph H. Fine.

49 CJCCCNA, CJCCF, ZA 1943, box 2, file 13: 'Canadian Jewish Congress Committee on Social and Economic Research and Post-War Planning, Interim Report to the Members of the National Dominion Council, 18 April 1944.

50 CJCCCNA, CJCCF, ZA 1944, box 4, file 84: Memorandum for Mr Caiserman with reference to anti-discrimination legislation, from David A. Freeman.

51 Ibid., L. Rosenberg to Ben Lappin, 24 February 1944; Ibid., H.M. Caiserman to J.H. Fine, Chairman, JPRC, 28 December 1944.

52 Ibid., 'Joint Public Relations Committee, Comment on Plan Submitted by Committee of B'nai B'rith, Re: Public Relations Program, n.d. Marked 'confidential.'

53 CJCCCNA, CJCCF, ZA 1943, box 3, file 27A: 'Memorandum on the Bill Proposed by J.J. Glass, Esq, MPP;' CJCCCNA, CJCCF, DA 1, box 8, file 17: 'Summary Report on Public Relations Work, 1942–1944.'

54 CJCCCNA, CJCCF, ZA 1943, box 3, file 27A.

55 CJCCCNA, CJCCF, DA 1, box 8, file 17: 'Summary Report on Public Relations Work, 1942–1944.'

56 James W. St.G. Walker, 'The "Jewish Phase" in the Movement for Racial Equality in Canada,' *Canadian Ethnic Studies* 34, no. 1 (2002), 1–29.

57 CJCCCNA, CJCCF, ZA 1944, box 4, file 84: 'Federal-Provincial Legislation on Discrimination,' Joint Public Relations Committee, Comments on Plan Submitted by Committee of B'nai B'rith, Re: Public Relations Program, marked 'confidential'; 'Orange Lodge Scents Insult in Anti-Discrimination Bill,' *Globe and Mail*, 9 March 1944, 5; 'Not to be Silenced Says Dr. Shields,' *Globe and Mail*, 31 March 1944, 5.

58 CJCCCNA, DA 1, box 2, file 23: Caiserman to Bercovich, 24 July 1942; Caiserman to Harvey Golden, 'Public Relations Matters' concerning favourable response from MP Hart Green, 7 August 1942.

59 CJCCCNA, CJCCF, ZA 1944, box 4, file 84: L. Rosenberg, Secty Public Relations Committee, Western Division, to Ben Lappin, Public Relations Committee, Central Division, 24 February 1944; CJCCCNA, CJCCF, ZA

1944, box 5, file 90A: Minutes of a meeting of the JPRC, Western Division, 29 February 1944.

60 CJCCCNA, CJCCF, ZA 1942, box 5, file 55: 'Some notes on activities of the Western Division of the Canadian Jewish Congress, 1933–1945.'

61 CJCCCNA, CJCCF, ZA 1943, box 2, file 13: 'Proposed program for Economic and Social Research Committee,' n.d.

62 AUA, WKP, box 47, file 6.

63 CJCCCNA, CJCCF, ZA 1943 and 1944, box 4, file 85.

64 'Ontario Legislature to Consider Anti-Discrimination Bill,' *Fellowship*, February–March 1943, 1–2.

65 JHSWC, Records of the CJC, Western Division, vol. 2, file: Dominion Council (Western Executive Committee), 1941–1945, Minutes of the JPRC of the CJC and BB, Montreal, 6 September 1940. In fact, the JPRC claimed to have created the Canadian Conference of Christians and Jews, under the direction of Dr C.E. Silcox.

66 CJCCCNA, CJCCF, ZA 1942, box 13, file 123.

67 CJCCCNA, CJCCF, ZA 1943, box 3, file 27A; CJCCCNA, CJCCF, ZA 1944, box 4, file 88: 'Report of the JPRC Conference, Central Region, 16 April 1944; CJCCCNA, CJC, CJCCF ZA 1944, box 4, file 84: Memorandum on Public Relations Program, M. Saalheimer to Saul Hayes, 21 November 1944.

68 CJCCCNA, CJCCF, ZA 1944, box 5, file 97: CJC Dominion Council, Memorandum by M. Saalheimer, 'Interview with Dr. H.H. Giles, Director, Bureau of Inter-Cultural Education,' 8 December 1944.

69 CJCCCNA, CJCCF, ZA 1944, box 5, file 97: CJC Dominion Council, Memorandum by M. Saalheimer, 'Research Committee of the American Jewish Committee,' 7 December 1944; Ibid., M. Saalheimer to Saul Hayes, 'Commission on Community Inter-Relations of the American Jewish Congress, 7 December 1944; Ibid., Interview with Professor M.A. Davie, 8 December 1944.

70 Ibid. For a discussion of the depoliticization of the American anti-discrimination campaign, see Stuart Svonkin, *Jews Against Prejudice*, 33–40.

71 Richard W. Steele, 'The War on Intolerance: The Reformulation of American Nationalism, 1939–1941,' *Journal of American Ethnic Studies* (Fall 1989); Clarence I. Chatto and Alice L. Halligan, *The Story of the Springfield Plan* (New York, 1945).

72 OA, *Annual Report of the Minister of Education, Province of Ontario*, 1946, 12; *Annual Report of the Minister of Education, Province of Ontario*, 1947, 15.

73 Svonkin, *Jews Against Prejudice*, 33–40.

3. Other Racialized Citizens

1 *Toronto Telegram*, 4 March 1944.
2 LAC, Mackenzie King Fonds: Correspondence, Shadd Philip, Afro-Canadian Advancement Association, to Prime Minister King, 1 December 1943.
3 Robin Winks, *The Blacks in Canada: A History* (Kingston and Montreal, 1997), 332–3.
4 *Canadian Tribune*, 19 June 1943, 4.
5 Winks, *The Blacks in Canada*, 423–4; Dorothy W. Williams, *The Road to Now: A History of Blacks in Montreal*, (Montreal, 1997), Chapter 5.
6 LAC, Records of the CBRE, MG 28 I 215, vol. 81, file: 'Race Issue – Can. Nat. Railways Employees 1940–1952,' J.A. Robinson to Mosher, 1 August 1945.
7 Agnes Calliste, 'The Struggle for Employment Equity by Blacks on American and Canadian Railroads,' *Journal of Black Studies* 25, no. 3 (January 1995), 297–317.
8 *Canadian Unionist*, September 1940, 86.
9 Calliste, 'Struggle for Employment Equity;' Sarah-Jane (Saje) Mathieu, 'North of the Colour Line: Sleeping Car Porters and the Battle Against Jim Crow on Canadian Rails, 1880–1920,' *Labour/Le Travail* 47 (Spring 2001), 9–41.
10 LAC, Records of the CBRE, MG 28 I 215, vol. 81, file: 'Race Issue – Can. Nat. Railways Employees 1940–1952,' D.A. Brown to J.E. McGuire, General Chairman, CBRE and Other Transport Workers, 21 Mar 1943.
11 Ibid., W.W. Overton to A.R. Mosher, 3 November 1942.
12 Ibid., J.A. Robinson to A.R. Mosher, 1 August 1945.
13 Ibid., J.E. McGuire to A.R. Mosher, 8 April 1942; CJCCCNA, CJCCF, ZA 1942, box 5, file 57: unidentified clipping.
14 LAC, Records of the CBRE, MG 28 I 215, vol. 81, file: 'Race Issue – Can. Nat. Railways Employees 1940–1952,' J. E. McGuire to B.G. Sullivan, Regional Superintendent, NSS, 11 March 1943.
15 'Unity Against Discrimination is Langston Hughes' Message,' *Canadian Tribune*, 1 May 1943, 22.
16 Harold Herbert Potter, 'The Occupational Adjustments of Montreal Negroes,' (master's thesis, McGill University, 1949), 70–1.
17 Potter, 'The Occupational Adjustments of Montreal Negroes,' 93.
18 OA, Alvin McCurdy Collection, F2076-9-0-5: the Amherstburg Community Club, Alvin D. McCurdy to Murray Clark, MP, 24 April 1943.
19 OA, Alvin McCurdy Collection: Alvin D. McCurdy to H.C. Stratton, manager of the Unemployment Insurance Commission in Windsor, 1 June

1943, and McCurdy to H.C. Hudson, Employment Service Division, Unemployment Insurance Commission, 26 July 1943.

20 'UAW condemns Race Hatred,' *Ford Facts*, 13 May 1943.

21 'Toronto Negroes Barred from Plants,' *Canadian Tribune*, 27 March 1943, 24.

22 LAC, Frank and Libbie Park fonds, MG 28 I 11, vol. 4, file 27: Minority Groups, Joint Council of Negro Youth, 10–11 March 1944; MHSO interviews, Daniel Braithwaite, 17 August 1978.

23 LAC, Frank and Libbie Park fonds, MG 28 I 11, vol. 4, file 27: Minority Groups, 'Findings of First Conference, Joint Council of Negro Youth, 10–11 March 1944.

24 *Report of the Proceedings and Addresses of the Ukrainian Teachers' Convention at Mundare, Alberta*, 16 November 1940 (Mundare: Basilian Fathers' Press, n.d.), 28.

25 *Ukrainian Teachers' Convention*, 13.

26 Rozsa Páll Kovács, 'Non-Preferred,' in *Canadian Overtones: an Anthology of Canadian Poetry Written Originally in Icelandic, Swedish, Norwegian, Hungarian, Italian, Greek, and Ukrainian*, edited and translated by Watson Kirkconnell (Winnipeg, 1935), 68–9.

27 Anthony W. Rasporich, *For a Better Life: A History of the Croatians in Canada*, 145.

28 *Ukrainian Teachers' Convention*, 6.

29 Ibid., 11.

30 Ibid., 12–13.

31 Canada. House of Commons, *Debates*, 1940, vol. 1, p. 380, cited in Thomas M. Prymak, *Maple Leaf and Trident*, 48–9.

32 See Thomas M. Prymak, *Maple Leaf and Trident*, passim, and Bohdan S. Kordan, *Canada and the Ukrainian Question*.

33 LAC, Vladimir Julian Kaye fonds, MG 31 D69, vol. 21, file 5: Correspondence with Nationalities Branch, W. Burianyk to Professor Simpson, 10 May 1942.

34 LAC, Mackenzie King fonds, 1943, Correspondence, vol. 345, p. 197124: note on article from *Ukrainian Voice* about why Ukrainians are drifting away from Liberal Party for PM.

35 *Ukrains'ke zhyttia*, 16 April 1942, 8.

36 'The Ukrainian Press,' *Canadian Foreign Language Press Survey*; Wartime Information Board, Ottawa, March 16–31, 1944, 29.

37 OA, Tester Collection, C-97 (AV 219-1): J.J. Billoki interview.

38 Interview with Ann Hunka, Welland, 21 February 1986. (Author's Collection.)

39 Fern A. Sayles, *Welland Workers Make History* (Welland, 1963), 136.

40　Interview with Ann Hunka.

41　OA, RG 4-1941, file 11-7: Memorandum by A.S. Wilson, Inspector, CIB, on Industrial unrest at Campbell Soup Company, New Toronto, Ontario, 14 September 1941, marked 'secret and confidential.'

42　LAC, Labour Canada, Strikes and Lockouts, RG 27, vol. 413, file 209: Campbell Soup Factory, New Toronto, September 1941. For another example of the support of Ukrainian Canadian workers for labour unions see *Organizing Westinghouse: Alf Ready's Story*, edited by Wayne Roberts (Hamilton, 1979), 14.

43　LAC, Tracy Philipps fonds, vol. 2, file 8: Tracy Philipps to Mr Wood, President of Sun Life Insurance Company, 29 August 1942.

44　Dreisziger Collection, Béla Eisner, 'Report of my Goodwill Visit to and Survey of the General Situation of Canadian Communities of Hungarian origin,' especially 14–15, 33–4. This collection has been deposited at the LAC since I consulted it.

45　'Canadians All,' *Kanadai Magyar Ujság*, 25 March 1941, 2.

46　'Minorities Speak Out,' *Kanadai Magyar Ujság*, 13 November 1943, 3.

47　'What Awaits Agitators?' *Kanadai Magyar Ujság*, 7 April 1939, 2.

48　'Freedom,' *Kanadai Magyar Ujság*, 23 January 1942, 2.

49　'Minorities Speak Out,' *Kanadai Magyar Ujság*, 13 November 1943, 3.

50　Ibid.

51　'The Ides of March,' *Kanadai Magyar Ujság*, 15 March 1940, 2.

52　Letter from István Juhász, *Kanadai Magyar Munkás*, 22 May 1941, 15.

53　*Kanadai Magyar Munkás*, 6 June 1940, 1–2.

54　Interview with Stephen Bornemissza and his daughter Helen Gerencser, 25 November 1986, Welland.

55　Museum of Civilization, Degh collection, interview no. 30.

56　*Głos Pracy*, 9 March 1940, 22 November 1941, 30 May 1942, 13 June 1942, 1 August 1942. I would like to thank Jerzy Borzecki for translating Polish sources for this project.

57　OA, RG 7-1-0-329, Minister of Labour's general correspondence and subject files: Strikes - Kitchener - Merchants' Rubber Company and Canadian Tire Company 1939, 13 February 1939, Resolution which was passed at the meeting of the women's section of the Polish People's Association at 544 King St. West.

58　LAC, TPF, file 29.

59　'From Workers' Life,' *Związkowiec* (The Alliancer), 5 May 1940.

60　Unpublished interview with UPWA organizer Charlie Borsk by Vanessa Chuvallo, 3 July 2002, cited in Wendy Elizabeth Cuthberton, 'Labour Goes to War: The CIO, the People's War, and the Construction of a "New Social

Order," Toronto, 1939–1945,' (PhD diss., University of Toronto, 2006), 88.

61 University of Saskatchewan Archives, Saskatoon, George Simpson papers: George Simpson to Watson Kirkconnell, 27 August 1942; LAC, RG 44, vol. 35, file: 'Bureau of Public Information – Foreign Section,' T.C. Davis to Hume Wrong, 16 October 1942; Ibid., G. Simpson to T.C. Davis, 24 August 1942; LAC, RG 26, vol. 2, file: 'Taraska, Peter.'

62 Wayne Roberts, *Baptism of a Union: Stelco Strike of 1946* (Hamilton, 1981), 14.

63 MacDowell, *Remember Kirkland Lake: The Gold Miners' Strike of 1941–42*, revised ed. (Toronto, 2001), 235–6.

64 OA, RG 4-2, Office of Attorney General, Correspondence, Subject Files: 'Further Information to Shareholders on the Kirkland Lake Labour Situation. January 16, 1942.'

65 *Miner's Life: Bob Miner and Union Organizing in Timmins, Kirkland Lake and Sudbury*, edited by Wayne Roberts, 6.

66 OA, RG 4-32, Attorney General Central Registry Criminal and Civil Files: Re: Kirkland Lake Strike Cases. Rex vs. Harken, Malarchuk, Maki, Rushton, Pysklywes, Radoman, Brown, Bluta, Piluka, Raymond, Henessey, Baxter, 1942, case no. 7, Special Report, Constable Charles Wheeldon, constable no. 12, 20 November 1941.

67 OA, RG 4, Provincial Police – Strikes, 1942, Memorandum to Wm. H. Stringer, Commissioner of Police for Ontario, Re: Miners' Strike – Township of Teck, 31 January 1942. Because of privacy regulations it is not clear who the informant was. However, since the memo bears the heading 'Police Department' it may well have been from a local police officer.

68 MacDowell, *Remember Kirkland Lake*, 253, note 64.

69 OA, RG 4: Provincial Police – Strikes, 1942, Memorandum to Wm. H. Stringer, Commissioner of Police for Ontario, Re: Miners' Strike – Township of Teck, 31 January 1942.

70 Ibid.

71 'Foreigners are in a tough spot,' letter from Colin Clarke, Kirkland Lake, *Saturday Night*, 24 January 1942, 2.

72 OA, *Proceedings of Select Committee to Inquire into Collective Bargaining between Employers and Employees*, vol. IX, 11 March 1943, 826. Witness John Mikituk, a strike participant who lost his job, reported 'Welland is full of Kirkland Lake strikers.' Interview with Nick Dzoibak, Welland, 21 February 1986.

73 Satzewich, 'Whiteness Limited: Racialization and the Social Construction of "Peripheral Europeans,"' *Histoire Sociale/Social History* 33 (November 2000), 271–91.

74 David Roediger, *Working Toward Whiteness*, chapters 7 and 8, and especially page 221.

75 LAC, NSS, CRF, RG 27, vol. 638, file 202: Canada Packers Ltd., Toronto, J.S. Willis, Personnel Director, Canada Packers Ltd, Toronto, to Prof. Gilbert E. Jackson, Montreal, 12 July 1941. Willis commented on such responses by 'foreign' workers as evidence of the new, aggressive behaviour that was fostered among them by the Packinghouse Workers' Organizing Committee.

76 CJCCCNA, CJCCF, ZA 1942, box 5, file 55: 'Some notes on activities of the western division of the CJC, 1933–1945.'

77 'Canadian Unity Council,' *Kanadai Magyar Ujság*, 4 June 1943, 3; 'The Unity Council Active Again,' *Kanadai Magyar Ujság*, 24 September 1943, 2.

78 Richard W. Steele, 'The War on Intolerance: The Reformulation of American Nationalism,' *Journal of American Ethnic History* 9, no. 1 (1989), 14–17.

79 *Kanadai Magyar Ujság*, 23 January 1945, 30 January 1945. For other articles from the Common Council, see 26 September 1944, 29 December 1944.

4. The Disenfranchised

1 LAC, LC, RG 27, vol. 421, file 279: Coal Miners, Chinese, Union Bay, G.R. Currie, Labour Relations Officer, to Chao-Wing Shee, Consul General of China, 21 August 1942. For a discussion of the National War Labour Board's role in adjudicating wage disputes in mining, see Michael Stevenson, *Canada's Greatest Wartime Muddle*, 92–3.

2 Harry Con et al., *From China to Canada: A History of Chinese Communities in Canada* (Toronto, 1982), 167; LAC, Comintern, MG 10-K3, Red International materials, reel 45, file 334: on CPC and Chinese workers, 1928.

3 LAC, LC, RG 27, vol. 998, file 2-114-15: 'NSS Aliens, Chinese,' translation of letter from Charles Woofay to Mobilization Board, Kingston, 4 February 1945.

4 Con et al., *From China to Canada*, 199; *Chinese Times*, 12 April 1942. All references to the *Chinese Times* are to the translated version in the Chinese Canadian Research Collection, UBC.

5 'Equal Pay Asked,' *The People*, 6 March 1943, 6.

6 *Chinese Times*, 6 July 1943, 7 July 1943, 15 July 1943.

7 'Roy Mah New IWA Organizer,' *The People*, 15 April 1944, 2; 'Two Unions Appoint Chinese Organizers,' *The People*, 17 June 1944, 2.

8 'Two Unions Appoint Chinese Organizers,' *The People*, 17 June 1944, 2.

9 Ibid.; Patricia Roy, *The Triumph of Citizenship: The Japanese and Chinese in Canada, 1941–67* (Vancouver, 2007), 151–2, 180; Alicja Muszynski, *Cheap*

Wage Labour: Race and Gender in the Fisheries of British Columbia (Montreal, 1996), 192.

10 Wendy Cuthbertson, 'Labour Goes to War: The CIO, the People's War, and the Construction of a "New Social Order," Toronto, 1939–1945,' (PhD diss., University of Toronto, 2006), 234.

11 *The Chinese Times*, the Chinese Freemasons' newspaper, reported approvingly of protests by unionized Chinese workers. See, for example, 6 July 1943, 7 July 1943, 15 July 1943, 12 April 1944, 1 May 1944, 20 May 1944, 24 April 1945.

12 'Labour Personalities: Darshan Singh Sangha,' *The People*, 11 March 1944, 7.

13 'East Indians Protest Pearson's Statement,' *The People*, 18 March 1944, 6.

14 Ken Adachi, *The Enemy That Never Was*, 53–4, 160–4; Stephanie Bangarth, *Voices Raised in Protest*, 116.

15 *Canadian Student*, February 1936.

16 Provincial Sound Archives, Regina, Saskatchewan, Interview with T.K. Shoyama, 4 November 1981.

17 Patricia Roy, *The Triumph of Citizenship*, 69–70.

18 Rolf Knight and Maya Koizumi, *A Man of Our Times* (Vancouver, 1977).

19 Patricia Roy et al., *Mutual Hostages: Canadians and Japanese during the Second World War* (Toronto, 1990), 112.

20 LAC, LC, RG 27, vol. 650, file 23-2-0-6, pt. 1: Road Camps, Mines and Resources, Kinzie Tanaka to BCSC, 26 May 1942.

21 David B. Iwaasa, 'The Japanese in Southern Alberta 1941–45,' *Alberta History* 24, no. 3 (1976), 8. On organizing Hungarian and other east-central European beet workers, see OA, Abella Collection, C82-1-0-103: Interview with William Repka, interviewed by S. Bourdon, Toronto, 29 December 1971.

22 F.E. Laviolette, *The Canadian Japanese and World War II* (Toronto, 1978), 132. LAC, LC, RG 27, vol. 170, file 614-02-11: 'Re: Placement of Certain Japanese Families in the Province of Alberta,' vol. 2, Geo Collins to MacNamara, 12 May 1943.

23 Laviolette, *The Canadian Japanese and World War II*, 131.

24 Laviolette, *The Canadian Japanese and World War II*, 132.

25 *The New Canadian*, 20 November 1943.

26 'This Curious Paradox,' *New Canadian*, 6 November 1943.

27 LAC, LC, RG 27, vol. 169, file 614-02-11: Memo from A.R. Brown, Department of Labour, to MacNamara, concerning farm work in Ontario, 5 May 1943.

28 LAC, DEA, RG 25, vol. 3005, file 3464-S-40: Status & Treatment of Japanese

in Canada in Wartime, General file, Fred Kayahara, West Hotel, Fort William, to Dr G. Hori, c/o Pigeon Timber Co., Neys, Ontario.

29 'Labour Organizations and Us,' *New Canadian*, 3 July 1943.

30 Laura E. Jamieson, 'Where White and Brown Men Meet,' *Canadian Forum*, August 1941.

31 'Labour Organizations and Us,' *New Canadian*, 3 July 1943.

32 *New Canadian*, 7 April 1945.

33 *New Canadian*, 3 June 1944.

34 Patricia Roy, *The Oriental Question*, 215.

35 Laura E. Jamieson, 'Where White and Brown Men Meet,' *Canadian Forum*, August 1941; UBC, Special Collections, Angus MacInnis Correspondence, Grace MacInnis, 'Wanted: A Country,' *The Canadian Forum*, June 1942.

36 Provincial Sound Archives, Regina, Interview with T.K. Shoyama, 4 November 1981.

37 UBC, Special Collections, Angus MacInnis Papers, H. Kitagawa to Angus MacInnis, 13 April 1939.

38 *New Canadian*, 3 June 1944.

39 LAC, LC, RG 27, vol. 169, file 614-02-11: Secret Report on Japanese Situation in BC, by RCMP intelligence section, 23 March 1943.

40 For a discussion of the mobilization of Native Canadians, see Michael D. Stevenson, *Canada's Greatest Wartime Muddle: National Selective Service and the Mobilization of Human Resources during World War II* (Montreal and Kingston, 2001), Chapter 2.

41 Hugh Shewell, 'Jules Sioui and Indian Political Radicalism in Canada, 1943–1944,' *Journal of Canadian Studies* 34, no. 3 (1999), 211–42; Shewell, *'Enough to Keep them Alive': Indian Welfare in Canada, 1873–1965*, 162; Scott Sheffield, *The Red Man's on the Warpath*, 46.

42 Hugh Shewell, 'Jules Sioui and Indian Political Radicalism in Canada, 1943–1944.'

43 LAC, DIA, RG 10, vol. 6769, file 452-20-6: Minutes of Six Nations Council, 4 February 1943.

44 LAC, LC, RG 27, vol.1485, file 2-153, pt. 1: NSS Native Indians, Robert George of Ravenswood, Ontario, to T.C. Davis, Assoc Dept Minister, Ottawa, 7 July 1941.

45 LAC, DIA, RG 10, vol. 6766, file 452-12: Correspondence Concerning the Nat. Sel. Ser. Bd. of Canada and the Indians, (On the file itself: Indian Affairs Branch, Dept of Mines and Resources, National Service and Labour Supply Council, file 452-12, vol. 2), Chief Richard to E. McPherson, 16 November 1942.

46 LAC, LC, RG 27, vol. 1485, file 2-153, pt 2: NSS – Native Indians, Gabriel

Sylliboy, Grand Chief, Eskasoni, Chapel Island, Cape Breton to Prime Minister King, 15 October 1942.

47 Shewell, 'Jules Sioui;' P.W. Luce, 'Paucity of Pickers and Packers for the Fruit of the Okanagan,' *Saturday Night*, 10 June 1944, 30; LAC, DIA, RG 10, vol. 6766, file 452-12: Correspondence Concerning the Nat. Sel. Ser. Bd. of Canada and the Indians; LAC, Indian Affairs Branch, Dept. of Mines and Resources, National Service and Labour Supply Council, 452-12, vol. 2: E. Arsenault, Agent, Restigouche, Que, to Indians Affairs Branch, 6 August 1945.

48 E. Palmer Patterson, 'Andrew Paull (1892–1959): Finding a Voice for the "New Indian,"' *The Western Canadian Journal of Anthropology* 6, no. 2 (1976), 67; LAC, LC, RG 27, vol. 605, file 6-19-1: A. Paull to Humphrey Mitchell, Minister of Labour, 10 July 1944.

49 LAC, DIA, RG 10, vol. 6769, file 452-20-8: C. Roberts, Indian Agent, Report on Kenora Agency for December, 7 January 1943.

50 'Indians of Many Tribes Gather for Pow-wow at North Battleford,' *Saskatoon Star Phoenix*, 12 August 1942.

51 Patterson, 'Andrew Paull,' 71. On Native longshoremen and Andrew Paull, see also Andrew Parnaby, *Citizen Docker: Making a New Deal on the Vancouver Waterfront, 1919–1939* (Toronto, 2008), Chapter 3.

52 *The People*, 27 February 1943.

53 'Native Indians See Labor as Ally,' *The People*, 11 December 1943, 11.

54 *The People*, 20 May 1944, 3.

Introduction to Part Three

1 'Emancipation Day,' *Toronto Daily Star*, 1 August 1942, 6.

2 'Racial Discrimination,' *Globe and Mail*, 8 October 1942, 6.

3 *Saturday Night*, 4 September 1943.

4 Ron Faris, *The Passionate Educators: Voluntary Associations and the Struggle for Control of Adult Educational Broadcasting in Canada, 1919–1952* (Toronto, 1975), 34–6.

5 LAC, Canadian Association for Adult Education (hereafter CAAE), MG 28 I 400, vol. 1, file: 'Group Findings: Canadian Jewish Congress, 1945–1946; Ibid., file: Macdonald College Conference, 15–17 June 1944, proceedings; Ibid., file: National Conference, 28–31 May 1945; OA, CAAE, Director's Files, 1935–43, box 1, file: Inter-Cultural Relations Toronto Committee.

6 Ontario Jewish Archives (hereafter OJA), National Joint Public Relations Committee (JPRC), reel 3, file: Fellowship for Reconciliation, Albert Watson to Rabbi Feinberg, 16 September 1947.

7 Ibid., A. Watson to B. Lappin, 3 July 1944; Fellowship of Reconciliation Summer Conference Agenda, 7–9 July 1944.

8 LAC, Fellowship of Reconciliation, MG 28 I 128.

9 Interview with Ben Kayfetz, 29 April 1997, Toronto.

10 United Church of Canada Archives, Board of Evangelism and Social Service, box 47, Records of the Corresponding Secretary, file 90: 'A Plan to Found a Permanent Organization to Study and Promote Inter-Cultural Relations,' December 1944. See also OJA, JPRC Correspondence, reel 1, file 70: Civil Liberties Association, 1942–46. For a detailed analysis of the relationship between civil rights and human rights activism see Ross Lambertson, *Repression and Resistance*.

11 The CNCR's origins and campaigns are discussed in Irving Abella and Harold Troper, *None is Too Many*, 44–6.

12 *Canadian Forum*, July 1945, 87.

13 LAC, MG 28 V7, vol. 2, file 4: Canadian Civil Liberties, 'A Record of the work of the Cooperative Committee on Japanese Canadians, June 1943 to September 1947.' Stephanie Bangarth offers a detailed examination of the CCJC in *Voices Raised in Protest*, Chapter 3. See also, Ross Lambertson, *Repression and Resistance*, Chapter 3.

14 Records of the Cooperative Committee on Japanese Canadians, McMaster University.

5. Mainstream Critics and the Burden of Inherited Ideas

1 Howard Palmer, *Multiculturalism as State Policy*. For a discussion of the changing understanding of race in the United States during the interwar period, see Jacobson, *Whiteness of a Different Color*, Chapter 3. For changes in the scientific explanations of race, see Elazar Barkan, *The Retreat of Scientific Racism* (Cambridge, 1992).

2 OA, Workers' Educational Association fonds, MU 4043, Drummond Wren files, file 164: Civil Liberties Committee, B. K. Sandwell to Drummond Wren, 30 November 1943.

3 Alan Davies and Marilyn Felcher Netsky, 'The United Church and the Jewish Plight during the Nazi Era, 1933–1945,' *Canadian Jewish Historical Society* 8, no. 2 (1984), 64.

4 Acadia University Archives, Watson Kirkconnell Papers, box 47, file 6.

5 Second Report of the Director of the Canadian Conference of Christians and Jews, 29 December 1944.

6 Claris Edwin Silcox, *The Challenge of Anti-Semitism to Democracy* (Toronto, 1939), 4.

7 CJCCCNA, CJCCF, ZA 1943, box 3, file 27A: Script for CBC programme 'Are Canadians Racially Intolerant?' 6.
8 United Church of Canada, Silcox Papers, 'Cultural Advantages Derived by Canada from the Admission of Refugees,' (Canadian National Committee on Refugees and Victims of Political Persecution, July 1939), 4, 7.
9 CJCCCNA, CJCCF, ZA 1943, box 3, file 27A: 'Are Canadians Racially Intolerant?' 8.
10 Ibid., 13.
11 'Statement by Rev. Dr. C.E. Silcox to accompany Special Report on Immigration,' *The Bulletin*, Council for Social Service, Church of England in Canada, 15 October 1941, 10–24.
12 Claris Silcox, 'Family Allowances,' *Food for Thought* 3, no. 3 (November 1942), 4–5. For a discussion of Silcox's views in the context of the Canadian eugenics movement, see Angus McLaren, *Our Own Master Race* (Toronto, 1990), 158.
13 CJCCCNA, CJCCF, ZA 1943, box 3, file 27A: 'Are Canadians Racially Intolerant?' 16 May 1944, 15.
14 Watson Kirkconnell, *A Slice of Canada: Memoirs* (Toronto, 1967), 175.
15 Kirkconnell, *A Slice of Canada*.
16 Ibid., 176. Kirkconnell estimated that between 1938 and 1941 he averaged 100 public addresses a year.
17 Kirkconnell, *A Slice of Canada*, 123, 128.
18 AUA, WKP, box 47, file 6: Rabbi M.N. Eisendrath and Dr C.E. Silcox to Professor Watson Kirkconnell, 29 February 1940.
19 Watson Kirkconnell, *Twilight of Liberty* (London, 1941), 75–6.
20 'The Agony of Israel,' *Canadian Jewish Review*, 11 June 1943.
21 Watston Kirkconnell, *Canadians All: A Primer for Canadian National Unity* (1941), 8–11.
22 Watson Kirkconnell, *Canadian Overtones* (Winnipeg, 1935), 4.
23 Kirkconnell, *Twilight of Liberty*, 80.
24 Watson Kirkconnell, *Canada, Europe and Hitler* (Toronto, 1939), 2, 203–4. Discussed in Angus McLaren, *Our Own Master Race*, 78–9, 151.
25 Kirkconnell, *A Slice of Canada*, 88.
26 Watson Kirkconnell, *Seven Pillars of Freedom* (London, 1944), 192.
27 AUA, WKP, box 56, file 18: J.R. Mutchmor to Watson Kirkconnell, 16 October 1943.
28 Kirkconnell, *Seven Pillars of Freedom*, 76; AUA, WKP, box 56, file 11: C.H. Millard, National Director, United Steelworkers of America to Watson Kirkconnell, 19 February 1943.

29 Robert England, *The Central European Immigrant in Canada* (Canada, 1929), 3.

30 Robert England, *Living, Learning, Remembering* (Vancouver, 1980), 46.

31 Robert England, *The Colonization of Western Canada: A Study of Contemporary Land Settlement (1896–1934)* (London, 1936).

32 England, *Living, Learning, Remembering*, 90.

33 For a discussion of the 'new pluralists' in Canada, see Howard Palmer, *Multiculturalism as State Policy* (Ottawa, 1976).

34 England, *Living, Learning, Remembering*, 90–3.

35 Ibid., 68f.

36 Ibid., passim.

37 England, *The Central European Immigrant*, 174–5.

38 Ibid., 183. See Kenan Malik, *The Meaning of Race* (New York, 1996), for a discussion of the Victorian understanding of the evolutionary ladder from which England's views appear to derive.

39 England, *The Central European Immigrant*, 189–90.

40 Ibid., 163.

41 Ibid., 176.

42 Ibid., 25–7.

43 Ibid., 70, 175.

44 Ibid., 49–50, 58, 168, 176.

45 Ibid., 166, 173.

46 England, *Living, Learning, Remembering*, 82.

47 Ibid., 57, 59, 95; England, *The Colonization of Western Canada*, 222–4.

48 J. Murray Gibbon, *The Conquering Hero*, 148. For a discussion of Gibbon's work, see Terrence Craig, *Racial Attitudes in English Canadian Fiction 1905–1980* (Waterloo, 1987), 8, 47.

49 John Murray Gibbon, *Canadian Mosaic: The Making of a Northern Nation* (New York, 1939), 3.

50 Ibid., 406.

51 John Murray Gibbon, *The New Canadian Loyalists* (Toronto, 1941), 20.

52 J. Murray Gibbon, 'Overcoming the Barrier of Language,' in *Poles in Canada*, edited by J.S.W. Grocholski; AUA, WKP, box 33, file 44: John Murray Gibbon to Watson Kirkconnell, 25 January 1943.

53 Gibbon, *Canadian Mosaic*, x–xii.

54 'Gwethalyn Graham: a Canadian Author with a Crusading Spirit,' *Saturday Night*, 28 October 1944.

55 Gwethalyn Graham, *Earth and High Heaven* (Toronto and Montreal, 1969), 43, 50.

56 Ibid., 48.

57 Barbara Meadowcroft, *Gwethalyn Graham (1913–1965): A Liberated Woman in a Conventional Age* (Toronto, 2008), 80–6, and Chapter 6.

58 Graham, *Earth and High Heaven*, 13.

59 UBC, Special Collections, Angus Family Papers, box 1, file 2: Henry Angus Autobiography, unpublished, 224.

60 Ibid.

61 Ibid., 235.

62 Ibid.; Ken Adachi, *The Enemy That Never Was*, 158.

63 'Immigration,' *International Journal: Quarterly of Canadian Institute of International Affairs* 1, no. 1 (1945), 65–7.

64 Henry Angus 'The Effect of the War on Oriental Minorities in Canada,' *Canadian Journal of Economics and Political Science* (November 1941), 507–8.

65 UBC, Special Collections, Angus Family Papers, box 1, file 2: Henry Angus Autobiography, unpublished, 321.

66 Angus, 'The Effect of the War on Oriental Minorities in Canada,' 515–16.

67 Philleo Nash, 'An Introduction to the Problem of Race Tension,' in *The North American Indian Today*, edited by C.T. Loram and T.F. McIlwraith (Toronto, 1943), 335.

68 C.W.M. Hart, 'The Problem of Laws,' in *The North American Indian Today*, 251–2.

69 Appendix A, *The North American Indian Today*, 349.

70 For an analysis of the public discussion of First Nations in the last years of the war see R. Scott Sheffield, *The Red Man's on the War Path*, Chapter 4.

71 *Saturday Night*, 23 September 1944.

72 Elazar Barkan, *The Retreat of Scientific Racism: Changing Concepts of Race in Britain and the United States between the World Wars* (Cambridge, 1992).

73 Ibid., 207.

74 Ibid., 240.

75 Ibid., 257–8.

76 Ibid., 297. On the British and American publications promoted by Canadian critics of racism during the war, see *The Problem of Race* (Canadian Council of Education for Citizenship & the Canadian Association for Adult Education, 1944).

77 Barkan, *The Retreat of Scientific Racism*, 299.

78 Matthew Frye Jacobson, *Whiteness of a Different Color*, 103.

79 C.W.M. Hart, 'The Race Myth,' *University of Toronto Quarterly* 11, no. 2 (1942), 187.

80 Ibid., 188.

6. Labour and the Left

1 Watson Thomson, *I Accuse: Call to Arms against the Enemy Within* (Contemporary Publishers, n.d.), 20.
2 Thomson, *I Accuse*, 6. See also Watson Thomson, 'Refugees and Minorities,' *Canadian Student*, November 1943; and 'The Jews in Europe,' a broadcast by Watson Thomson over the National Network of the CBC, from Winnipeg, Man., on Easter Sunday, 1943.
3 *Food for Thought*, September 1943.
4 Harvey Forster, *The Church in the City Streets* (Toronto, 1942), 140, 147–53; *Welland–Port Colborne Evening Tribune,* 22 February 1943.
5 *The Church in the City Streets*, 149.
6 United Church Archives, Annual Report, All People's Missions, Niagara Peninsula, 1942; *Welland–Port Colborne Evening Tribune,* 22 February 1943.
7 United Church Archives, Harvey Forster Papers; Acadia University Archives, Watson Kirkconnell Papers, box 56, file 18: J.R. Mutchmor to Watson Kirkconnell, 21 October 1943.
8 Claris Silcox, 'Foreword,' in *What About the Jews?* by Norman Black (Toronto: Canadian Association for Adult Education, 1944).
9 Norman F. Black, *A Challenge to Patriotism and Statesmanship* (Toronto: The Christian Social Council of Canada, July 1944).
10 Regina Manifesto, Programme of the Co-operative Commonwealth Federation, adopted at first national convention, Regina, July 1933, 1.
11 LAC, Co-Operative Commonwealth Federation Papers (hereafter CCF), vol. 13, National Conventions and Inter-Provincial Conferences, 1932–60, file: 1944 Convention – Resolutions; 'We Are All Canadians,' *Commonwealth*, 17 April 1946; LAC, CCF, vol. 53, CCF Provinces, 1932–58, Ontario – Education, 1943–51.
12 Christopher MacLennan, *Toward the Charter*, 70.
13 LAC, Francis Reginald Scott fonds, MG 30 D211, vol. 14, file: Year of Human Rights, 1946–49; Frank R. Scott, *What Does Labour Need in a Bill of Rights?* (Summary), Dalhousie Labour-University Committee, Institute of Public Affairs, Dalhousie University, 1959.
14 *Canadian Forum*, July 1940, September 1941.
15 *Canadian Unionist*, March 1941, 245.
16 G.M.A. Grube, 'Civil Liberties in War Time,' *The Canadian Forum* 20 (July 1940), 106–7.
17 LAC, CCF, vol. 59, Ontario – Policy and Research: General, 1942–47, Provinces, 1932–58, 1954 Statement on Bill of Rights under Fed.-Prov. Relations.
18 LAC, CCF, vol. 13: Resolutions, 1944 Convention, National Conventions

and Inter-Provincial Conferences, 1932–60, 'We Are All Canadians.' The article refers to statements by Alistair Stewart.

19 Saskatchewan Archives Board, T.C. Douglas Papers (hereafter TCD), vol. 197, file: Pamphlets; M.J. Coldwell, *Am I My Brother's Keeper?*; Paul H. Christensen to Douglas, 5 December 1945.

20 Saskatchewan Archives Board, TCD, vol. 255: Angus MacInnis to Douglas, 8 April 1946.

21 Saskatchewan Archives Board, TCD, vol. 58: Norman Black and Bruce York to Douglas, 3 March 1945.

22 *Commonwealth*, 17 April 1946.

23 UBC, Special Collections, Angus MacInnis Papers, folder 54A–9: Angus MacInnis to A.R.M. Lower, 14 September 1938.

24 Saskatchewan Archives Board, TCD, vol. 37: Grace MacInnis to T.C. Douglas, 6 April 1946; Patricia Roy, *The Triumph of Citizenship*, 120–1.

25 LAC, CCF, vol. 174, file: Oriental-Canadians, George Grube to Lloyd Fell, 6 October 1943. For a discussion of the response of British Columbia's political left to the persecution of Japanese Canadians, see Werner Cohn, 'The Persecution of Japanese Canadians and the Political Left in British Columbia, December 1941–March 1943,' *BC Studies* 68 (Winter 1985–6), 3–22.

26 Bill Waiser, *Saskatchewan: A New History* (Calgary, 2005), 247–52, 332–3.

27 LAC, MG 28 V114, Jewish Historical Society of Western Canada Collection, Records of the CJC, Western Division, vol. 7, file: Regina Executive Correspondence, A. Samuels – L. Rosenberg 1944–45, H. Frank, Acting Exec. Dir., to Pearl Halman, 11 December 1945.

28 Laurie Barron, *Walking in Indian Moccasins: The Native Policies of Tommy Douglas and the CCF* (Vancouver, 1997); James M. Pitsula, 'The Saskatchewan CCF Government and Treaty Indians, 1944–64,' *Canadian Historical Review* 75, no. 1 (March 1994), 21–53; 'The CCF Government and the Formation of the Union of Saskatchewan Indians,' *Prairie Forum* 19 (1994), 131–51; Morris C. Shumiatcher, 'Indian Smoke on the Western Sky,' *Canadian Forum* (March 1946), 283–84.

29 Saskatchewan Archives Board, TCD, vol. 878(58), file: Japanese Canadians, Douglas to Donald Ewing, 18 December 1945.

30 Ibid., file: Attorney General J.W. Corman to Premier Douglas, 16 January 1946.

31 LAC, Communist International fonds (hereafter Comintern), MG 10 K3, Profintern, reel K-313, file 334: Tim Buck to A. Losovsky, Exec. Secty. Profintern, Moscow, 11 January 1928.

32 See, for example, Carmela Patrias, *Patriots and Proletarians*, 208.

33 LAC, Comintern, MG 10 K3, Communist Party of Canada, reel K-288, file 164: 'Oriental Labor in Canada,' 1934.

34 LAC, Comintern, MG 10 K3, Communist Party of Canada, reel K-290, file 179: Proposals of Central Committee on work in National Fractions, 'The Italian Workers' Paper,' 1935.

35 *Kanadai Magyar Munkás*, 11 March 1943.

36 'Ne hallgassunk a társultati ügynökökre, be a C.I.O.-ba!' (Don't Listen to Company Agents, Join the CIO!), *Kanadai Magyar Munkás*, 7 January 1943.

37 Judy Fudge and Eric Tucker, *Labour Before the Law: The Regulation of Workers' Collective Action in Canada, 1900–1948* (Don Mills, ON, 2001), 247; LAC, Comintern, MG 10 K3, Young Communist League of Canada (YCL), reel K-310, file 1759: Letter from Rose Brahen, July 1939.

38 See, for example, OA, RG 7-30-0-217: Industrial Disputes Inquiry, 'Atlas Steels Limited, Welland, Ontario and vote of employees,' 2 June 1943 to 22 June 1943. See also, MacDowell, *Remember Kirkland Lake*, 90–1.

39 'Windsor – City of Unity,' *Canadian Tribune*, 10 April 1943, 12.

40 LAC, Comintern, CPC, reel K-283, file 131: Trade Union and Unemployed Work of the Party, 12 September 1932.

41 LAC, Comintern, CPC, reel K-288: *The Shingle Worker* 1, no. 5 (July 1934), 2, Issued by the Militant Groups of Rank and File Union Shingle Workers; LAC, Comintern, YCL, reel K-310, file 1759: Letter from Rose Brahen, July 1939.

42 'The Blubber Bay Victory,' *B.C. Lumber Worker*, 15 September 1937, 8.

43 See, for example, *Kanadai Magyar Munkás*, 25 April 1940, 23 May 1940, 30 May 1940, 20 February 1941, 1 May 1941, 4 June 1941.

44 Mrs Lottie Black, '"Jim Crow" Stalks Windsor Streets,' *Canadian Tribune*, 20 March 1943, 18; 'Toronto Negroes Barred from Plants,' *Canadian Tribune*, 27 March 1943, 24; Wm. H. Trott, 'Porters' Union Leader Hits Racial Discrimination Here,' *Canadian Tribune*, 19 June 1943, 4.

45 LAC, Comintern, MG 10 K3, YCL, reel K-310, file 1762: Memorandum on Developments in the Finnish-Canadian Youth Movement.

46 LAC, Comintern, MG 10 K3, YCL, reel K-311, file 1769: The Opinions and Program of Canadian Young People as Expressed, Reported and Adopted by the 5th Canadian Youth Congress, Montreal, July 1940; Cynthia Comacchio, *The Dominion of Youth* (Waterloo, 2006), 202–3; Paul Axelrod, 'The Student Movement of the 1930s,' in *Youth, University and Canadian Society*, edited by Paul Axelrod and John G. Reid (Kingston and Montreal, 1989), 216–46.

47 'Treatment of Canada's Indians Is Cause for Shame, Sorrow,' *Canadian Tribune*, 15 July 1944, 14. See also 'Algonquin Indian Lumber Workers, Golden

Lake Reserve,' *Canadian Tribune*, 23 October 1943, 10; 'Six Nations Indians Vigorously Object to RCMP "Guardianship,"' *Canadian Tribune*, 13 May 1944.

48 'Oriental Minorities Vital to Canada's War Effort,' *Canadian Tribune*, 9 May 1942, 6.

49 'Appeal to Prejudice Is No Answer,' *The People*, 15 April 1944, 4.

50 'What About the Japanese?' *The People*, 20 May 1944, 4.

51 *Special Committee on Reconstruction and Reestablishment. Minutes of Proceedings and Evidence*, no. 9, 24 May 1944, 302.

52 Ibid., 297.

53 Ivan Avakumovic, *The Communist Party in Canada* (Toronto, 1975), 38.

54 LAC, Comintern, MG 10 K3, reel K-276, file 64: 'A Declaration by the Minority of the Central Executive Committee and the National Ukrainian Agitpropcom of the CPC.'

55 LAC, Comintern, MG 10 K3, reel K-274, file 39: Minutes of joint meeting of Political Com and Org Com, 7 June 1926; LAC, Comintern, MG 10 K3, reel K-274, file 39: Minutes of Central Executive Committee meeting, 31 September 1926. See also Brian Palmer, *Working Class Experience*, 228.

56 LAC, Comintern, MG 10 K3, reel K-286, file 152: Information Material, Estimated work in District no. 3.

57 *Workers' Unity*, Official Bi-Monthly Organ, Workers' Unity League of Canada, Canadian Section RILU, vol. 1, no. 1, 15 July 1931.

58 Carmela Patrias, *Patriots and Proletarians*, 224–5.

59 'New Canadians Express Loyalty to Canada,' *The Guide* 1, no. 11 (November 1939), 3.

60 LAC, Kossuth Sick Benefit Federation fonds, vol. 1, file 9: Minutes and Reports of the National Conventions, Minutes of the 14th National Convention of the IMBF, Hamilton, 7–9 April 1944, 7.

61 'Grand Council Report to the 14th National Convention of the IMBF,' *The Guide* 4, no. 20, 9.

62 See also, Walter Reuther Library, UAW, Region 7, Canadian Regional Office, box 85: By-laws of Local 195, UAW-CIO, Windsor, 1943.

63 University of Pittsburgh Libraries, Archives of Industrial Society, UE/Labor Archives (UELA), box 55, local 529, Constitution and By-Laws, Article XIII: 'Initiation Oath,' 11.

64 *Montreal Gazette*, 2 October 1939, 10.

65 *Canadian Unionist*, September 1940, 86.

66 CJCCCNA, DA 1 box 2, file 23: Memorandum on Public Relations, 8 May 1942.

67 CJCCCNA, ZA 1942, box 5, file 57: clipping.

68 LAC, Frank and Libbie Park fonds, MG 31 K9, file 147: W.A. Tuttle, Vancouver Labor Council, to W.L. Mackenzie King, 2 August 1943.

69 OA, RG 49 116, vol. IX: Proceedings 11 March 1943, Testimony of R.J. Smith of the Packinghouse Workers' Organizing Committee.

70 The Trades and Labour Congress of Canada, Report of Proceedings 1944, 336.

71 CCL resolutions against anti-Semitism and discrimination in *Labour Gazette* September 1944, 1087 and November 1944, 1440; OA, RG 7-60-0-74, Constitution of the United Gas, Coke and Chemical Workers, 12 September 1942, 19–20: Members Obligations – 'I will do all in my power to defend my fellow workers against discrimination because of color, creed or nationality...'

72 *Canadian Tribune*, 11 December 1943.

73 OA, Drew Papers, box 434: Burt to Drew, 23 March 1944.

74 The CIO pamphlet was based on *They Got the Blame* by Kenneth Gould, and published by the International Committee of the YMCA.

75 OA, WEA fonds, vol. 242, file 13, 1943–45, pt. 3.

76 'Young Auto Worker to Study in Britain,' *The Oshawa Labor Press*, 25 August 1938, 1.

77 OA, RG 7-30-0-151: Arbitration – McKinnon Industries, Case of Joseph di Mercurio, St Catharines, 3 June 1942.

78 LAC, United Steel Workers of America, vol. 1, file: SWOC, Conference of the Local Unions in basic steel plants (Ottawa), Proceedings, Reports circulars, 3–5 December 1941.

79 *Canadian Tribune*, 23 January 1943, 21.

80 *Magyar Szakasz* was *Melting Pot*'s Hungarian version.

81 Archives of Labour and Urban History, Wayne State University, Walter Ruether Library, Detroit, UAW, Local 199 Collection, box 23: Executive Minutes 1944–45.

82 'Népgyülés vitatta a p. colborni magyarság teendöit.' (Mass Meeting Discusses Plans of Hungarians of Port Colborne), *Kanadai Magyar Munkás*, 3 June 1943, 15.

83 *New Canadian* 4 (1943), 3 June 1943, 8 January 1944.

84 LAC, Labour Canada, RG 27, vol. 644, file 23-2-3-7-1, pt. 1: clipping dated 14 September 1943.

85 LAC, United Steel Workers of America, Canadian National Office, National Director's Office, Corresp. and Related Documents. MG 28 I 268, reel C-13109,vol. 14, file: Cabinet Members Federal Govt. Correspondence, C.H. Millard to W.L. Mackenzie King, 14 July1944.

86 UBC, Special Collections, records of the Hotel, Restaurant and Culinary

Bartenders Union, box 5, Local 28, Vancouver, 1 November 1935 to 4 August 1943; Minutes of Meeting, Local 28, 29 January 1945.

87 Walter Ruether Library, UAW Toronto Sub-Regional Office, box 11, file: Meeting Nov. 1942, Minutes and Report: Minutes of District Council 26, 7–8 Nov 1942.

88 'Demand Grows to Curb 5th Column,' *Montreal Gazette*, 22 May 1940, 11.

89 LAC, Labour Canada, RG 27, vol. 650, file: Lumbering Employment, unidentified clipping, 7 February 1942.

90 LAC, Labour Canada, RG 27, vol. 170, file 614-02-11: Re: Placement of Certain Japanese Families in the Province of Alberta, vol. 2, A.E. Russell, BCSC to the Secty., Edmonton TLC, 21 Jan 1944.

91 LAC, DL, RG 27, vol. 644, file 23-2-3-7-1, pt. 1: Provincial Coaters Union Local 481, Georgetown, Ontario, to A. MacNamara, Deputy Minister of Labour, 18 September 1944; *New Canadian*, 18 March 1944, refers to rebuttal in Lethbridge Herald.

92 LAC, DL, RG 27, vol. 644, file 23-2-3-7-1, pt. 1: British Columbia Security Commission, International Brotherhood Pulp, Sulphite and Paper Mill Workers to Humphrey Mitchell, Minister of Labour, 16 September 1944; Provincial Coaters Union Local 481, Georgetown, Ontario, to A. MacNamara, Deputy Minister of Labour, 18 September 1944.

93 Pamela Sugiman, *Labour's Dilemma: The Gender Politics of Auto Workers in Canada* (Toronto, 1994), 89.

7. Anglo-Saxon Guardianship

1 LAC, RF, MG 27 III B11, vol.115, file: Manpower, NSS and Civilian Work, July–Nov. 1941, Feb. 1942–Mar. 1943, Confidential analysis of report of Labour Supply Investigating Committee, 4.

2 University of Saskatchewan Archives, George Simpson fonds (hereafter GSF): G.M. Simpson, Memorandum to Citizenship Division, 1960, 2.

3 LAC, DNWS, RG 44, vol. 36, file: 'German and Italian Unemployable,' Norman Robertson, Memorandum of the Interdepartmental Committee on the Treatment of Aliens, 13 August 1940.

4 University of Saskatchewan Archives, GSF: Summary of discussion of the first meeting of the CCCC, 10 January 1942.

5 Leslie Pal, 'Identity, Citizenship and Mobilization: The Nationalities Branch and World War II,' *Canadian Public Administration* 32, no. 3 (Fall 1989), 407–26.

6 N.F. Dreisziger, 'The Rise of a Bureaucracy for Multiculturalism: The Origins of the Nationalities Branch, 1939–1941,' in *On Guard for Thee: War,*

Ethnicity and the Canadian State, 1939–1945, edited by Norman Hillmer, Bohdan Kordan, and Lubomyr Luciuk (Ottawa, 1988), 1–29.

7 William R. Young, 'Chauvinism and Canadianism: Canadian Ethnic Groups and the Failure of Wartime Information,' in *On Guard for Thee*, 45; John Herd Thompson, *Ethnic Minorities during Two World Wars* (Ottawa, 1991).

8 Mark Kristmanson, *Plateaus of Freedom: Nationality, Culture and State Security in Canada, 1940–1960* (Toronto, 2002), Chapter 1, and p. 231.

9 Ivana Caccia, *Managing the Canadian Mosaic in Wartime* (Kingston and Montreal, 2010).

10 LAC, DNWS, RG 44, vol. 36, file: 'German and Italian Unemployable,' Excerpts from Minutes of Meeting of National Labour Supply Council, 30 December 1940.

11 LAC, RF, MG 27 III B11, vol. 113: Manpower Labour Supply Investigation, Committee's report to the Labour Coordination Committee, October 1941, 'Recommendations,' 4–5. See also LAC, Privy Council Office, RG 2, vol. 6, file M5: 'Re: Armed Services Industry 1941,' A.D.P Heeney's analysis of Manpower Supply for Cabinet War Committee.

12 LAC, DNWS, RG 44, vol. 36, file: Foreign Section Committee on Cultural-Group Cooperation, Memorandum on the Establishment of a Committee on Cultural-Group Cooperation to advise the Minister of National War Services.

13 Ibid.

14 LAC, DNWS, RG 44, vol. 36, file: 'Foreign Section CCCC,' Interdepartmental meeting on organization of proposed committee on cultural-group cooperation under Ministry of National War Services, by S.F. Rae, 1 November 1941.

15 LAC, Boards, Offices and Commissions (hereafter BOC), RG 36, vol. 13, file 8-9-1: Memorandum from W.E. Halliday to Mr Heeney, Re: Foreign Language Group – Wartime Information, 14 May 1943.

16 LAC, TPF, MG 30 E350, vol. 2, file 1: Summary of discussion of the first Meeting of the Committee on Co-operation in Canadian Citizenship, 10 January 1942.

17 *Hansard*, 27 May 1942, 2806.

18 Thomas M. Prymak, 'George Simpson, the Ukrainian Canadians and the "Pre-History" of Slavic Studies in Canada,' *Saskatchewan History* 41 (1988), 53–66.

19 University of Saskatchewan Archives, GSF: G.W. Simpson to J.W. Arsenych, 23 March 1944. The shifting membership of the CCCC had to do with Professor Simpson's illness, and with confusion and changes in NWS. At least one of the members, however, Isabel Skelton, also believed that

the committee was ineffectual, serving as window dressing for the DNWS, and she resigned in October 1943. But even if Skelton's assessment was accurate, for our purposes the ideas and actions of those who stayed are important in what they reveal about state views of minorities.

20 University of Saskatchewan Archives, GSF: Simpson to Walter Katrenchuk, 3 March 1944.

21 University of Saskatchewan Archives, GSF: Summary of the discussion of the first meeting of the Committee on Cooperation in Canadian Citizenship, 10 January 1942; University of Saskatchewan Archives, GSF: Summary of the discussion of the fourth meeting of the Committee on Cooperation in Canadian Citizenship, 25–26 November 1943.

22 LAC, Inter-Departmental Committee on Labour Coordination, MG 28, vol. 144, file 3-L-1, no. 4: A.W. Crawford and W.J. Couper to Labour Co-ordination Committee, Re: Discrimination in Employment of Certain Nationality Groups by War Industries, 13 January 1942, 2.

23 AUA, WKP, box 48, file 22: Note from George Simpson appended to Summary of discussion of the first Meeting of the CCCC, 10 January 1942.

24 LAC, TPF, MG 30 E350, vol. 2, file 1: Recommendation from J.S. Thorson, Minister of National War Services, to Governor General in Council for the establishment of CCCC, 27 January 1942

25 LAC, LC, RG 27, vol. 1500, file 2-K-184: NSS, Orientals, B.C. Div K, 'Report on Recommendations of Special Committee on Orientals in British Columbia, December 1940,' 22.

26 LAC, TPF, MG 30 E350, vol. 2, file 1: Summary of the Discussion of the First Meeting of the CCCC, 10 January 1942.

27 UBC, Special Collections, Angus Family Papers, box 1, file 2: Henry Angus Autobiography, unpublished, 319–20.

28 LAC, DNWS, RG 44, vol. 36, file: 'Foreign Section Committee on Cultural Group Cooperation,' T.C. Davis to George Simpson, on Canadian Jewish Congress, 7 April 1942; and Davis to Simpson, 7 April 1942; LAC, TPF, MG 30 E350, vol. 1, file 29: Rev. Dr W. Kushnir, President, and J.W. Arsenych, Secretary, Ukrainian Canadian Committee, to Prime Minister King, 13 November 1943.

29 LAC, DNWS, RG 44, vol. 36, file: Foreign Section CCCC, J.T. Thorson to Davis, 26 March 1942; Davis to Simpson, 7 April 1942; LAC, TPF, MG 30 E350, vol.1, file 29: Deputy Minister Chester Payne to Major General LaFlèche.

30 University of Saskatchewan Archives, GSF: L. Rosenberg, Corresponding Secretary, National Unity Council to J.T. Thorson, Minister of National War Services, 23 March 1942.

31 LAC, TPF, MG 30 E350, vol. 2, file 1: 'Summary of the discussion of the first Meeting of the Com. on Coop. in Can. Cit.,' 10 January 1942. When Major Bois suggested representation of 'ethnic groups' particularly concerned, Simpson explained the difficulties of getting representation since the groups varied so greatly in point of numbers and in some cases were 'split into many conflicting factions. It was believed that the composition of the Committee was a satisfactory safeguard against such a presumption.' See also, LAC, TPF, vol.1, file 29: Payne to LaFlèche, 14 December 1943.

32 LAC, TPF, MG 30 E350, vol. 1, file 16: 'Tour of Western Canada, November – December 1941.'Tracy Philipps, Dept. of National War Service, European Advisor, Correspondence, January 1941.

33 University of Saskatchewan Archives, GSF: G.W. Simpson, to J. T. Thorson, Minister of National War Services, 28 July 1942.

34 LAC, Citizenship and Immigration, RG 26, vol. 1, file: 'Arts and Crafts Interdepartmental Committee on Canada's Homecrafts,' Report by the General Publicity Agent of the CPR, Murray Gibbon, to the Canadian Handicraft Guild about Canadian handicraft work that he came across on his recent trip west. Cover letter to George Simpson, 16 September 1942.

35 Ibid.

36 Watson Kirkconnell, *Seven Pillars of Freedom* (Toronto: Oxford University Press, 1994), 76.

37 Donald Avery, *Dangerous Foreigners: European Immigrant Workers and Labour Radicalism in Canada, 1896–1932* (Toronto, 1979); Howard Palmer, *Patterns of Prejudice*, 53–60.

38 AUA, WKP, box 56, file 29: Rod Kennedy, Editorial Department, *Family Herald Weekly Star*, to Watson Kirkconnell, 29 January 1945; and Kirkconnell to Kennedy, 31 January 1945.

39 AUA, WKP, box 56, vol. 48, file 23: Summary of Discussion of the third meeting of the Committee on Cooperation in Canadian Citizenship, 23 September 1942.

40 LAC, Citizenship and Immigration, RG 26, vol. 9, file 50-3: 'Correspondence with the Dept. of Mines and Resources,' Ann Grant, Editorial Assistant, Department of National War Services, to Director of Mines and Geology, Department of Mines, 3 September 1942.

41 University of Saskatchewan Archives, GSF, Citizenship Division, Department of National War Services, Report to the Minister of National War Services of the meeting of the CCCC, 25–26 November 1943.

42 'What It Means To Be Canadian,' *Kanadai Magyar Ujság*, 8 December 1943, 3.

43 LAC, TPF, MG 30 E350, vol. 1, file 29: 'It's Women's War Too!'
44 LAC, DEA, RG 25, vol. 2977, file 3426-40, pt. 2: 'Taras Shevchenko, Greatest Ukrainian Poet.'
45 Queen's University Archives, Isabel Skelton Papers, box 1: Correspondence, Committee on Cooperation in Canadian Citizenship, V.J. Kaye to I. Skelton, 27 June 1944.
46 LAC, Citizenship and Immigration, RG 26, vol. 9, file: National Registration, G.H. Lash, Director, to A.A. McIntosh, 22 December 1941.
47 See Chapter 5.
48 LAC, Robert England fonds, MG 30 C-181, vol. 3, file: 'Report on the Reorganization of Nationalities Branch,' Department of National War Services, by Robert England, 12 June 1944.
49 My thanks to Professor Ning Wang, Department of History, Brock University, for translating this poster.
50 NFB Archives, 'Peoples of Canada,' The Canadian Committee Film Program Notes, no. 1.
51 NFB Archives, 'Peoples of Canada,' Gordon Sparling to Stewart Legg, 24 May 1940.
52 University of Saskatchewan Archives, GSF: G.W. Simpson, Memorandum to Citizenship Division, 11–12.
53 CJCCCNA, CJCCF, ZA 1943, box 3, file 26: Stanley Jackson, National Film Board of Canada, to Mr Caiserman, CJC, 17 October 1942.
54 LAC, National Film Board of Canada, Still Photography Division, R1196-14-7-E, WRM 4036.
55 William R. Young, 'Chauvinism and Canadianism: Canadian Ethnic Groups and the Failure of Wartime Information;' N.F. Dreisziger, 'The Rise of a Bureaucracy for Multiculturalism;' and Bohdan S. Kordan and Lubomyr Y. Luciuk, 'A Prescription for Nationbuilding: Ukrainian Canadians and the Canadian State, 1939–1945, all in *On Guard for Thee*; N.F. Dreisziger, 'Tracy Philipps and the Achievement of Ukrainian-Canadian Unity,' in *Canada's Ukrainians: Negotiating an Identity*, edited by L. Luciuk and S. Hryniuk (Toronto, 1991); Bohdan S. Kordan, *Canada and the Ukrainian Question* (Montreal and Kingston, 2001); Thomas M. Prymak, *Maple Leaf and Trident: The Ukrainian Canadians during the Second World War* (Toronto, 1988); Mark Kristmanson, *Plateaus of Freedom*, Chapter 1.
56 LAC, TPF, MG 30 E350, vol. 2, file 1: 'Summary of the discussion of the first meeting of the Committee on Cooperation in Canadian Citizenship, 10 January 1942, 3.
57 University of Saskatchewan Archives, GSF: G.W. Simpson, Memorandum to Citizenship Division, 1960, 4.

58 LAC, DNWS, RG 44, vol. 35, file: Bureau of Public Information – Foreign Section, T.C. Davis to Paul Reading, Press Attaché, Canadian Legation, Washington.

59 LAC, RG 25, vol. 2977, file 2426-40, pt. 1: Memo to LaFlèche from T.C. Davis, Re: Committee on Cooperation in Canadian Citizenship, 13 November 1942.

60 Caccia, *Managing the Canadian Mosaic*, 69.

61 Kordan, *Canada and the Ukrainian Question*, 201, note 102.

62 AUA, WKP, box 48, file 44: Tracy Philipps to 'Deputy Minister', 15 March 1944.

63 AUA, WKP, box 48, file 35: 'Reply to an official Request to foresee and forestall all possible senior staff questions which could occur in parliament.'

64 Ibid., box 49, file 6: Tracy Philipps to Watson Kirkconnell, 26 February 1944.

65 LAC, Robert England fonds, MG 30 C181, vol. 3, file 1: Dept of National War Services: Nationalities Division, Corresp. 1944–47, Memorandum, Robert England to Deputy Minister of DNWS, 15 May 1944; Acting Undersecretary of State for External Affairs to Robert England, 4 May 1944.

66 LAC, TPF, MG 30 E350, vol. 2, file 4; LAC, Vladimir J. Kaye fonds, MG 31 D69, vol. 21, file 2.

67 Kordan, *Canada and the Ukrainian Question*, 40–1.

68 LAC, TPF, MG 30 E350, vol. 1, file 6: Tracy Philipps to Commissioner Wood, 24 June 1941.

69 LAC, TPF, MG 30 E350, vol. 2, file 4: 'V.J. Kaye, Toronto, Correspondence from Tracy Philipps, 1940.'

70 LAC, TPF, MG 30 E350, vol. 1, file 6: Tracy Philipps to Commissioner Wood, RCMP, 20 May 1941.

71 LAC, TPF, MG 30 E350, vol. 1, file 19: Correspondence April 1941; Ibid., file 20: Memorandum to S.T. Wood, RCMP, n.d. 'Hemisphere Defence. Foreign-born populations of the Americas;' Ibid., file 20: Tracy Philipps to Sir Esmond Ovey, British Ambassador to Argentina, 28 May 1941; Ibid., file 24: Tracy Philipps to T.A. Crerar, 23 September 1941.

72 Kristmanson, *Plateaus of Freedom*, 3.

73 LAC, LC, RG 27, vol. 125, file 601.3: Tracy Philipps to W.J. Couper, 1 October 1942.

74 LAC, TPF, MG 30 E350, vol. 1, file 24: Report from Sudbury, 4 September 1941.

75 LAC, TPF, MG 30 E350, vol. 1, file 22: Correspondence July 1941, A. Cross, President, Dominion Steel and Coal Corporation Ltd. to Tracy Philipps, 30 July 1941; and Ibid., file 23: Correspondence August 1941, Memorandum

dated 1 August 1941. See also AUA, WKP, box 48, file 41: Monthly Report for August, Internal Affairs, Canadians of recent European origin, 6 September 1943, 5.

76 LAC, DEA, RG 25, vol. 2977, file 3426-40, pt. 1: Tracy Philipps, Observations on a visit to the coal fields of New Brunswick, August 1942.

77 LAC, Citizenship and Immigration, RG 26, vol. 1, file: 'Canadian Institute of International Affairs,' Memorandum from Tracy Philipps to Deputy Minister, NWS, Re: October activities.

78 LAC, DEA, RG 25, vol. 3040, file 4174-40: S.F. Rae, 'The Pan-Slavic Mov't in Canada,' 31 July 1942

79 LAC, Citizenship and Immigration, RG 26, vol. 2, file 28-1: Correspondence with the Dept. of Labour, Tracy Philipps to N.A. Robertson, U.S. Ext. Aff., 24 June 1942.

80 LAC, TPF, MG 30 E350, vol. 1, file 24: 'Foreign-Born New Canadians from the Continent of Europe,' 7 July 1941; Ibid., file 25: 'Proposed European Section for War Services and Canadianization of Immigrant Europeans.'

81 Ibid., vol. 2, file 13: CCCC Correspondence Jan., 1943, Nationalities Branch. Methods.

82 Ibid., vol. 1, file 6: T. Philipps DNWS Secret RCMP Correspondence, 1941, Tracy Philipps to S.T. Wood, RCMP Commissioner, 4 May 1941.

83 LAC, Robert England fonds, MG 30, C181, vol. 3, file 1: Memorandum from Robert England to Deputy Minister, 15 May 1944, Telegrams exchanged between Ottawa and High Commissioner of Canada in London, April–May 1944. Davis claimed that he requested a background check from the DEA and received a report that he was reliable. LAC, DNWS, RG 44, vol. 35, file: 'Bureau of Public Information – Foreign Section' T.C. Davis to Paul Reading, Press Attaché, Canadian Legation Washington, n.d. On a copy of a memorandum from Davis to the same effect, someone, presumably from the DEA, scribbled 'no' next to Davis's claim that the DEA recommended Philipps. LAC, DEA, RG 25, vol. 2977, file 3426-40, pt. 1: Memo to LaFlèche from T.C. Davis, Deputy Minister, Re: CCCC, 13 November 1942.

84 LAC, BOC, RG 36, vol.13, file 8-9-1: Committee on Cooperation in Canadian Citizenship, Donald Cameron to T.C. Davis, 21 November 1942.

85 LAC, LC, RG 27, vol. 630, file 26: Correspondence concerning employment of Aliens, Sept. 1939–Nov. 1941, Joseph P. Jonusza to Colonel Mess, President of the Association of Canadian Clubs, 7 May 1941.

86 LAC, TPF, MG 30 E350, vol. 1, file 16: 'Tour of Western Canada, November–December 1941.'

87 Ibid.

88 LAC, TPF, MG 30 E350, vol. 1, file 6: T. Philipps DNWS Secret RCMP Corresp. Jan.–June 1941, Tracy Philipps, Confidential, 20 June 1941.

89 LAC, TPF, MG 30 E350, vol.1, file 24: 'Report from Fort William, 16 September 1941.'

90 See, for example, LAC, LC, RG 27, vol. 125, file 601-3: Tracy Philipps to W.J. Couper, 'Job Discrimination, morale and patriotism,' 1 October 1942; University of Saskatchewan Archives, GSF, Memorandum for the Deputy Minister (DNWS) and the Committee, Tracy Philipps, 25 September 1942.

91 LAC, TPF, MG 30 E350, vol.1, file 24: 'Report from Fort William, 16 September 1941.'

92 LAC, TPF, MG 30 E350, vol.1, file 9: Tracy Philipps Secret RCMP Correspondence, 1943, Brief Monthly Report of Internal Affairs, Canadian communities of recent European origin, 2 August 1943.

93 LAC, TPF, MG 30 E350, vol. 1, file 26: Correspondence, November 1941, Record Notes, 'Jews.'

94 Ibid.

95 LAC, TPF, MG 30 E350, vol. 1, file 24: Report from Fort William, 16 September 1941.

96 LAC, TPF, MG 30 E350, vol. 1, file 22: Correspondence, July 1941, Tracy Philipps, Confidential report, dated 25 July 1941.

97 LAC, DEA, RG 25, vol. 2977, file 3426-40, pt. 1: Tracy Philipps, Observations on a visit to the coal fields of New Brunswick, August 1942.

98 LAC, TPF, MG 30 E350, vol.1, file 22: M. Black, RCMP to Tracy Philipps, 25 July 1941.

99 See Chapter 1, p. 24.

100 LAC, Citizenship and Immigration, RG 26, vol. 5, file: 'Fossati, Dr. Alfred,' Fossati to Tracy Philipps, 29 March 1943; and clipping from *Montreal Star*, 30 March 1943.

101 LAC, Citizenship and Immigration, RG 26, vol. 6, file: Mazzini Society, Carlo Lamberti to Tracy Philipps, 16 June 1943; and Ibid., file 24-L-1: 'Carlo Lamberti.'

102 LAC, TPF, MG 30 E350: Tracy Philipps to Mr Wood, President of Sun Life Insurance Company, 29 August 1942; LAC, RG 44, vol. 35, file: Bureau of Public Information, K.D. Macaulay, Assistant Comptroller, Sun Life Assurance Company of Canada, to TP, 3 September 1942.

103 Eisner Papers, 'Report of my Goodwill Visit to and Survey of the General Situation of Canadian Communities of Hungarian origin in certain Industrial Areas of the Province of Ontario and Districts of the Prairie Provinces,' by Béla Eisner, 3 March 1943, 14.

104 AUA, WKP, box 44, file 30: Brief Report, as asked, for the personal in-

formation of General LaFlèche, on the Origin, Aim and Functions of the Nationalities Branch, Tracy Philipps, 28 December 1942.

105 Ibid., box 44, file 6: Peter Taraska to Watson Kirkconnell, 16 October 1943.

106 LAC, Citizenship and Immigration, RG 26, vol. 6, file: 'Peter Taraska,' Peter Taraska to G.W. Simpson, 25 September 1942.

107 LAC, Citizenship and Immigration, RG 26, vol. 2, file: Correspondence with the Department of Labour, Tracy Philipps to W.J. Couper, 1 October 1942.

108 LAC, LC, RG 27, vol. 125, file 601-3: Tracy Philipps to W.J. Couper, Department of Labour, 1 October 1942.

109 *Canadian Tribune*, 20 February 1943, 15.

110 *Hansard*, 27 April 1944, 2407. For examples from other communists in other minority groups see *La Vittoria*, 27 November 1943, translation in LAC, BOC, RG 36, vol.13, file 8-9-2.

111 LAC, TPF, MG 30 E350, vol. 1, file 29: Rev. Dr W. Kushnir, President, and J.W. Arsenych, Secretary, Ukrainian Canadian Committee, to Prime Minister King, 13 November 1943.

112 University of Saskatchewan Archives, GSF, W.J. Lindal to J.T. Thorson, 20 March 1942.

113 LAC, TPF, MG 30 E350, vol. 1, file 29: H.W. Winkler to L.R. LaFlèche, 5 November 1943; Blair Fraser, 'New Canadians in Wartime,' *Montreal Gazette*, 19 October 1943.

114 LAC, BOC, RG 36, vol. 13, file 8-9-2: 'Ethnic Groups Canada,' R. Fletcher, President, H. Markus, Vice-President, National Unity Council, to John Grierson, Director, Wartime Information Board, n.d.; Ibid., John Grierson to Major General L.R. LaFlèche, 28 October 1943.

115 LAC, BOC, RG 36, vol. 13, file 8-9-2: 'Ethnic Groups Canada'. See also University of Saskatchewan Archives, George Simpson Papers, L. Rosenberg, Corresponding Secretary, National Unity Council, to J.T. Thorson, Minister of National War Services, 23 March 1942.

116 LAC, BOC, RG 36, vol. 13, file 8-9-2: 'Ethnic Groups Canada' J. Grierson to H.R.L. Henry, Private Secty, Office of Prime Minister, 5 March 1943.

117 LAC, BOC, RG 36, vol. 13, file 8-9-2: Translation of Editorial from 5 October 1943. Special report for Press Censors of Canada.

118 LAC, BOC, RG 36, vol. 13, file 8-9-2: Translation of Editorial from Polish Newspaper *Czas* (Winnipeg), 5 October 1943.

119 'Ukrainian Speaks,' *Montreal Gazette*, 8 November 1943.

120 *Welland–Port Colborne Evening Tribune*, 22 February 1943.

121 Watson Kirkconnell, *Our Ukrainian Loyalists*, 8.

122 University of Saskatchewan Archives, GSF, G.W. Simpson to T.C. Davis, 17 November 1942.

123 *Hansard*, 27 April 1944, 2417.

124 Blair Fraser, 'New Canadians in Wartime,' *Montreal Gazette*, 19 October 1943.

125 Kordan, *Canada and the Ukrainian Question*, Chapter 4.

126 LAC, DEA, RG 25, vol. 2977, file 3426-40, pt. 2: Canadian Minister to the USSR to Secretary of State for External Affairs, 17 May 1943.

127 LAC, DEA, RG 25, vol. 3040, file 4174-40: S.F. Rae, 'The Pan-Slavic Mov't in Canada', 31 July 1942.

128 LAC, DEA, RG 25, vol. 2977, file 3426-40, pt. 2: RG Rid, Memorandum, Re: CCCC, 7 June 1943.

129 LAC, BOC, RG 36, vol.13, file 8-9-2: John Grierson to H.R.L. Henry, Private Secretary, Office of the Prime Minister, 5 March 1943.

130 LAC, TPF, MG 30 E350, vol. 1, file 29: C.H. Payne, Deputy Minister to LaFlèche, Minister, Memorandum: Nationalities Division, 11 August 1943.

131 University of Saskatchewan Archives, GSF: Robert England to G. Simpson, 12 May 1944.

132 Ibid., 18 May 1944.

133 University of Saskatchewan Archives, GSF: C.H. Payne, Deputy Minister, DNWS, to George Simpson, 23 February 1944.

134 LAC, Robert England fonds, MG 30 C181, vol. 3, file: Report on the Reorganization of Nationalities Branch, Department of National War Services, by Robert England, 12 June 1944.

135 Ibid., 10.

136 Ibid., 13.

137 LAC, Vladimir J. Kaye fonds, MG 31 D69, vol. 11, file 10: Kaye to Jean Bruchesi, Secretaire adjoint de la Province de Quebec, 24 April 1944.

Conclusion

1 'Discrimination in Employment,' *Winnipeg Free Press*, 31 March 1945.

2 'Views on Nationality and Employment,' *Winnipeg Free Press*, 31 March 1945.

3 The Senate of Canada, *Proceedings of the Standing Committee on Immigration and Labour* (Ottawa, 1946), 222, 224.

4 'Racial Bill Not the Cure,' *Globe and Mail*, 10 March 1944.

5 'FEP Act Works a Conversion,' *Globe and Mail*, 15 March 1951.

6 LAC, Robert England fonds, MG 30 C181, vol. 3, file: Report on the Reor-

ganization of Nationalities Branch; Leslie Pal, *Interests of State: The Politics of Language, Multiculturalism, and Feminism in Canada* (Montreal, 1993), Chapter 3.

7 MacLennan, *Toward the Charter*, especially chapters 3 and 4; Lambertson, *Repression and Resistance*, Chapter 8.

8 Carmela Patrias and Ruth Frager, '"This Is Our Country, These Are Our Rights": Minorities and the Origins of Ontario's Human Rights Campaigns,' *Canadian Historical Review* 82 (March 2001), 12–14.

9 Carmela Patrias, 'Socialists, Jews, and the 1947 Saskatchewan Bill of Rights,' *Canadian Historical Review* 87, no. 2 (June 2006), 279.

10 MacLennan, *Toward the Charter*, 111.

11 Ross Lambertson, *Repression and Resistance*, 382 and passim. On the advantages of an incrementalist approach, see R. Brian Howe, 'Incrementalism and Human Rights Reform,' *Journal of Canadian Studies* (Fall 1993), 29–44.

12 For a detailed discussion of this complex topic see Ruth A. Frager, 'Class and Ethnic Barriers to Feminist Perspectives in Toronto's Jewish Labour Movement, 1919–1939,' *Studies in Political Economy* 30 (1989), 143–65.

13 'Discrimination: Right résumé, wrong name,' *Globe and Mail*, 21 May 2009, L1, L3.

14 *Not One of the Family: Foreign Domestic Workers in Canada*, edited by Abigail Bakan and Daiva Stasiulis (Toronto, 1997); Vic Satzewich, 'The Canadian State and the Racialization of Caribbean Migrant Farm Labour, 1947–1966,' *Ethnic and Racial Studies* 11, no. 3 (July 1988), 282–304; Nandita Sharma, 'On Being Not Canadian: The Social Organization of "Migrant Workers" in Canada,' *Canadian Review of Sociology and Anthropology* 38, no. 4 (2001), 415–39.

15 Interview with Kalmen Kaplansky, Ottawa, 30 June 1995.

16 See Dominique Clément, *Canada's Rights Revolution: Social Movements and Social Change, 1937–1982* (Vancouver, 2008), 10–11; Miriam Smith, *Lesbian and Gay Rights in Canada: Social Movements and Equality-Seeking, 1971–1995* (Toronto, 1999).

17 Nelson Lichtenstein, *Labor's War At Home* (2003), 209.

18 See, for example, Larry Savage, 'Workers' Rights as Human Rights: Organized Labor and Rights Discourse in Canada,' *Labor Studies Journal* 34, no. 1 (March 2009), 8–20; and for the United States, Nelson Lichtenstein, *State of the Union: A Century of American Labor* (Princeton, 2001); and Lichtenstein, 'The Rights Revolution,' *New Labor Forum* 12, no. 1 (Spring 2003), 61–73.

19 On similar developments in the United States, see Nelson Lichtenstein, *Labor's War At Home* (2003), xiv, xvi–xx.

Index